Sand Creek—A Childhood Legacy

Carl Soren Hoveland

VANTAGE PRESS
New York

FIRST EDITION

Published by Vantage Press, Inc.
419 Park Ave. South, New York, NY 10016

Manufactured in the United States of America
ISBN: 978-0-533-16134-8

Library of Congress Catalog Card No.: 2008908204

0 9 8 7 6 5 4 3 2 1

To my mother, who made it possible to realize my potential

Contents

Preface

It was an early October day in northwestern Wisconsin with bright sun and blue skies that showed off the spectacular autumn tree leaf color. I ambled slowly on the soft bluegrass sod of Zion Lutheran Cemetery about a half mile north of Sand Creek, enjoying the scenery, and peering thoughtfully at gravestones with names like Arne Eyk, Oscar Anderson, Lena Larson, Gerhard Gregarson, Maren Noer, Garfield Ness, Soren Hoveland, Margaret Anderson, John Hanson, and Gilbert Severson. Reading the names brought up rich memories of growing up in the Sand Creek community during the 1930s and early 1940s, I'm wrapped up in a cocoon of contentment.

My immigrant great-grandparents and grandparents settled here in the 1860s along with others from rural Norway. They were mostly poor, hard-working people who had struggled to eke out a living on tiny subsistence farms in their homeland. America, with its promise of cheap land, offered an opportunity for a new life. They worked hard cultivating former forests and eventually developed a sustainable agriculture and life that fulfilled their dreams. These people did not expect to become rich; they were contented with the farming community they had built. The second generation inherited the strengths of their parents and triumphed over the hardships of the Great Depression and severe droughts during the 1930s. These were the people I knew and lived with. They were strong, honest people, tolerant of hardship, frugal, patient, hard-working, uncomplaining, and able to enjoy the life they had together in this close-knit, loving community.

Today, many of the people I knew have moved away. Most are dead; so I come to the cemetery to visit them and recall my wonderful childhood. I was so fortunate to have grown up in the Sand Creek community. After living away from here so long, it was good to be back home again with friends. These people buried here and in three other local cemeteries had given me pleasure, molded my character and work ethic, and contributed to any success that I have had in life. It was a rich childhood legacy from this community and its people.

This book is about the Sand Creek community that I knew. It reviews some history of the area, the environmental resources, the Norwegian immigrants who settled it, and the agriculture. My immigrant ancestors were typical of the many who settled here. Mostly, this book is about the people and farming community I knew and my personal childhood experiences during the 1930s and early 1940s, most of which encompassed the Great Depression.

In writing this book, I received help from many sources, both written and oral. I owe a great deal to cousins Aldred Gunderson, Gertrude Sparby, and brother-in-law Gaylon Greenhill for their diligent genealogical work. Swanhild Rasmussen kindly provided countless details on people and events while Aaron Hanson, now deceased, furnished background information. I am indebted to Don Ball, Paul Toycen, and Lillie Sauer who critically reviewed and greatly improved the manuscript. The University of Georgia and University of Wisconsin libraries and the Dunn County Historical Museum supplied historical material. However, the personal stories that I tell about people and my characterization of them are my own. Any errors are mine.

Sand Creek—A Childhood Legacy

The Beginning

The Native People

Glaciers left much of what is now northeastern Dunn County, Wisconsin, covered with deep sand, resulting in acid, infertile soil that supported white pine forests interspersed with oak and maple trees in more fertile areas. The first inhabitants of this area migrated from Asia across a land bridge to Alaska and eventually moved southward. Two stone dart points typical of the Clovis people 11,000 to 12,000 years ago were found in Dunn County and are on exhibit at the county historical museum in Menomonie. These points were likely used to kill mammoths and musk oxen for food during that period. Since then, various Indian tribes have lived in this area, with frequent wars among them during the 1600s and 1700s. Eventually, the Chippewa (Ojibwe) conquered the Dakota tribe and dominated the area (Bieder, Robert E. 1995. *Native American Communities in Wisconsin, 1600–1960.* Univ. of Wis. Press, Madison). French fur traders from Quebec traveled through the area during the 1600s and 1700s to buy beaver furs from the Indians, establishing trading stations at places such as Eau Claire. Beaver pelts were in great demand for making men's hats in Europe, making the fur trade a highly profitable venture. Beaver were abundant in this area and the Indians were good trappers, allowing them to trade with the French for guns, tools, cloth, trinkets, and liquor. The Chippewa people generally were not farmers, instead obtaining most of their food by gathering wild rice, berries, and maple sap for syrup and sugar. Fishing provided much of their diet, especially sturgeon, which were abundant in streams. Dogs were their only domestic animal and a favorite dish at feasts. They rarely used horses or hunted bison. Deer hunting provided limited amounts of venison. A few villages were more permanent and squaws cultivated some corn, squash, beans, and tobacco. Birch bark was a valuable item as it was used for utensils, canoes, and to cover their elliptical dome-shaped houses.

After the fall of Quebec City in 1760, French involvement in the fur trade declined, and eventually it was dominated first by the English and after the Revolution by Americans. Over the years, heavy slaughter of beaver and other fur animals resulted in fewer pelts being harvested; as Indian income declined, so their desire for trade goods resulted in large debts at trading posts. The debt problem was widespread and the traders prevailed upon the government to help them. After the Blackhawk War in 1832, negotiations with the Indians resulted in the Chippewa tribe ceding most of northern Wisconsin to the USA government in 1842. Expulsion of most Indians opened up the area for "palefaces" to exploit the rich forest resources.

The Logging Era

The landscape of the Red Cedar and Chippewa river areas must have appeared to contain limitless supplies of virgin white pine and Norway pine timber. Many of the trees were 120 feet tall and 3 or 4 feet in diameter (Raney, W. F. 1935. Pine Lumbering in Wisconsin. *Wisconsin Magazine of History*, 19:71–90). Wisconsin Congressman Ben Eastman optimistically extolled in an 1852 speech, "Upon the rivers which are tributary to the Mississippi, and also upon those which empty themselves into Lake Michigan, there are interminable forests of pine, sufficient to supply all the wants of the citizens for all time to come." (C. E. Twining, 1963. Plunder and Progress: The Lumbering Industry in Perspective. *Wisconsin Magazine of History* 47:116–124).

The limitless forests and growing demand for lumber in expanding cities offered a rich opportunity for individuals who could harvest the trees and convert them into lumber. The first sawmill in what is Dunn County was built in 1831 on the Red Cedar River at what would become the city of Menomonie (Anon. 1925. History of Dunn County, Menomonie, WI). This mill was later acquired by Knapp Stout Co., the largest lumber company in the world (R. F. Fries. 1989. *Empire in Pine: The Story of Lumbering in Wisconsin 1830–1900*. Caxton Ltd., Sister Bay, WI). It was a stunning business opportunity as they bought pine land for $2 to 5 per acre from the federal or state government. They utilized cheap French-Canadian, Irish, Norwegian, German, and other immigrant labor to cut the trees into logs and float them down the Red Cedar and Chippewa rivers to sawmills in Menomonie and Eau Claire. From 1846 to 1896 this highly profitable company produced nearly two billion feet of lumber. The company also operated a machine shop, merchandise stores, gristmills, as well as five farms on 6,000 acres of good land at places like Menomonie and Prairie Farm that produced wheat, potatoes, beans, beef, and pork.

Dunn County was created out of Chippewa County in 1854. Census figures for Dunn County show only 1796 people in 1855, growing to 5,170 by 1865 and 16,859 in 1880. Logging of the pine timber was wasteful with hardly more than 40% of wood in the trees reaching market as lumber (Raney, 1935). The loggers left an ugly wasteland of huge stumps, tree limbs, and scattered undesirable trees that the timber companies offered for sale at low prices as potential farmland to immigrant settlers. The fertile flat land soon attracted settlers, and through hard work was slowly developed into productive farms during the 1840s and 1850s. However, the sandy infertile soils of the Sand Creek area in northeastern Dunn County were less attractive and settlement came later.

The settlers faced an enormous task in converting this wasteland by hand into tillable land just to produce enough food for their own household. Tree limbs had to be gathered into piles and burned. Fires were set in centers of large stumps and burned when possible or simply left to rot, and the land around them tilled and cropped. On some land, stones were abundant and had to be gathered and made into fences or dumped in piles. Oxen were used to plow bits of land around the big stumps. It must have been an exhausting task just to grow enough wheat, rye, corn, beans, and potatoes to feed a family. Commonly, men spent their winters working in northern Wisconsin logging camps to obtain some income, then came back to their family farm to work at clearing additional land and cropping in the summer (Fries, 1989). Great Grandpa Soren Hovland was probably typical of many new settlers; he spent 14 years working during winter at logging camps and sometimes at an Eau Claire sawmill while his sons worked on the farm. In summer he would often walk and carry some groceries the 45 miles from Eau Claire to spend Sunday with the family. His eldest son, my grandfather Soren, worked for seven winters in logging camps, starting at age 16, earning $16 per month during the late 1870s and early 1880s.

The Immigrants

A desolate cutover landscape in the Sand Creek area faced the first settlers, the Sven Toycen and Andrew Myran families. These Norwegian immigrants arrived in 1865 and built the first cabins, meanwhile living in their covered wagons. More immigrants followed so that the area became a Norwegian-speaking farm community. Many came from the same Norwegian counties such as Telemark, Setesdal, and Hedmark; so had similar cultural ties.

It is likely that these people were the product of generations that had lived in the same area of Norway for many centuries. Their gods were Odin, Loki, Thor, Freyr, and others to whom animal or sometimes human sacrifices were offered on an altar or "hov", from which comes the name "Hovland", the land on which the altar was located. Although King Olav decreed in the year 1000 that Catholicism would be the religion of Norway, it was many decades before people in rural areas completely adopted the new faith. There was no doubt a mixing of religions as evidenced by both Christian crosses and dragon heads decorating the elegant wood stave churches built in the 1100s, many of which survive and are still used for worship. Norway remained staunchly Catholic until the mid-1500s Reformation when King Christian III of Denmark-Norway ordained that the church should become Lutheran. This decree took time to accomplish as monasteries and convents were closed, church relics and statuary removed, church wealth sent to the king in Copenhagen, and priests were retrained or removed, but eventually the people adopted the changes.

Why did these people come to America? The Hovelands were typical of most that emigrated. They came from generations of small farmers who eked out a living on tiny mountain farms in the Hjartdahl area of Telemark "fylke" or county. A large county museum at Skien, Telemark has a magnificent collection of old farm buildings and indoor displays depicting the long history of this large county in southern Norway. Today this scenic mountain area has a small population, but in the 1860s it was densely populated with large families. The eldest son inherited a tiny farm, but for the other children in large families there was no other land available, and Norway had no industrial sector to provide city jobs. Norway was a poor country in the mid-nineteenth century. Thus, letters from immigrants in America and advertisements by shipping companies about cheap or free land offered opportunity for young people. This resulted in "America fever" where massive numbers of young people left their parishes in spite of Lutheran priests generally advising against this folly. Over the years, Norway lost over one-third of its population to emigration. Wisconsin was settled by European immigrants from many countries, with Norwegians being the second most populous nationality after German. Norwegian immigrants first settled in southern Wisconsin during the early 1840s with settlements father north in succeeding decades.

The decision to emigrate must have been agonizing as they knew they would likely never again see their homeland, parents, and other relatives. It also must have been a struggle to get sufficient money for the ocean ticket and travel to Wisconsin. The long ocean voyage, six weeks for Grandpa Hoveland, must have been an awful experience. Old sailing ships, formerly used for freight, had immigrants packed into poorly ventilated holds with little privacy and the air stinking of human waste. Seasickness and communicable diseases were commonplace, often resulting in deaths, so some ended their journey by burial at sea. Each immigrant family provided its own food, which deteriorated during the long journey. After surviving this ordeal and arrival in New York City, new trials greeted them. With no knowledge of English, they were dependent on Norwegian-speaking agents who were not always honest in arranging travel to Wisconsin. One wonders how many of them at this point wished they had stayed in

Norway. There must have been many family arguments and tears during this awful journey.

Weeks of travel via train, lake boat, and wagons were needed before the immigrants could arrive at their Sand Creek destination. The cutover timber land that would be their new home must have been a depressing sight. No open fields for farming, only stumps, brush, and some scattered trees near a river. With few resources, they had to construct a crude log house and till a bit of ground and grow some grain and potatoes to feed the family. A wood chest or two carried all their personal belongings of clothes, kitchenware, tools such as an axe, the Bible, and a few treasured mementoes of Norway. A fortunate few brought chests covered with colorful rosemal painting by talented Telemark artists.

It must have been an awesome feeling for these people to be in this strange place so far from home. Wild game and fish were a potential source of food, but there was little to be gathered from wild plants except some berries. Money for flour, sugar, salt, and other essentials necessitated the man finding employment part of the year cutting timber or working in the sawmills. The wife undoubtedly had the hardest life as she bore children, cared for family, and worked on the farm. Alone in this new world, they bonded with their fellow Norwegian neighbors to form a new community. These immigrants were remarkable people, molded by poverty and adversity in Norway, toughened by an awful trip, and able to take on the struggle to achieve a better life in America.

One wishes that these early Norwegian immigrants had left written records on their trip to America: what the settlement area looked like, their experiences in developing farms, and family life; however it is easy to understand why they did not. Most of them had little education and were barely able to read Norwegian sufficiently to master Luther's Small Catechism for church confirmation. Writing was not one of their skills. They had little sense of history. Most of all, every day these people were faced with grueling work to put food on the table for a growing family. Exhausted after a hard day of work, writing a diary was not an appealing task. Also, these people had a long oral tradition in Norway where stories about earlier times were retold in conversation from one generation to another rather than written. Thus, we lack any intimate written accounts of these people during the early settlement period.

All four of my grandparents were born in Norway and came to the Sand Creek area with their parents during the 1860s. My mother's paternal grandparents, Niels Juel Noer and Pauline Olsdatter Gruseth emigrated in 1863 and settled in the hills of the Trout Creek area south of Sand Creek. They had ten children, eight of them born in Norway. They apparently were more affluent than most immigrants as Pauline was a remarried widow who had come from a large farm in Hedmark County in east Norway which probably provided the means to transport their children to America where they had the advantage of cheap labor for land clearing and growing crops.

Amazingly, four of the children obtained university educations. We are not sure how the eldest son Ole, who became a pharmacist and owned a drug store at Colfax, paid for his education. However, two bachelor brother farmers, Arne and Martin, assisted two brothers in getting through medical school. Peter Juul became a surgeon in Wabeno, WI, and Julius was a physician who did graduate work in Vienna, Austria before practicing first in Stoughton, WI and later in Berkeley, CA. A younger brother, Olaf, became a pharmacist and owned a drug store in Menomonie.

My mother's maternal grandparents, Martin Isakson and Sophie Konsgaarden Pedersdatter, emigrated about 1864 and also settled in the hills of Trout Creek south of Sand Creek. They had eleven children, three of them born in Norway. Both Martin and Sophie came from relatively affluent families who owned large farms in the flat river valleys of Hedmark, east Norway. Martin was a graduate of the Norwegian military college and served as an officer in the army for several years. He soon tired of army routine and came home to serve as overseer on the farm and also worked as a surveyor. There must have been some personal difficulties with this arrangement as eventually his parents sent Martin and his family to settle in Wisconsin. Life as a pioneer in Trout Creek was especially hard for Martin who believed menial labor needed to clear land and grow food for his growing family was beneath him. He tried opening a country store but it failed. Life was hard, but when his son Paul and the other boys grew old enough to work, they managed to survive on the farm. Ma had a strong dislike for her Grandpa Martin Isakson who remained an arrogant strong-willed man who survived for ninety-eight years doing a minimum of work.

My father's maternal grandfather, Halvor Halvorson, emigrated from Hedmark County in east Norway in 1864 to Beloit, WI where he worked as a shoemaker. In 1866 he sent money to his wife, Olea Ovidea Engen, and daughter Minda to bring them to Beloit and then to Eau Claire where he worked as a shoemaker. Later, the family settled on a farm just across the Barron County line north of Sand Creek. They had ten children of which only Minda was born in Norway.

My father's paternal grandparents, Soren Sorenson Hovland and Torgun Oldsdatter Lofthus, were both born on tiny farms near Hjartdal, Telemark County, Norway. They emigrated in 1865 and settled near Red Wing in Goodhue County, Minnesota. In 1867 they moved, via a hired covered wagon, to Wisconsin and settled on 160 acres along the Red

Cedar River just southwest of Sand Creek. They had fourteen children, four of whom were born in Norway. For some reason, many of the children ended up with the surname "Hoveland" rather than "Hovland" as used in Norway. The most commonly used version in Sand Creek, "Hoveland," will be used for all family members in this book.

My great-grandparents were prolific people, producing forty-five children from these four couples. Babies were born about two years apart. My ancestors were of good genetic stock as they survived longer than most people of that time. Great-Grandma Hovland bore fourteen children and survived to the age of 78. She must have been a lot tougher than Great-Grandma Isakson who only made it to age 65 after birthing eleven children. The men survived about fifteen years longer than the women of that generation. These folks truly practiced the Biblical command in the Book of Genesis "to be fruitful and multiply"; so it didn't take long to populate the Sand Creek area and provide labor for farm work. In those days, children were an asset as cheap farm labor.

Sand Creek Settlement and Agriculture

As more land was cleared and farms developed, the main cash crop of the Sand Creek area was wheat. In 1872 Hiram Graham, Robert Tolles, and Samuel White constructed a dam across the Sand Creek and built a water-powered flour mill to process local wheat (Russel, J. *Dunn County News*. Dec. 13, 1998). However, a severe flood in 1884 destroyed the mill and it was never rebuilt. After that wheat was transported by horse-drawn wagons to the Eau Claire market. Later in the century, potatoes became a cash crop and were hauled on wagons to New Auburn where they were shipped by train to various cities.

A serious limitation for farming in the Sand Creek area was the poor soil. Glaciers had covered most of the area with deep sandy or gravely soil that did not hold moisture and plant nutrients well. Thus, crops suffered from lack of moisture during periods of low rainfall. More importantly, continuous cropping with no fertilization resulted in nutrient exhaustion and yields declined. The introduction of red clover as a rotation crop furnished some nitrogen and boosted yields, but its growth was hurt by the acid low-fertility soil. We now know that fertilizers and lime were needed, but they were not available to these settlers. The area desperately needed a source of manure, but the only farm animals were a milk cow or two, oxen and horses for farm work and transportation. Thus, the amount of manure produced was far less than needed to restore the fertility of these soils. Wheat, the main crop, was profitable until the late 1880s when a combination of low prices, declining yields, Hessian fly, and diseases such as smut and rust devastated this crop. Sand Creek settlers were in a bad way for farm income.

The cow that supplied milk for the family was decidedly a poor relation and certainly not regarded as a source of income. Norwegian immigrants had no concept of dairy farming as a business. Men considered a cow as part of the household and care of lactating cows was women's work. Men did not milk cows. This attitude of men resisted introduction of dairying as a way of life and income. Thus, dairy farming was not introduced to Wisconsin by Norwegian immigrants, but by New York state farmers who moved to the state, bringing their expertise in keeping cows for milk to produce butter and cheese (Lampard, E. E. 1963. *The Rise of the Dairy Industry in Wisconsin*. State Historical Society of Wisconsin, Madison, WI).

During most of the 1800s New York was the leading USA dairy state. Wisconsin dairying started in the southern part of the state during the 1870s with most of the milk being used for butter and later for cheese. As wheat yields and farm income declined, dairying moved northward during the late 1880s and 1890s. Desperation was probably the stimulus for these Sand Creek settlers considering dairying as an option. Farm-made butter from a few cows was traded at a local store for other items. As cow numbers increased, a creamery was established in Sand Creek to process cream from farms into butter, gradually resulting in a more uniform and better quality product.

Milk production on these farms was low in the early days of dairying. Most cows were not dairy breeds but Shorthorn, Devon, or unknown breeds often selected for their draft potential rather than milk production. Pastures and hay were generally of low quality. Animal health was a problem. Hoof and mouth disease was prevalent during the 1800s and early 1900s. Brucellosis was widespread and caused abortion in cattle and undulant fever in humans. Tuberculosis was a serious problem in cattle and was spread via unpasteurized milk to humans. Sanitation was often poor both in production and processing of the milk. Thus, early dairying had many problems and farmers had few solutions. However, increased numbers of dairy cows on a farm furnished a source of manure to fertilize their feed crops so yields increased.

Three major factors helped grow the dairy industry. First, the invention of small affordable mechanical cream separators in Sweden by Carl de Laval in 1885 allowed easy separation of the cream in milk on the farm instead of tediously skimming it off the top. Second, development of the Babcock butterfat test at the University of Wisconsin in 1890 allowed rapid and dependable results, so farmers could be paid for their milk on the basis of fat content rather than by volume. It also allowed testing of individual cows for butterfat output to permit selection and breeding of more productive cows. Third, a major innovation was the silo where high quality chopped green forage such as corn was pickled like sauerkraut and stored for use during the long winter period.

The ability to feed cows adequately during the winter extended the lactation period and increased milk flow. In 1877, a farmer near Fort Atkinson was the first one to use a silo in Wisconsin, ensiling green corn in a 6-foot deep trench. Over time, upright silos made of wood staves, brick, stone, or cement became the norm. The value of silos was heavily promoted by W. D. Hoard, editor of the *Hoard's Dairyman* magazine, resulting in wider use of this innovation in dairy cow feeding. Silos were probably late in coming to the Sand Creek area. In 1904 a silo census showed there were only 716 in the entire state of Wisconsin (Lampard, 1963). By 1915 there were 55,990 and by 1924 over 100,000 in the state, resulting in silos becoming commonly used to provide high quality dairy cow feed in winter on farms.

Adoption of dairying as a way of life was difficult for most farmers as they had to learn how to improve forage and feed quality, cattle breeding, health care, and milk sanitation as well as accept a new discipline of milking a herd of cows twice daily seven days a week. The main reason that dairying became a way of life on Sand Creek farms was that it provided a dependable source of monthly income year after year, even on sandy, infertile soil. As farmers discovered, dairying was an exercise in soil conservation.

Red clover in rotation with corn supplied nitrogen to the soil. Most of the crops raised on the farm were fed to livestock and the manure was used as fertilizer. A book published for farmers in 1908 made a strong case for dairy farming, "It is estimated that whereas a ton of wheat worth $22 removed $7.50 of plant food from the soil, a ton of butter worth nearer $500, removed less than $0.50 from the soil" (G. H. Benkendorf and K. L. Hatch, 1908. *Profitable dairying: A Manual for Farmers and Dairymen*. Madison, WI).

13

The development of dairy farming required butter creameries or cheese factories to be built in a community; so people skilled in butter and cheese making had to be found. Farmers had to get their milk to the factory on roads that were often little more than muddy or dusty trails. It is no wonder that much of the early butter and cheese produced was often of wretched quality, produced from milk in unsanitary barns and not properly cooled before being taken to the creamery. Wisconsin cheese and butter had a poor reputation in markets during the 1880s and 1890s, often resulting in prices half that of New York state dairy products (Lampard, 1963). Even Illinois or Iowa butter was more appreciated in the marketplace. But by 1909, ten western Wisconsin counties, including Dunn, were the top butter producers in the state. Cheese production in this area remained low with the main cheese areas being in southern and eastern Wisconsin.

It is difficult to determine when dairying became an important part of Sand Creek agriculture, but it probably started in the late 1890s after the collapse of wheat farming. The first creamery was built in the little hamlet of Sand Creek in 1901, which already had a Farmers Store that had been established in 1892. The first creamery manager was Peter M. Scott, followed by Bob Worman. Roy Rathbun was the first buttermaker. Originally, farmers separated cream from milk on the farm and brought it to the creamery where it was made into butter, a commercial product shipped and sold elsewhere. Skim milk and buttermilk were valuable for feeding to pigs. As dairy cow numbers expanded and creameries grew larger, they installed large cream separators that allowed farmers to deliver whole milk for processing.

Sand Creek provided a creamery and served as a trade town for families on the small, mostly 80- to 160-acre dairy farms covering the flat to rolling countryside. Large families provided needed labor for dairying which was profitable until the 1930s when low milk prices and a succession of severe droughts sharply reduced incomes for both rural and towns-people. Somehow these frugal people managed and lived their simple lives with dignity even during those difficult years.

Our Family

Grandparents

Grandpa Soren Samuel Hoveland, born in Norway, gew up on the family farm across the Red Cedar River from Sand Creek and just over a mile south of Our Savior's Lutheran Church. He never attended school since there was none. Despite this, he eventually learned to read Norwegian and later some English. He never learned to write and always signed his name with an "X". From age sixteen he worked in logging camps, spring log drives on the rivers, sawmills, and railway construction until 1884. The death of his father brought him home that year to marry Grandma and operate the home farm for two years until he left to manage the 200-acre Ole Noer farm north of Sand Creek along the Red Cedar. In 1891, he bought this farm and another 80 acres, farming it for twenty-seven years. Grandpa was an enterprising fellow as he also operated, with T. S. Peterson, a grain threshing machine, a bean thresher, and a sawmill, all powered by a steam engine, doing custom work for other farmers in the community. He also served as the local undertaker, building wooden coffins and laying out the dead. A good natured man with a fine sense of humor, Grandpa was a great story teller and well liked in the community.

Grandma Minda Halvorson Hoveland, also born in Norway, came from a family of eight girls and two boys on a farm north of Sand Creek. The girls known for their beauty and ambition were in demand as wives. Unfortunately, the sisters also were strong-willed and humorless, making life difficult for their husbands. Grandma was a stern, dutiful woman who worked hard, and she expected those around her to do the same. Pa said that when Grandpa was working away from the farm, Grandma was a tough boss who assigned jobs to each child and made sure they got done.

Grandpa Carl Noer, likewise born in Norway, was raised on a farm in Trout Creek between Colfax and Sand Creek. He married Grandma in Eau Claire in 1882 and moved to a 160-acre farm about three miles north of Sand Creek where he farmed until he died of throat cancer in 1912 when Ma was fifteen years old. Carl Noer was a kind, gentle man and well liked by his neighbors.

Grandma Maren Isakson Noer, born in Norway, was also raised on a farm in Trout Creek. She worked as a maid in the elegant home of a timber baron in Eau Claire before marrying Carl Noer. She was proud to tell how she had saved enough from her small maid's wages to buy a treadle sewing machine. Grandma Noer was a wonderful story teller, outspoken, and strong-willed, but she had a better sense of humor than Grandma Hoveland.

Pa and Ma

My Pa, Herman, was born in 1890, and grew up on the family farm north of Sand Creek with sister Ona and his brothers Art, Elvin, Oscar, Torphin, and Albert. Educated in seven grades at the local school, at age sixteen he began working winters in a northern Minnesota logging camp and on the farm in summer. At age twenty he was tempted by Canadian Pacific railway advertising to homestead 160 acres of free land on the prairies of western Saskatchewan in 1910. Pa built a tiny wood shack and later a horse barn on this bleak open land where he spent his long winters in solitude. He said that he would entertain himself by singing, patching clothes, and visiting nearby neighbors. His brothers, Elvin and Torphin, also homesteaded land in that bleak, treeless area; his brother Art started a commercial dray stable in the little nearby town of Kindersley.

Pa, who became a Canadian citizen, apparently did well wheat farming during World War I and was able to purchase a steam engine, breaking plow, and threshing machine to do custom work for other farmers. He was satisfied with his new life, but after ten years, he reluctantly agreed to come back to Wisconsin to become a naturalized US citizen and take over the 80-acre dairy farm on which his parents resided, having sold their larger farm to my Uncle Sophus Noer. Living on the farm with Grandpa and Grandma, Pa built a new house and courted Ma who lived on the adjoining farm. They eloped to Stillwater, MN and were married in the Lutheran parsonage of Pastor C. E. Benson on December 3, 1926. Grandpa and Grandma Hoveland then bought a house in Sand Creek and moved there to retire.

My Ma, Caspara, was born in 1897 on the Noer farm north of Sand Creek and had a sister Laura and brothers Sophus, Fritjof, and Arnold. Ma and Arnold, twins, were the youngest. Julius died as a baby. Ma lived on the farm with her mother and brothers until her marriage, except for one year when she worked in Minneapolis as a maid in the home of a state executive.

My parents were handsome people when they married and retained their fine appearance into old age. Both were older than average when they married, Ma being twenty-nine and Pa thirty-six. It was probably not a highly romantic courtship but more likely a practical arrangement for life on the farm. They were not well suited for one another as both were strong-willed, outspoken people with set opinions that were not easily dislodged. These traits did not soften during the years I was growing up but often exploded, resulting in periods when they did not speak to each other. During those periods, they would give me instructions to tell the other parent what they needed to convey, and the other parent would reply similarly. It was a painful experience for me as a child to serve as a communication transmission center for my parents as I loved both of them and knew I was loved by each parent. These non-speaking periods would last for a week or two, then fade away to longer periods of tolerance and finally to actual good will toward each other.

Pa only had seven grades of school, but his creative mind and high level of intelligence made him highly competitive with people who had more education. He had only studied arithmetic, but had a mathematical mind much like that of an engineer that was good at problem solving. Pa had superb mechanical skills and great ability to repair machinery and operate it efficiently. Raised on the farm, he had learned to take pride in the work he did. Four winters working in logging camps, starting at age sixteen, hardened his strength and endurance. Pa was a physically strong, muscular man who could hold his own at any task and confident that he could compete with anyone.

The Pa I knew was a person I looked up to, knowing that he could do anything better than anyone else. I was proud of him and willingly let him dominate me. He was not a mean person but drove himself hard at work and expected the same of others. I worked hard but could not match his skills or ability to work. Work dominated life. He loved to work and took pride in each day's accomplishments. Unfortunately, he expected me to be the same, but I had many of my mother's attributes. He was well organized and ruled by the clock, always on time and irritated by those who were not.

Pa viewed the environment in practical terms of what it could be used for—such as trees for lumber, land to grow crops and livestock. Everything was looked upon as to how it could be best used to produce profitability. As I grew older, I realized that I too was a part of this work system. Pa had little appreciation for the beauty of song birds, wild flowers, or scenery. I noticed at an early age that some neighbors would sometimes stop their horses and farm implements to enjoy looking at wildlife or at vistas of billowing clouds. Pa never let beauty interfere with farm work. Recreation was not part of his system.

Ma's clever letters written in mixed English and Norwegian reached me for over seventy years as we each corresponded weekly from the time I left the farm until her mid 90s. Had she been better educated it is likely she would have become a highly successful professional woman. Ma had her own ideas, but most did not jibe with those of Pa. He was an early riser, she was a late riser, although this had to be modified to meet Pa's expectations. Her sense of time was not the same as his; she was quite willing to have a flexible schedule for meals, but that was impossible in our house that was ruled by the clock. Pa was an ardent church goer whereas the Noer family where Ma grew up was more lax. She enjoyed sitting down with a cup of coffee to chat with friends on the phone or with someone who stopped by, while Pa viewed these things as intrusions on the work day. Ma was not lazy and got her work done, but she just had a different sense of time than Pa and could enjoy watching a sunset or a wren family build a nest under our porch eaves. I liked Ma's system better.

Pa was the head of our household and made major decisions, handled the money, and expected the household to operate under his rules. Ma's task was to operate the house efficiently, put timely meals on the table, raise me when I was small, help milk cows, and assist on outside jobs in haying or grain harvest. Ma had no money of her own except for small handouts that Pa gave her from time to time. It was a humiliating position for Ma, but not uncommon in our community. Pa never understood that marriage was a shared enterprise and not a dictatorship. I do not think Pa wanted to be unkind to her, but his failure to consider her feelings and needs simply antagonized her further. In a later era, their marriage would never have survived and a divorce would have been inevitable. However, as they grew older and entered retirement, both mellowed and their relationship greatly improved so that life became more enjoyable for both of them.

My Early World

I entered this world in my parents' tiny bedroom in our farmhouse on October 25, 1927. Ma was thirty and Pa thirty-seven. Dr. McCormick from New Auburn and Grandma Noer were present at this event. The delivery was a difficult one, not surprising since I weighed over ten pounds. It was followed by a serious infection and long illness which may explain why Ma chose to have a nine-year gap before the birth of my sister. I was named Carl Soren after my two grandfathers and baptized by Rev. Ingel Hovland (no relation), pastor of Zion Lutheran Church in Sand Creek.

I was a fat little baby and afflicted with exzema rash. Carrots were supposed to improve this condition; so Ma fed me lots of this vegetable; in fact, so much that I hated carrots and did not want to eat them until later in life. My first language was Norwegian as that is all that I was exposed to at home and with close neighbors. There were no nearby children who could have introduced me to English, which my parents knew but did not use at home.

As I learned to walk, I soon discovered that it was fun to punch my fist into the glass windows and break them. This habit continued, and to save our windows, they nailed boards across them. Another thing I enjoyed was to take hold of the oil cloth on our kitchen table, preferably when it had dishes and food on it; then pull it off. This must have been great fun as the dishes made a great noise as they crashed to the floor. The solution for this was fastening the oil cloth to the table with thumb tacks. I had a lot of curiosity, which often got me into trouble. One day, Ma had just hung a load of wet laundry on the clothes line and returned to the kitchen where she washed. She found me with my shoes and stockings standing in a washtub of rinse water that was sitting on a wood bench next to the washing machine. Another time, she caught me entertaining myself by holding on to wet clothes on the line and swinging until they fell down. I had pulled down a number of items on the grass, enjoying myself immensely. Ma was not pleased.

I had a wonderful day once when visiting the farm of Uncle Sophus and Aunt Clara. They were in the dining room enjoying coffee with my parents when I disappeared from the room and things became very quiet. Ma and Aunt Clara walked into the kitchen and found me standing on a counter merrily throwing toothpicks all over the room. Aunt Clara and cousin Swanhild had a good laugh, but Ma was not pleased. Of these events, I remember only the boards nailed across our house windows, denying me access to a source of entertainment. Ma tried spanking my bottom with the lefsa turner, but this didn't have much effect. A lefsa turner is a very thin flat piece of wood about three feet long, which can be used to inflict a sharp sting on a little boy's bottom. Ma soon learned that I was hard headed.

One early event in my life was especially memorable. It was twilight during a summer evening as trees cast long, dark shadows on the nearby hay and corn fields. The aroma of new mown hay filled the air. Tall grass and weeds grew along the side of the narrow sandy road which I later learned was known as "Lovers Lane," about a half mile from our farm house. I was around two years old, probably dressed in my usual striped coveralls. As daylight diminished, I was getting scared, trudging alone on this road.

A Model T Ford touring car with side curtains off for the summer chugged slowly toward me and stopped. The neighbor couple sitting high in their car, Leonard and Helen Toycen, recognized this chubby little blond kid. Helen, a large husky woman in her usual dark print dress got down out of the high car seat and grabbed me. I began to cry and tried to get away but I was caught. Squeezing me to her ample bosom and stomach, I struggled. I wanted Ma! Helen smelled different. Back in the car, she scolded me for running away and being so bad to my parents. I was scared and angry, hating this awful person. Leonard, a patient, kind man much smaller than Helen, didn't say much and just smiled as he drove to our farm. My frantic parents, who had been looking for me, gave me a warm welcome. When Helen finally let me go, I rushed to Ma who gave me warm kisses and pats with her hands. Then she folded her arms around me and held me close. She smelled so good! I was safe again.

One would think that after my Lovers Lane experience that I would end my solitary travels. Apparently, exploration was interesting because I continued my adventures. I recall another time I was at the far end of a cow pasture about a quarter mile from the house, again at twilight. The grass was fairly high. This time, neighbor Casper Field had been over to our house in the evening with his blue Chevrolet flat bed truck. Ma suspected that I might be in this pasture as she had seen me playing by the fence earlier. So Ma rode in the truck cab with Casper while Pa stood on the flat bed looking for me as they drove in the pasture. Finally, I was spotted and Pa scooped me up and put me into Ma's arms. Again, the end of another trip. Ma didn't think my explorations were much fun and was afraid that I would get run over in the gravel highway past our house. The solution to this problem was tying a rope around my middle and attaching it to a big maple tree near our house. A photo shows me pouting at my new equipment, preventing my exploring the wider world.

Books and Language

As a child, I was intrigued with books. We didn't have many, but in one closet upstairs were a number of old books, some of them in Norwegian. I recall a small flexible ABC book printed on linen-like paper from which I learned the Norwegian alphabet. This was a big help, but did cause some problems later in learning to read English as the Norwegian alphabet has three extra letters. Anyway, I spent many happy hours putting letters together to make words, asking Ma for help, and eventually teaching myself to read simple Norwegian words. It was wonderful discovering that these alphabet letters made words that I could use to make up stories! Books became my new world. I also figured out English words and learned to read. It was no doubt a miracle for Ma as I completely changed from a troublesome child into a little boy engrossed with reading. Ma said that after I discovered books, I became a well behaved child and her problems with me were over. I recall it was such fun to spend hours upstairs in a storeroom at Grandma Noer's house where there were more old books to enjoy. Also, there were many cards with double photos of places in different parts of the USA and foreign countries that one looked at through a steropticon, making objects and people in them look alive. I was fascinated with all these exotic views so different from my world in Sand Creek.

I grew up content as an only child even though I had no one else to play with since there were no children who lived adjacent to our farm. Norwegian was my first language, and I knew only a few words of English. When visiting the John and Laura Hanson farm, my seven older cousins, Andrew, Martin, Julian, Philip, Daniel, Aaron, and Frederick, all spoke and used fluent Norwegian which was fine with me. It was the same with my cousin Swanhild Noer. It was different at Uncle Oscar and Aunt Margaret Hoveland's farm where cousins Kenneth, Aldred, Orville, and Venonah spoke only English, resulting in me being left alone or listening to Pa and Uncle Oscar as they generally conversed in Norwegian. The same language barrier was true for Toddy (Robert) and Billy, sons of Uncle Art and Aunt Vearl Hoveland in Sand Creek. These English-speaking cousins didn't quite know what to do with me when I was little. It was the end of an era and I happened to be one of a few children in my age category to have Norwegian as my first language. The result was that I had a closer association with older people who always complimented me on my Norwegian, making me feel superior to other children who only spoke English. It was a strange situation as it alienated me from most other kids my age and certainly delayed my development in many ways, making me somewhat of a loner. I was a peculiar little kid, content to live in my own little world of books and make-believe.

We Norwegian speakers around Sand Creek naively assumed that we spoke the language fluently as in Norway. In reality, the language we used was that spoken in rural Norway when our immigrant ancestors came to Wisconsin in the 1860's. Thus, language changes in Norway were not incorporated in that spoken by any of us. As new inventions or products appeared in common use, people in Norway developed a name for them while the immigrants simply used the English name and added a Norwegian ending or pronunciation. For instance, in Norway they used "bil" to describe a car while we incorrectly spoke of "kaar" in the singular and "kaarn" in plural. In addition, many English words with Norwegian endings or pronunciations were blended into our speech. The result was that by the 20th century a peculiar "immigrant Norwegian" was spoken by second and third generation Norwegians in Wisconsin and differed considerably from that of the homeland (Joan N. Buckly and Einar Haugen, ed., 1984. *P. J. Rosendahl. Han Ola og han Per: a Norwegian-American Comic Strip.* Univ. of Oslo, Norway).

Our Farmhouse

My early world was our 80-acre farm. Along the east side of the short driveway from County Highway I (eye) was a row of large old maple trees, and several more of these gnarled giants shaded the west side of our house. Our small house was a typical two-story 1920s bungalow with gray cement stucco walls and rust-brown trim on the wood. A small uncovered porch extended out from the back door, under which the dog usually slept. Inside was a tiny room with a small medicine cabinet and enamel wash basin for washing one's hands and face since there was no indoor plumbing and bathroom. Cold water from the water pump in the basement was piped to a faucet in the entry room. A slop bucket for wash water and kitchen waste water stood on the floor. Wall hooks held a collection of overall jackets, mackinaws, caps, and hats, while the floor held rubbers and overshoes.

As one entered the kitchen, built-in-cabinets, counters, and a sink-cabinet (with another cold water faucet but no drain) covered the wall. On one's left was the General Electric drum-top refrigerator and directly ahead was the wood stove, complete with warming ovens and a hot water reservoir. A wood box stood beside it. In the center of the room was the kitchen table where we ate our meals, entertained drop-in guests for coffee, and talked over farm business. The next room was supposed to be the dining room, but it was where we spent our time reading, listening to programs like Lum and Abner on the Philco dome-shaped table radio, and entertaining neighborhood visitors. The dining room table was set with fancy china and silver for dinner or coffee only when we had special guests. Pa had a leather rocker chair where he spent his few hours of leisure. The party line telephone (our ring was a long and a short) was on one wall. Ma often took down the receiver and listened in when she heard the ring of a neighbor who might have interesting news.

The living room was always referred to as the "front room," as the exterior door faced the highway at the front of the house. It contained a sofa, two stuffed chairs, several wood chairs, a small octagon-shaped table, and an upright piano that no one in the family could play. The front room was rarely used except when we had guests during a holiday or for city relatives such as Pa's Uncle Sewell and Aunt Mabel Hoveland from Chippewa Falls, or Ma's Uncle Olaf and Aunt Ida Noer from Menomonie. I loved both of these couples as they were such fun. Uncle Sewell, assistant county highway commissioner, was such a good story teller and had an infectious smile. Uncle Olaf was special as he always brought me oranges and old National Geographic magazines, both treasures on the farm during the Depression. A tiny entry hall connected to the rarely used front door which opened onto the open porch facing the lawn and highway. My parents' tiny bedroom, where I was born, completed the first floor except for a small hall room at the center of the house where we took our baths in a round, steel laundry tub filled with hot water from the stove reservoir.

The second floor had two bedrooms; another room was used as a storage area since it was often oppressively hot in summer because the tiny dormer windows could not be opened. Each bedroom had two large walk-in closets where all sorts of interesting old stuff was stored. The hall at the top of the stairs had a tall elegant mahogany Victrola phonograph with a lot of vinyl records that I played, a gift of some city relatives who did not want it any more. The basement contained the pipe furnace that supplied heat to each room on the first floor. Supposedly, heat would reach the second floor, but on a very cold winter night that didn't seem to happen. Heavy frost covered the second floor windows, even with storm windows. In one corner of the basement was an electric water pump attached to a "point" driven into the water-bearing sand. One area was reserved for Ma's canned goods, potatoes, rutabagas, and the remainder of the basement held sawmill slabs and wood chunks used to feed the furnace.

The Farm Buildings

A clothes line hung between the house and a small brooder house for chicks, beyond which was a garage for our car. An old unpainted hay shed had a red side barn attached to it for our small herd of Guernsey cows. A small chicken house stood near the fenced barnyard with a moss-covered wood-stave water tank under a bur oak tree. Next to it was the milk house with a concrete water tank for cooling milk cans, a rack to store clean milk cans, and an electric water pump. Nearby was a metal roofed granary. Behind the car garage was a corn crib, beyond which was a machine shed where the old black Chevrolet flat bed truck was kept along with various horse-drawn farm implements such as a corn planter, drill, mower, rake, hay loader, and binder plus unused items like a buggy. Next to it was the shop with a forge, anvil, electric emery wheel grinder, lots of tools, machinery parts, and junk. Outside was a hand-cranked grindstone for sharpening hay sickles, scythes, and axes. Behind was an open shed that covered our McCormick-Deering threshing machine. Nearby was the tractor shed with wood shaving-insulated walls, housing our big dark blue 22–36 McCormick-Deering tractor with steel lug rear wheels, which was used for plowing, land breaking, threshing, and silo filling. Just behind the tractor shed was a small unused ice house filled with sawdust to insulate ice cakes sawed from the nearby Red Cedar. Since Wisconsin Hydro Electric had run a power line to our farm the year after I was born, we had the luxury of an electric refrigerator in the house to cool perishable food so we had no need for ice. Behind the ice house were about ten acres of good-sized white pine trees extending to the highway across which was the Myran farm. On one side of the woods was our sawmill used for trees cut from our land and custom sawing for neighbors. Near our corn crib were two rows of lumber piles from the sawmill waiting for buyers.

Obviously, our place had a lot of buildings for an 80-acre dairy farm. As I learned much later, this size farm would support only a small dairy herd, so Pa had invested in additional enterprises such as custom threshing, land breaking, and saw milling to increase our income. For a small child the farm offered a lot of things to explore, increasing my knowledge of the world around me. There was the fascination of watching a spider build a web, ants carrying seeds into their nests, squirrels burying acorns from a nearby oak tree, butterflies feeding on flowers, fluffy dandelion heads distributing their wind-borne seed, a wren mother feeding its hungry little ones in the nest, little fuzz ball yellow chicks trying to run and falling over, and tree leaves fluttering in the breeze. It was fun to get on the high seat of the tractor and imagine driving this massive blue machine, crank the grindstone, tap on an empty milk can to make different sounds like a drum, float pieces of wood or bark as a boat in the outdoor water tank, play like a fish in a bin of oats, or lie in the grass to watch the fluffy white clouds and imagine them as people or animals. I had a vivid imagination and played all sorts of fantasy games alone and with make-believe friends. Early childhood alone on the farm was a happy time and I never felt lonely.

There was a small lawn between our house and the highway, beyond which was a thick pine forest owned by Annie Myran that extended a short distance to steep banks sloping down to the slow flowing Red Cedar River. As I grew older, the river became a great attraction for fishing and scenic enjoyment. Sand Creek lay about three miles south of our farm. My early travels were made in our family car, a tiny 1926 dark green 2-door Chevrolet. These outings on the dusty or muddy gravel or dirt roads were always a delight whether they were for shopping in town, church attendance, or visiting neighbors and relatives.

Sand Creek—the Town

What was Sand Creek (pronounced "San Crik") like in the 1930s? The flat- to gently-rolling landscape surrounding Sand Creek was covered with small family dairy farms except for mixed pine and hardwood forests on steep knolls and along streams. A simple county highway sign with black letters "Sand Creek" on a white background announced this on each entrance road. It apparently wasn't considered much of a place since it didn't have the population number on the sign or designation "city" as with Chetek, or even "village" as with nearby Colfax. During the 1930s this hamlet of maybe 200 people contained a busy creamery, stores, repair services, two Lutheran churches, bank, post office, telephone exchange, barber shop, and an elementary school. Although there were taverns in the early days of Sand Creek, there had been none since National Prohibition as the Township of Sand Creek voters chose to keep it dry.

The town, situated on a ridge, was named for the squiggly little stream which entered the tranquil, tree-shaded Red Cedar River. A road led across the rust-red iron girder bridge over the river to the local park and beyond to a pond with Tom Pruzek's water-powered mill that ground corn and oats for feeding cows of local dairy farmers. Farther on was Our Saviour's Norwegian Synod Lutheran Church, a white building with a tall steeple. The Sand Creek homes of these staunch Republican residents were plain little wood-siding houses of nondescript architecture, mostly painted a conservative white, with a few venturesome folks using tan or cream colored paint. I sometimes wondered why people didn't paint their houses bright red, blue, or green as it would have looked much more cheerful against the snow during the long winter. Most had a vegetable garden but many houses lacked indoor bathrooms so had outdoor toilets. Each house had its own well for water. Streetlights and sidewalks lined the main street which ran parallel to the river, originally graveled and later asphalted. Side streets were sand. It was not a pretty town, but maple and elm trees enhanced it and provided welcome shade in the heat of summer. Lilac and peony blooms provided color in late May and June.

Entering Sand Creek from the north one would see several tiny wood houses on the right, and on the left a brick elementary school with two classrooms, a small library on the top floor, and a large game room on the ground floor. Two teachers taught eight grades here. Outside were swings, teeter totters, and a softball field that was used for winter games in the snow. Beyond, several small houses lined both sides of the block before a little street turned off by the Farmers Store to Zion Lutheran Free Church and the parsonage. It was a typical white board Norwegian Lutheran church with a tall bell steeple. The basement, used for Sunday School, Ladies Aid luncheons, Young People's meetings, and other events, was mostly above ground, necessitating many steps to reach the sanctuary door for worship services. It must have been hard for old people to climb those steps, especially in winter when there could be ice.

The Farmers Store

Pa did our grocery shopping, usually at the Farmers Store. I always was glad to ride along in the car on those trips to Sand Creek. The Farmers Store in Sand Creek, managed by Theodore Nelson, was one of a chain located in towns like New Auburn, Dallas, Chetek, Barron, Prairie Farm, Colfax, Eau Claire, and Menomonie, but the biggest and busiest was in Bloomer where the clientele were mainly prosperous German farmers, whose farms were mostly located on excellent loam soil. The Farmers Store across the street from the creamery was the biggest store building in Sand Creek and also had a small farm machinery parts shed behind it. At one point they also sold merchandise from the second floor, but during my time it was mostly a place to store various unused items.

Outside the Farmers Store, one walked up several concrete steps to the front door located on the corner of the building. Huge windows covered the front of the store. There was space for displays, but rarely was there anything there as customers were more interested in getting what they needed inside the store. Indoors, on one's left were glass cases and open counters with hardware, tools, overalls, work shirts, mackinaws, gloves, underwear, socks, work shoes, rubber overshoes, and hardware items. On one counter stood what I imagined to be a ferris wheel, which was actually a rotating rack of eyeglasses for customers to try on. Many residents, including Grandpa Hoveland, bought their reading glasses there rather than from an optometrist. Shelves and drawers were stacked along the wall nearly to the ceiling. A high stepladder that could be moved along a track allowed a clerk to reach desired items for the customer. On the right side of the store were swivel stools along a counter where women could sit and look at print dress material from bolts in many colors stored on shelves along the wall. After a decision was made on what print would look best for a farm or a Sunday church dress, Ona Lien or another clerk would measure the desired length and tear it off. Women sitting here would socialize with Ona and learn local news as well as buying "piece goods," spools of colored thread, and a Butterick or Vogue dress pattern.

Groceries were sold at the back of the store, which was the busiest place for customers. Clerks like Henry Nelson with his distinctive moustache (he always wore a necktie and white bib apron) stood behind the counter and wrote down on a pad what you wanted and then assembled those requested such as C&H sugar packages, Arm and Hammer baking powder, Karo syrup pails, Del Monte canned peas, Ivory soap, sauerkraut, Hills Bros coffee, and Copenhagen snuff (called snus) off the shelves and brought them to the counter. A long hooked stick allowed the clerk to pick items off the higher shelves. Nabisco cookies were dug by hand out of big boxes, pickles and apples out of barrels, and Pillsbury or Gold Medal flour was sold in 50-pound bags stacked on the floor. Most people baked their own bread instead of buying white flavorless Taystee bread from Eau Claire which Ma derisively called "bomull" or cotton. Small wooden pails contained pickled herring imported from Norway. Fresh sides of beef and pork were kept in a cooler and sawed or cut as needed by the customer. Hamburger, baloney, wieners, summer sausage, and liver sausage were also available.

In winter, frozen salmon and halibut from Washington state, and in late autumn and at Christmas dried slabs of lutefisk from Norway were available. Cheese selections were limited and generally cut from wheels of cheddar or Swiss. Few fresh vegetables and fruit were available. There was no ice cream or other frozen foods. Most important for a little boy was the glass front candy counter containing many kinds of loose candy, suckers, sticks of licorice and horehound, Baby Ruth, Butterfinger, and Hershey candy bars, and Wrigley's chewing gum which could be bought at one cent per stick. After the grocery list was totaled on the pad, the clerk gave the bill to the customer who took it to the bookkeeper sitting encircled on three sides by counters too high for a little boy to see up to the top. She took the bill and the money, totaled it on her noisy mechanical adding machine, and made change. Irene Hoff, an orphan who had grown up with the Ness family, was the pleasant lady who had this job for many years when I was a child. Going to the Farmers Store was always a big event with all sorts of nice smells and things to see. Farmers in their bib overalls liked to stand in the store, or outside on the steps during nice weather, spitting tobacco, visiting with each other (often in Norwegian) about politics, the weather, crops, and cows.

The Creamery

Across the street was the two-story creamery that made butter, with steam pouring out of pipes, the clang of milk cans, and surrounded by milk trucks waiting to unload during the morning hours. In the early 1930s, Chevrolet, Ford, or International trucks had wooden racks that held the cans on a flat bed, but later regulations required enclosed canopies to keep road dust off the milk cans. Milk truck drivers covered a set route each morning, collecting 10-gallon cans of milk from each farm and leaving empty clean cans to be filled. It was hard work as each full can of milk had to be lifted out of the tank of cold water and up on to the truck bed. At the creamery, cans had to be lifted off the truck and the milk dumped into a receiving tank, weighed, and samples collected for butterfat test. Then cans went through a hot water washer, and the clean empty cans with the correct number for each farm painted on the shoulder were collected and loaded onto the truck.

In nice weather it was pleasant work and often allowed the milk hauler to get the job done well before noon unless he had two routes. Winter was often another story, with bitter cold and snow drifts. Many drivers had small snow plows on the front of their trucks to clear driveways, but when a serious blizzard came, there was too much snow and farmers had to haul their cans to the main road with horses and a sleigh. Delays could make milk pickup take all day. During a big blizzard roads might remain unplowed so milk could not be collected for a day or two, thus the need for a farmer to have extra milk cans. In spring, gravel or dirt roads would have frost boils and mud with trucks bogging down and having to be pulled out by a farmer with horses or tractor. It was a seven-day-a-week job as milk was picked up daily unless roads had deep snow drifts. Milk truck drivers didn't get to attend church except for an afternoon funeral or wedding.

Milk truck driving was considered a glamorous job by farm kids in the 1930s. Drivers wore long leather bib aprons split and buckled around their legs to keep their overalls dry as they pulled wet milk cans out of cooling tanks. Shiny visor caps were often perched at an angle on their heads. Frugal drivers who saved their money often were able to buy their own truck and sometimes own several trucks. With all the heavy lifting they did, back problems were common. Drivers generally wore wide leather belts above their waists for back support, something we kids thought was impressive and added to their heroic stature.

After unloading milk, they parked their truck nearby and headed for the café next door for pie and coffee, or if it was around noon it would be a dinner of meat, potatoes, bread, butter, and canned peas, corn, or sauerkraut. Milk truck drivers typically sat and hashed over the day's news on their routes and exchanged jokes with other drivers. The café, owned at various times by Karl Hansen, Art Hansen, and Edmerald Olson, was a busy place, and waitresses hustled to feed the hungry crowd. The café gained a reputation for its huge rich malted milks, prepared at a marble soda fountain.

Just north of the creamery was Conrad Gilberts' Skelly gas station, a bustling place where the trucks were refueled, lubricated, tires fixed, and minor repairs made. Conrad was a short, cheery, hard-working man with a visor cap and leather bow tie who rushed around waiting on customers. At the gas pumps, everyone got full service on a vehicle—windshields washed, and oil, radiator, and tire pressure checked. It was fun for a little farm kid to stand and look at all this activity. Just inside the station, tires and small parts were stored in a room pungent with a rubber smell. Another room served as a local club house for farmers and retired men who sat in old Chevrolet or Ford bench seats to smoke, spit tobacco, exchange local gossip, and tell stories. In pleasant summer weather, they would often sit outside on benches and nail kegs.

Downtown

Down the street from the Sand Creek café was Henry Nelson's house, then the telephone exchange, and Bill Lyon's little white barber shop. Bill was a big talker and kept folks entertained as they sat in the barber chair. He was a heavy smoker and generally had a lighted cigarette parked on an ash tray as he worked. He was open for business six days a week. On Saturday evenings it was a busy place with lots of story telling as farmers came to town and shopped. I had my first haircut there, sitting on a board placed across the barber chair arms. I was scared stiff and cried, afraid of Bill's fast moving shears and the noisy electric shaver buzzing around my head. Bill liked to have a glass or two of wine each day so kept a number of bottles stored in a cabinet. One Saturday evening as he was closing up the shop, several young men who often played tricks on Bill came in and said that this time they wanted to do something decent for him. They brought several bottles of wine and suggested they drink them together. Bill was surprised, but enjoyed an evening of free wine and conversation. On Monday, Bill went to his wine cabinet for a drink and found it empty. He was furious; his generous Saturday night friends had somehow pilfered his wine and then enjoyed drinking it with him.

Next door was an old two-story building where Selmer Severson operated a grocery store. Selmer grew up on a poor sandy dairy farm in the Pine Creek area across the Red Cedar River. Life was hard during the Depression, but Selmer managed to leave the farm and borrow enough money to start a store in this old empty building. He and his wife Beatrice worked long hours and prospered, aided by being the only grocery store in town that gave short-term credit, which was mighty attractive to many poor people at that time. Of course, his prices were higher than the Farmers Store which did not give credit. Selmer, a quiet friendly man, was frugal and "squeezed the nickel mighty hard" as folks would say. One day, Edsel Peterson was chatting with him in the store when Selmer suddenly stopped talking and dashed around the end of the counter to pounce on a penny he'd spotted on the floor. He held it up, asking if Edsel had dropped it. He replied, "No." Selmer unlocked the cash drawer and dropped in the penny, all the while whistling a happy tune. Selmer did well, managing to buy a house and an airplane which he enjoyed flying. Later he took a trip to Norway. He also learned to play a violin and enjoyed performing for folks.

On the other side of the street next door to the Farmers Store was an empty lot and then the Bank of New Auburn, Sand Creek Branch. Margaret Anderson, a tall, lean spinster lady with glasses, was the manager, teller, and accountant.

This is where Pa did his bank business, depositing milk checks and any others from his threshing, saw milling, lumber sales, and land breaking businesses. At an early age, Pa had me bring the pennies, nickels and dimes from my small cast-iron lion savings bank to Margaret where I opened a savings account and received a pass book to record future savings and interest from my tiny accumulation of money. Another room served the bank and other local folks for business meetings. During tax season, Margaret's father, Oscar Anderson, the township tax assessor, held court here for farmers to come and discuss their tax assessments with him.

Adjacent to the bank was Uncle Art's garage where he repaired cars and trucks. Outside, were two Standard Oil Red Crown gas pumps with big colored glass crowns on the tops. Gas was pumped by a handle on one side of the pump. A wooden bench stood outside, inviting folks to sit and visit in nice weather. Just inside through the wide double doors on the left was the office filled with auto parts, fan belts, tires, inner tubes, a desk piled with papers, a large ash tray filled with cigar butts and pipe ashes, two old leather car seats for folks to sit and talk while spitting tobacco into several old metal oil cans. The place appeared to have been cleaned rarely, although the worn unpainted wood floor was occasionally swept by sons Toddy or Billy.

The main part of the building had one room where a few cars awaiting repair were parked, and some others that obviously had not been moved for quite awhile. The next room at the rear was the repair shop with several cars or trucks in various stages of repair. The concrete floor had an uneven, thick layer of old grease and dirt, that had accumulated over many years. The place was a shambles with wrenches, hammers, screwdrivers, electric drills, and old parts scattered in disarray on tables and counters. It was a wonder that Uncle Art could find anything.

Uncle Art was a large bulky man with a ruddy face who filled out his greasy bib overalls and wore a grimy cloth visor cap. He usually looked like he needed a shave. Uncle Art was a jovial man with a fine sense of humor who was a good mechanic so he had no lack of customers. Unfortunately, he was an alcoholic and sometimes had days when he wasn't in shape to do repairs. During Prohibition, he had a fellow deliver bootleg booze which he shared with other folks. He never had any money to buy a house so his family moved around and lived in various rental places. His drinking problem got worse in the late 1930s and eventually ruined the business; so he and Aunt Vearl moved to Indiana where he worked in a machinery factory during World War II. Eventually he moved to Homestead in south Florida to join their two sons who lived there.

Next along the street lived Oscar and Ona Lien and their blonde daughter, Beulah. Oscar, a tall, lean ruddy-faced fellow, was the service man for the local telephone company and known as "Lien the line man." He was a crusty, independent, outspoken fellow who sometimes irritated telephone customers. Ona was a large, buxom, blonde lady who worked at the Farmers Store. Oscar lived frugally but he had one indulgence; he would buy a new Chrysler car every few years even though he put few miles on it.

A tiny house between the Lien's and Grandpa Hoveland was occupied by Carl and Magda Trosvig who had retired there after a life of farming. Sand Creek had a number of retired farmers who had worked hard, lived frugally, and saved for retirement among old friends. Other retired farm couples lived in a second house on the farm they loved, sometimes helping their son and wife in farm tasks. It was a common sense solution since there were no retirement homes at that time. There was a county poor farm at Menomonie for

40

indigent old folks, but most people felt it was a disgrace to end one's days there.

Grandpa and Grandma Hoveland

Grandpa and Grandma Hoveland owned a two-story white board house with a garage, an outdoor toilet, wood-shed, and a small unused barn. A cast-iron water pump was near the back door. Grandpa (often called Bestefar as we conversed in Norwegian) was a large erect, ruddy-cheeked man with thick silver-speckled hair and a splendid sense of humor that showed in his twinkling eyes. Grandpa sat in a rocking chair by a kitchen window, often drinking coffee and visiting with old farmer friends who were in town. Everyone knew Grandpa, and many stopped at the house for a visit with him. He did not use snus but enjoyed the occasional cigar furnished by a visitor. In warm weather he sat in an arm chair on the back porch entertaining visitors.

As a little kid, I would often sit in his lap while we talked Norwegian and he entertained me with stories of his six-week trip crossing the Atlantic in a sailing ship, and old days in Sand Creek. He had some scary tales, too, such as laying out dead folks in the wooden coffins he made and how some of the corpses moved. Grandpa was interested in all sorts of things and always had plenty of time for me when we came to town. At some point during most visits, he pulled a long soft leather purse out of his pants pocket and opened the metal clasp top, reached in and pulled out a nickel for me to get an ice cream cone. This was a real treat as I rarely had ice cream, and it was my favorite dessert.

There were three places in town to buy an ice cream cone: the café, Worman's IGA, or Selmer Severson's across the street. One soon learned which place had the biggest ice cream cones; it usually was the café where the waitress behind the old marble soda fountain counter laid on a big cone of rich Gustafson's ice cream. In addition to the usual vanilla, chocolate, and strawberry, they often had special flavors like butter pecan, cherry, and black raspberry. Receiving one of Grandpa's nickels was a memorable event for a little boy during the Depression.

Grandpa spoke English but his reading skills were poor. Reading was easier in his native language so he subscribed to the "Skandinavian," a Norwegian-language weekly newspaper published in Minneapolis, and read it with his Farmers Store reading glasses. Others in the community subscribed to the weekly Norwegian newspaper "Decorah Posten" from Decorah, Iowa, which contained the popular comic strip Ola and Per written in immigrant-style mixed Norwegian and English.

Grandma, a lean lady with beautiful silver white hair in a bun, was severe and dutiful; always cooking, baking, mending, or knitting. Grandma was most comfortable speaking in Norwegian but conversed adequately in English. She read a little English and could write with difficulty. Grandma was not much fun. Best of all was when she was busy baking lefsa. This Norwegian delicacy was commonly made during the winter months and especially around Christmas. Dough made of mashed potatoes, flour, and milk was rolled thin on the kitchen table with a ribbed rolling pin, then floured, and the big sheets lifted with a wood lefsa turner onto the top of a wood stove where it was browned, then flipped over to do the other side. Hot lefsa from the stove, spread with butter, and then rolled up into a tube was heavenly eating. Many people put sugar on their lefsa, but I liked mine with just butter. Grandma Hoveland was the best lefsa maker in our family. Ma was not much of a lefsa maker, so we usually got our supply from my two grandmas.

Grandpa and Grandma Hoveland had over twenty-five years of retirement living in Sand Creek after they left the farm. Because Grandpa was an enterprising fellow and had saved money, he was relatively prosperous by Sand Creek standards. He was a generous man and had loaned money for farm mortgages. Some of these farmers went broke in the Depression, resulting in Grandpa owning several less than desirable sand farms. Fortunately, he continued to receive dividends on Farmers Store stock, which he had held since the formation of the company in the late 1800s. Grandpa died peacefully in 1951 at age ninety-three, having never spent a day in a hospital. At Grandma's death a year later, their estate was a little over $4,000. Their savings and frugality had given them a long, satisfying life with freedom from want.

South Sand Creek

Down the hill the street ended, and side streets went left and right. Mrs. Worman's IGA grocery store, containing the post office, was located at this point. The road to the right went across the river, while the one to the left passed Ingolf Hansen's gas station and trucking business. Just across the creek were two little former shops now combined into a residence. Next, just off the street, was Ole Engen's carpenter shop. Ole was a skilled craftsman who could make fine furniture, but there was no demand for this in Sand Creek, so he made a living making and repairing single trees, implement tongues, and other wood parts on farm machinery or buildings. Because Pa respected his skills, he had him make my first pair of skis. They were beautifully finished and served me well.

Turning south past Karl Hansen's house and dairy barn, one came to Tom Iverson's blacksmith shop where Pa made frequent visits during spring and fall to get shares for the moldboard plow reworked. Worn plow shares were not thrown away, but brought here so the blacksmith could weld on a new strip and extend the life of this tool. Tom was a good-natured, husky, ruddy-faced man with snow white hair. It was a busy place with Tom and another worker in blackened overalls standing by anvils pounding hammers noisily on hot iron from the forge. Adding to the scene was the sizzle of dipping a hot item into water to harden it, amid the smells of an acetylene wedding torch and coal burning in the forge. Across the street was the Iverson house and the parsonage for the pastor of Our Saviour's Lutheran Church west of Sand Creek. Near the end of town lived Ludvig and Hannah Gustum where they raised two husky sons who later started a plumbing business. Ludvig, a cheerful, kind man, was a talented hard-working carpenter well liked for his skills. Melvin Nelson's farm with a big, round, white barn was at the end of town past which the road headed south two miles to Highway 64. A little side street went past the Woodman hall and more homes before passing Bert and Clifford Nelson's farm on the way to New Auburn.

How We Lived

Food

Family life was centered in our farm house. As I grew older, the names I used to address my parents changed from "Papa" to "Pa" and "Mama" to "Ma" as was common in our community. I was always called "Carl" except when I had been naughty and then Ma called me "Carl Soren" with strong emphasis on my middle name. Pa was a timely man, controlled by the clock, and expected others in our family to be the same. Thus, the most important object in our house was a large Seth Thomas clock in our dining room. It was held in great respect by me, and I knew that when it was 5:15 pm Pa would immediately rise from his leather rocking chair to depart for the barn to milk the cows. Pa always carried an Elgin pocket watch in the bib pocket of his overalls and consulted it frequently during the day. Meals were at a set time. Dinner was exactly at noon when Pa came in from the fields. He quickly shoveled in the food before sitting five or ten minutes, to clean his teeth with a toothpick before abruptly heading out the door to work. Ma was much less inclined to live by the clock, but she had no choice in this household. On the rare times when she missed having food ready on the minute, it was not a pleasant scene. I preferred Ma's more leisurely approach, but soon conformed to Pa's system and became a timely person though not a slave to the clock.

Food was an important part of our day. We ate five times a day: breakfast, mid-morning coffee, dinner at noon, mid-afternoon coffee, and supper at night. If someone was visiting us in the evening, coffee, cookies, cake, and sometimes sandwiches would be served. With our high caloric intake, it was fortunate that hard physical work was a large part of our lives. Breakfast consisted of bread, butter, fried or boiled eggs, fried potatoes, sometimes sausage or bacon, and always coffee. As a child I often had hot "Malt-o-meal" oatmeal, or sometimes, "Wheaties." I didn't drink coffee like Ma and Pa so I had one or two glasses of whole unpasteurized milk with a "cowy" flavor. Often, cake or pie was available. Sometimes we had pancakes or waffles with maple or cane syrup. Morning and afternoon 'coffee' was a cheese or meat sandwich and cake or cookies eaten in the kitchen if Pa was working nearby, but if he was in the field, it was carried in a lunch box with a thermos for the coffee. Dinner typically was fried or roast beef or pork, fried or boiled potatoes, maybe canned rutabagas, peas or corn, bread and butter, and for dessert we often had home canned sweet fruit sauce and sometimes cake or pie. Water and coffee were also served.

Supper was often a repeat of noon, or we might have pickled herring, blood sausage, or liver with potatoes. Ma and Pa loved liver, but I couldn't stand it, especially pork liver, which has such a strong taste. Liver sausage, and especially homemade black evil-looking blood sausage, were in the same category for me. I looked forward to suppers where Ma fixed a hot casserole dish we all called "Dago" which was a mix of pasta shells or tubes, canned tomatoes, hamburger, onion, bay leaves, and oregano. Pa wanted potatoes on his plate three times a day, served boiled, fried, and occasionally mashed, but rarely baked. Sweet potatoes were a special treat usually reserved for a holiday. Bread and butter were always on the table and so was a jar of home-canned jam or jelly. Vegetables were served occasionally, mainly canned green peas or corn. I hated rutabagas and boiled cabbage, favorites of Ma and Pa. Fried onions and sauerkraut were both a treat for me. Salads were non-existent except when prepared for company when Ma served chopped apples, walnuts, and raisins in whipped cream. Lettuce did not exist at our house. Occasionally, we would have milk mush for supper, one of my favorites, smothered with butter, sugar, and cinnamon.

Chicken was not a common item on our table, maybe because it involved such effort. Ma and I would go out to the chicken house and catch an old hen; then I would grab the legs and hold its neck on a stump and chop off the head. The blood would spurt out and I hoped the neck didn't turn and spray me. Sometimes I let go, and the headless chicken would go hopping away for some distance, spraying blood all over until it collapsed. Then, Ma would pick it up and dunk it into a hot pail of water to loosen the feathers so we could pluck that stinking mess. Hot chicken feathers have a sickening smell. Next, Ma would remove the insides, saving the heart, gizzard, and liver which she loved to eat. I hated eating innards. After cutting up the chicken, she would dust it with flour and seasoning, then fry it. Other times she would bake it in the oven or boil it. When we had some old chickens that weren't laying eggs, Ma would have a chicken slaughter day for canning. Pa hated this job as much as I did. After a day of chicken killing, feather plucking, and gutting, we all smelled bad and were in no mood at supper to eat chicken. Baloney sandwiches were a better bet then.

Fish was my favorite food. When I caught sunfish or rock bass and occasionally black bass in the nearby Red Cedar River, I gladly dressed them for Ma to fry. Pa shared my love for fish but Ma was less enthusiastic. Occasionally, in years when there was a bit more money, we ʼ ᵊnjoy frozen halibut or salmon from the Farmers Stor
ter. During the worst of the Depression, mar
would spear fish from the river at night. Spe

but we consoled ourselves because money was hard to come by and there were plenty of fish in the river, so the law was to be ignored. We never saw a game warden and I knew of no one being arrested for spearing. I, often with Bennie Myran, would illegally spear suckers in the Red Cedar at night using an underwater light. It was easy to see them and get a nice harvest of fish. Suckers, a large fish, were normally ignored for food by many people as bones were scattered throughout the abundant flesh. However, suckers provided an opportunity to make our own fish balls instead of wishing for unaffordable canned ones from Norway. We would grind suckers in a power meat grinder, mix the finely ground flesh and bones with some mashed potatoes, form them into balls, and can them for future suppers where they were served in a butter cream sauce with dill and boiled potatoes. I looked forward to these delicious sucker fish ball meals with great pleasure.

We ate a lot of bread with our main meals and in morning and afternoon sandwiches as well as my school lunch box. Ma baked bread once a week, a big task using Pillsbury flour, water, and Fleischman's dry yeast cakes. Baking was done in the wood-fired cook stove where one needed experience to know how much wood to put in the firebox to have a suitable oven temperature. Fresh hot bread from the oven generously covered with butter was always a treat, but was less appealing by the end of a week. Old dry bread was used to make French toast or milk toast for breakfast. A special treat for Pa was to buy a pint of cream from the creamery and pour this over slices of dry bread, then sprinkle brown sugar on top of it. Cream and bread, an old Norwegian tradition, were eaten by many older people like Grandpa Hoveland, but I never learned to appreciate it. During hot humid summer weather, mold would develop on the bread. Ma would cut off the exterior mold but it imparted an unpleasant smell and flavor to the remaining bread. We ate it anyway. Spreading strawberry, blackberry, or raspberry jam on it helped.

Ma made a lot of cakes as they were a staple both in everyday eating as well as feeding drop-in company. Basic pan cakes were chocolate, white, spice, devil's food, and lemon, all topped with a frosting. Angel food was a fancy round cake for special company. Basic cookies were molasses, white sour cream, oatmeal, or sometimes chocolate brownies or date bars. Pies were made from home-canned fruit such as blueberry, apple, peach, blackberry, and rhubarb. An important dessert item was home-canned fruit sauces, just called "sauce," made from plums, prunes, apples, pears, blackberries, blueberries, raspberries, or rhubarb, which was commonly known as pie plant. These very sweet fruit sauces, served in a small dish at the end of a meal, were a common dessert on most tables in the area. Rhubarb sauce was especially relished except by a few people like me who found the oxalic acid unpleasant as it had a tart taste that puckered my mouth.

We didn't realize that our high intake of sugar caused a lot of dental cavities. The problem was made worse because we never brushed our teeth. Pa and Ma never used a toothbrush, and I didn't until I began occasionally using one while in high school. We never went to a dentist until we had tooth cavities that caused pain. Toothaches were common with adults and children. Delayed dental care often resulted in extraction of teeth at an early age. Most old people, and some in middle age, had lost all their teeth and wore dentures or "false teeth."

Clothing

Our clothes were simple. Pa and I wore blue denim bib overalls and blue long-sleeved chambray shirts. We never had short-sleeved shirts, but rolled up our long sleeves in summer. Some men wore striped overalls. Underneath we wore cotton undershorts. A wide-brimmed straw hat was always worn in summer. In winter we wore long wool underwear that itched. For the barn or field, we wore a denim overall jacket that could be unlined or lined with cotton flannel. When it was really cold, we wore a heavy wool mackinaw that was rough and scratched my tender neck and cheeks. A wool cap with ear flaps was essential. After starting school I wore barn overalls for milking and other chores, then changed to newer clean overalls for school. When we went to town, we put on new overalls. Uncle Sophus often wore a necktie and white dress shirt with his new overalls when visiting neighbors on a Sunday afternoon. As overalls aged, Ma patched holes with denim cut from old overalls. It was common to see farmers working in overalls covered with patches. Cotton and wool socks were darned to fill holes. For church, Pa would wear a suit and necktie. Since I rarely had a suit until I was confirmed, I wore pants, shirt and a sweater if needed. I had a heavy coat for school and church. Pa wore work shoes all week except for dress shoes at church. In winter, high buckled rubber overshoes were worn. During the Depression years I often did not have a pair of dress shoes as I would grow out of them before they were worn out.

Ma wore shapeless cotton print dresses for everyday wear. She put on a "barn dress" when she was milking cows or doing other outside farm chores. Some women wore men's overalls when milking or doing other farm work, but Ma never did. When picking blueberries or blackberries Ma would wear a pair of Pa's overalls. She thought women should not wear pants and was critical of those who did. Ma had only a few fancy dresses for church or visiting people. She had one winter coat. Women wore hats to church, so Ma had a winter hat and a summer hat. A scarf or wool cap was worn on the head when it was cold. She usually had only a few pair of shoes for work and dress. Our clothing expenditures were low.

Cleanliness

Washing clothes was a big job, usually done every couple of weeks, and generally less often in winter when we wore soiled clothes longer because they didn't get sweaty and dirty as in summer. In winter we often wore the same long under-wear, socks, and shirts all week. In summer, especially when sweating hard during haying or threshing, we changed clothes more often. Ma was lucky that we were on the electric line and owned a gray Maytag square-tub wringer washing ma-chine. On wash day, she wheeled the washer into the center of the kitchen, set up a bench with two rinse tubs on it, and went to work. Washed and rinsed clothes were squeezed and then tossed into the woven wood basket, carried outside, and hung on the clothes line with wooden clothes pins. On a sunny summer day, it could be pleasant as the clothes dried fast, especially with a breeze. Ironing was a big job as cotton clothing of that era wrinkled badly and needed a lot of press-ing. In winter, washing was an awful job as one waded through often deep snow to hang up clothes that quickly froze on the line. Then, Ma carried frozen boards of overalls, shirts, and long underwear back to the house and hung them on folding wood racks to thaw out and dry.

Our personal cleanliness left something to be desired by today's standards. Daily cleansing consisted of washing one's hands, face, and neck in the entry room basin. Deodorants were unknown. Pa used to shave once or twice a week using a safety razor. Not having a bathtub with running water, we used a round galvanized wash tub filled with hot water from the wood stove reservoir. Baths were taken in the stairs hallway where doors could be closed for privacy. Also, there was a heat register from the furnace so this room was warm in winter. Often, Pa and I used the same bath water to avoid having to dump and refill the tub twice. Usually, in summer we had a bath on Saturday night unless the river was warm enough for us to drive down and wash ourselves off with soap while wearing our swim suits. Sometimes we would visit the river two or three times a week for baths.

During bitter cold winter weather, our tub baths might come only at two- or three-week intervals. Ice and snow had to be scraped or pounded off the tub before it could be brought from the back stoop into the house. When the ice cold tub was filled with warm water, the icy tub rim could give one's back a jolt while sitting in the warm water. Taking a bath involved a lot of effort, especially in winter. Ma and I wanted a bathroom so badly and told Pa how much he would like it too. His usual answer was that times were hard and bathrooms didn't make any money for us to live on. In the late 1930s and early 1940s when we were more prosperous, Pa's answer was that we might not be on the farm too many more years so it didn't pay to invest that much money in a bathroom. Ma and I didn't think much of his reasoning as we still wanted a bathroom! Pa never installed a bathroom on the farm. It was one of the first things the new owner installed after he bought our farm.

Toilets

We, like nearly all other farmers at that time, lacked indoor toilets so had an outside privy, politely referred to as the toilet. Other, more colorful names were used in casual conversation. Pa and I did not use the toilet to pee; when near the house we emptied our bladders more conveniently in a private place on the north side of our garage. Persons making a visit to the toilet to defecate usually said they were going to "take a dump" although more crude words were also used.

Toilets varied a great deal from rather elaborate, clean, well-painted structures to crude unpainted shacks that were rarely cleaned so stunk to high heaven, especially on a hot day. Our toilet behind two large honeysuckle bushes was a well made, painted building with two holes in the wood bench. A hinged door opened at the rear to facilitate cleaning out the accumulation of feces and catalogue paper. We did this several times a year, a most unpleasant job. Some people spread this stuff on a field, but we buried ours in a hole to avoid having catalogue pages blowing around the farm. Small screened openings in the wall provided light for the occupant. Toilet paper rolls were rarely used on farms. Several old thick Sears Roebuck, Montgomery Ward, or Spiegel catalogues were tucked into a wall holder. This paper served two purposes, wiping oneself and providing recreational reading during one's meditations. On a warm day with crickets chirping and birds singing outside, it could be pleasant for the occupant to sit and peruse catalogue pictures of bicycles, tools, toys, tires, sewing machines, chicks, and models outfitted in the latest clothing styles.

There were several potential hazards for the sitter. In summer, yellow jackets could be nesting in the toilet or feasting on excreta and might decide to sting one's exposed rear end. In winter, frost often formed on the seat and added to the stimulation of exposing one's bare rear end to 20 below zero or lower temperatures. One did not linger long under those conditions. During extreme cold periods, Ma used a chamber pot in the bedroom which had to be emptied daily outside. Pa and I had an advantage in that we could quickly go outside just before bedtime and empty our bladders in the snow. The only problem was that Ma hated seeing yellow urine splotches in the snow right near the house where day-time visitors would see our imprint. She tried to get us to pee farther away where it would be less visible, but that meant a longer walk in extreme cold. Pa and I usually won on that except when we knew special company was coming and then I had to shovel snow over our yellow art work. Another approach was to take care of our excretory functions in the warm barn squatting in the straw of an empty stall. That meant that we needed to keep another catalogue in the barn during winter.

Coffee

Coffee was a necessity in our Norwegian culture. It is surprising that this addictive stimulant beverage, native to the tropical highlands of Ethiopia and popularized by Arabs should have been adopted to such an extent by the Nordic peoples. Even today, the Nordic countries have some of the highest per capita consumption of coffee in the world. The Norwegian immigrants in America arrived with a strong taste for coffee which remained with them.

In the Sand Creek community, coffee was an essential part of any table setting. Coffee was served at breakfast, din-ner, supper, and two or three additional times each day. Any social occasion required coffee. Virtually all adults consumed coffee, and children often started drinking coffee liberally mixed with milk at an early age. As a result, consumption was very high. I was unusual in that I did not care for coffee as a child and rarely drank it as an adult until later in life. Several brands of coffee were available in stores, but Hills

Brothers in bright red cans was the dominant one in our area. When serving company, hostesses would often mix egg with the ground coffee as a special treat. Coffee time was a sacramental occasion in our community.

Tobakk

Tobacco, or "Tobakk" as Norwegians called it, was used by most men in the community. Tobacco had been grown for their own use by early settlers around Sand Creek. As a child, I recall tobacco being grown in tiny fields just north of Colfax. The main tobacco production area was located in southern Wisconsin, all done by Norwegian farmers. Around Sand Creek, tobacco was a staple of life and an essential part of grocery shopping. Overwhelmingly, tobacco meant "snus," pronounced "snoose." Snus was finely ground moist tobacco in a flat round Copenhagen can. When the metal lid was lifted, it exuded a pungent aroma as a man dipped a pinch between two fingers and inserted it between gums and cheek of either upper or lower jaw and sometimes both. As saliva moistened it, a sharp kick of nicotine flowed into the user's body to give him a good feeling. Swallowing a mouthful of spit was a revolting experience unless one was used to it. Confirmed snus addicts said that swallowing it didn't bother them at all. They must have had strong stomachs.

Brown bits of tobacco remained between teeth and gums among users even without a pinch of Copenhagen in their cheek. A side effect was spitting brown snus saliva, some of which usually remained on lips of the spitter. Some spitters were distinguished by brown spit seeping down from the corners of their mouth to the chin. Men with beards were even worse with browned facial hair around their mouths. It is difficult to imagine a woman enjoying kissing one of these fellows. But then, Norwegian couples didn't normally express much romantic ardor in public. Spitters always sprayed some on themselves, something apparent when they wore white shirts to church. One did not walk on the grass near the steps leading up to the door of Zion Lutheran church as it would be littered with spit clumps of tobacco from the mouths of men deposited before they went in for morning worship. It was even more unsightly in winter when the tobacco offering was displayed on the snow. It was all a disgusting spectacle.

It was easy to understand why women did not use snus; they smelled and tasted enough of it from their menfolk. Wives had to be tolerant to put up with men having brown mouths, a strong snus smell, and their frequent spitting. In the house, they had a spittoon or can on the floor with a newspaper underneath to catch spit that missed the container. Spittoons were available in banks and other public places. Outside of businesses and along sidewalks in town, brown splotches of tobacco spit were common.

Cars and trucks created a special problem for spitters. In summer, they could drive with the window open and spit outside. One soon learned as a child riding in the back seat just behind the driver not to sit too close to the open rear window as spit might hit one in the face. Of course, there would be a nice spatter of tobacco spit on the driver's car or truck door. If this was not washed off frequently, the paint would be damaged, indicating the corrosive effect of tobacco juice. During colder weather when windows were frozen shut or kept closed, the driver spat into a can held in his hand or on the floor. This worked reasonably well unless the spit can was on the floor and tipped over. Tobacco spitters could be a hazard for the person riding in the seat next to the driver as I discovered once as a boy. We were in northern Minnesota visiting Pa's old foreman in the logging camp where he had worked. Pa and Uncle Art were riding in the back seat while I was up front with this man driving a new Chevrolet car. Chewing tobacco, he spit on the floor with relatively poor aim as the car bounced around on a rough dirt road.Tobacco juice sprayed on the dash and also on my clothes even as I tried to sit close to the right door. It was not an enjoyable ride.

As a small child, I recall Pa and his snus addiction, probably acquired at age sixteen when he started working winters in logging camps. Finally, Ma had enough of it and prevailed upon him to quit. Surprisingly, he finally listened to her and broke the habit although it was a struggle. Snus is highly addictive and it is not easy to stop using it. From heavy snus consumption, he substituted smoking a pipe during the evening when at home and a cigar on special occasions. In later years, he said the pungent smell of snus always made him miss it. I was so glad that my Pa didn't use snus any more.

Snus consumption was considered a passage to maturity in becoming a man. Boys had to experiment with it to show others they could handle it. The first big pinch in the mouth gave a good nicotine jolt as it was powerful stuff. Of course experimenting in a group they would continue consuming more snus which soon gave them nausea and often induced vomiting. This first experience could be wretched, but most boys would continue trying snus until they finally could handle it. I tried it once and that was enough to convince me that it was wretched stuff. I apparently never became a real man as I had no urge to master snus!

It was easy to spot snus users. Most carried a Copenhagen can in the bib pocket of their overalls, leaving a distinct circle in the denim. Others carried their can in a rear overall pocket where it left the same mark. Snus users bought a gray paper-wrapped roll of Copenhagen cans at the Farmers Store to replenish their supply. Although most men were snus users, some chewed tobacco. Most carried a soft pouch of Beech Nut or Plow Boy chewing tobacco in a back pocket of their overalls. This loosely cut tobacco was heavily flavored with a sweet syrup, which improved the smell and taste, as well as reducing the sharp bite of snus. Tobacco chewers produced more saliva so were better at spitting than snus users. As a child it was interesting to watch expert spitters hit their target with remarkable aim. Our neighbor, John Harrington, was one of the best and enjoyed showing off his skill to me. Pipe smoking was less convenient to use while working at many farm jobs. Still, there were quite a few men who carried a tin of Prince Albert or Velvet or a pouch of Raleigh smoking tobacco in the top pocket of their bib overalls and would light up between farm jobs or when talking to friends at the store. Some used hard composition pipes, but many stuck to old fashioned corn cob pipes. I always thought pipe smoke smelled a lot better than cigarettes.

Nearly all of my male relatives used tobacco. Most of my uncles used snus. Uncles Arnold and Fritjof next door kept a big red can of Prince Albert smoking tobacco in the house to make hand-rolled cigarettes and also to stuff in their mouths for chewing. Pa's Uncle George was one of the most impressive tobacco users. After eating, he would load his mouth with tobacco for several hours of work outside. From a big metal can of George Washington chewing tobacco he would stuff big wads in both his cheeks, then sprinkle snus on top. With cheeks bulging, it was difficult to understand him when he talked but he was an expert spitter. Other great tobacco chewers were cousin Julian Hanson, Uncle Art Hoveland, Pa's uncles Ole Hoveland and Dave Bonkrude, who had especially good aim when they spit. All of my male cousins used tobacco, mostly cigarettes, although most quit later in life. In our neighborhood, the only male non-tobacco users were Norman Anderson, Leonard Toycen, and Andrew and

Oscar Myran. There were several others in the Sand Creek area, but they were few.

Cigarette smoking was confined to younger men and increased greatly during the 1930s. Tobacco use among women was almost non-existent in the early 1930s. Thurina Myran smoked a corn cob pipe. I heard of several women who smoked cigarettes, but I never saw them smoke in public. One time I was at Selmer Severson's store and saw a young Thompson woman buy a couple packs of cigarettes which surprised me. I always hated the irritating stink of cigarette smoke and wondered why anyone wanted to suck that vile stuff into their lungs. Several of my cousins tried to introduce me to the delights of cigarettes, but I never succumbed.

Cigars cost more so were reserved for special times. Pa liked to smoke a King Edward cigar on Sunday afternoon. When our income got a little better, he would sometimes buy Dutch Masters cigars which cost more, but the second-hand smoke smelled a lot better to me than King Edwards. Cigars were commonly smoked by men when families got together for dinners or weddings. When Uncle Sewell and Aunt Mabel from Chippewa Falls drove up for a Sunday visit, he would always bring Pa some cigars so they would puff away together in the living room after dinner. By our standards, Uncle Sewell was prosperous as he was Chippewa County assistant highway commissioner. When we were invited to Sunday dinner with Uncle John and Aunt Laura with their seven grown sons, it was a lively affair. After dinner, cigars would be distributed and soon the living room would be blue with smoke as they told stories and laughed together. It was always a jovial affair at their house. Fathers of a new baby were expected to hand out cigars to other men. At a wedding reception it was customary to have cigars available for each man attending. Cigars were an important part of the celebration. I even saw some women puff on the cigar of a male companion during wedding festivities.

Tobacco was a close companion for most Sand Creek men of that era. Once hooked, they rarely ever quit. Even during the hard days of the Depression, money was available for snus, chewing tobacco, and even cigarettes. Camel, Lucky Strike and Chesterfield cigarettes were relatively expensive; so cheap brands such as Marvel appeared on the market and sold for as little as ten cents. Many didn't even buy cheap brands but bought cans of Prince Albert or Velvet tobacco and rolled their own cigarettes, twisting the ends to keep the tobacco from falling out. One can only guess what effect the high tobacco consumption had on health of male tobacco users around Sand Creek. Surely it must have increased the incidence of mouth, stomach, and lung cancers. No one worried about it during those years when tobacco was such an integral part of our culture.

Neighbors

Myrans

It was a community of small dairy farms, so neighbors lived in close proximity to each other. Our closest neighbors were the Myran family just across the road to the west of our farm. They were an extended family of eight adults living in a white wood-siding house with screen porches on both the front and back entrances. The elderly parents, Ole and Thurina, would often sit on a sofa smoking their corn cob pipes and refilling them from a pan of loose tobacco between them. Betsy, a thin, elderly spinster sister who wore drab-colored long dresses, helped in the house and was referred to as "Tante" or aunt. Of the children, only Minnie married, and she lived on a farm near Colfax with her husband Guy and four daughters. Andrew and Annie did the farming on the place. Andrew was a short spare fellow with a big Adam's apple and a small head that bobbled around as he talked or laughed. His overalls seemed to be several sizes too big as they hung on his thin frame. They both milked cows and performed other barn chores while Andrew did much of the field work. Annie had tightly bobbed hair and was always dressed in blue bib overalls, blue chambray shirt, and heavy laced high-top boots usually spattered with cow manure. Her overalls were rolled up to mid-calf, and the legs were usually shiny and hard from milk that had spilled on them during hand milking of the cows. The only time I ever saw Annie wearing a dress was at a funeral.

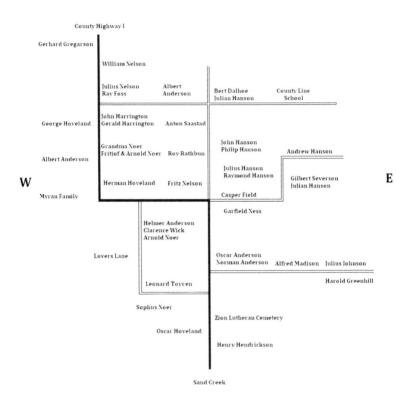

N

County Highway I

Gerhard Gregarson

William Nelson

Julius Nelson   Albert
Ray Foss   Anderson   Bert Dalhoe   County Line
                                       Julian Hanson   School

John Harrington
George Hoveland   Gerald Harrington   Anton Saastad

Grandma Noer   John Hanson
Fritjof & Arnold Noer   Roy Rathbun   Philip Hanson   Andrew Hanson
Albert Anderson
                                        Julius Hanson
                                        Raymond Hanson   Gilbert Severson
W   Herman Hoveland   Fritz Nelson   **E**
                                                           Julian Hanson
Myran Family   Casper Field

                                        Garfield Ness

                   Helmer Anderson
                   Clarence Wick
                   Arnold Noer

                   Lovers Lane   Oscar Anderson
                                        Norman Anderson   Alfred Madison   Julius Johnson

                                                                           Harold Greenhill
                   Leonard Toycen

                   Sophus Noer
                                        Zion Lutheran Cemetery
                   Oscar Hoveland
                                        Henry Hendrickson

                   Sand Creek

S

My World
Owners of farms in our area during my childhood

Oscar, a tall emaciated man, was the intellectual in the family. He didn't work on the farm or do much else except visit with people and think about all sorts of things. He was proficient at arithmetic and had developed tables for scaling logs to determine their lumber content. Pa used a set of the tables at his sawmill and was impressed with Oscar's ability. Oscar died young from tuberculosis in spite of drinking goat milk which his mother Thurina believed would help him. His brother Bennie was a stocky man with black hair and beard stubble, who always wore greasy overalls. A jovial face reflected his good sense of humor and kind gentle nature. Everyone liked Bennie. Bennie didn't do any farm work but operated a shop near the barn where he repaired farm machinery and did welding for other farmers. All sorts of junk machinery surrounded the shop, and a nearby shed was filled with old machinery and several old dust-covered cars in which I played as a child. It was an interesting place to visit when Pa was there to get a part welded with the acetylene torch. In later years, Bennie started a sawmill closer to the river and powered it with a Case steam engine that he loved to operate. Bennie took pride in owning a big car like an old Packard or LaSalle.

Bessie, a warm-hearted, lean lady who wore her hair in a bun and usually wore a simple dark long dress, worked hard cooking, cleaning, and washing clothes for this big household. She knew a lot of local history and genealogy, corresponded with relatives in Norway, and enjoyed the wild flowers that grew on the farm. Bessie had to do all the housework in a house that had no running water, cook on a wood stove, and entertain many coffee guests each day. Consequently, house cleaning was not a high priority. The house lacked modern conveniences except for ceiling electric lights, and personal needs were met in a two-hole toilet behind the house. The social center was a large dining room that opened to the back door where visitors were welcomed for morning or afternoon coffee served by Bessie in old brown-cracked mugs along with cookies or fresh doughnuts.

As a small child I loved running over to the Myrans to sit with all the adults around the big table covered with figured oilcloth. A sofa and other worn chairs provided seating elsewhere in the room for the big family and the many guests who wandered in. A big black dog always greeted guests before returning to his place on the blanket-covered leather sofa flecked with dog hair. Conversation was usually in Norwegian and covered local events, humorous stories, and weather. It was a jolly place, and the members of the family genuinely loved each other. Ma liked the Myrans, but disliked eating there as she doubted their cleanliness. If people did not match her standards of housekeeping, she would describe them as being "lortet" or dirty. She was sure that I would catch some sickness drinking milk out of those old cracked cups, but I never did and I loved my time spent with the Myrans. At noon, the family regularly listened to the radio for H.V. Kaltenborn and his news report.

One day when I was there, a salesman drove up to the house in a new Ford car. After enjoying coffee in the house and making his sales pitch for some unwanted product to Andrew and Annie, he realized that no sale was forthcoming. We all followed him outside where Thurina's small flock of milk goats wandered around the yard. All of a sudden, the salesman spotted two goats standing on the hood of his shiny new Ford and dashed to chase off the animals. He got into his car and roared off, obviously angry, while Andrew laughing said to us, "That salesman won't bother us any more." The Myrans didn't usually buy stuff from salesmen but got groceries mostly from Jorstad's store in Dallas and ordered overalls, other clothes, tires, hardware, and tools from the Sears Roebuck or Montgomery Ward catalogues.

The Myrans belonged to Our Saviour's Lutheran Church, but didn't attend worship regularly. Nevertheless, they were some of the kindest, loving neighbors we had. They welcomed everyone. Often people stayed with them for a few days or weeks. They would help Bennie in the shop and saw mill or Andrew on the farm. They even welcomed gypsies, whom other neighbors disliked because they were reputed to be thieves or dishonest in their trading as they traveled around.

One summer evening the Myrans had allowed a gypsy group to camp overnight near the river on their farm. I knew they were there and was desperately curious to see what they looked like as I had never seen gypsies. Ma told me never to get near them, telling me they were dishonest and might even steal children. As the sun went down, I told Ma I wanted to go out and watch the fireflies for awhile, a lie which was partly true. Once outside, I quickly walked toward the gypsy camp where a number of old cars were parked by their tents. As I got closer, I heard music and saw people sitting in a big circle near a bonfire. In the darkness I crept closer to watch them. A man was playing an accordion, and people were singing exotic melodies. Several women in colorful long dresses and lots of jewelry were dancing on the grass. This was exciting! I was entranced by the scene but scared I might be found and caught by the gypsies. I continued to watch this spectacle for some time but finally decided I had better get home before Ma became worried. Walking home, I was so thrilled that I had seen this world of the gypsies but couldn't tell anyone. Arriving home, I told Ma there were lots of fireflies which were especially bright that night!

Grandma Noer

Grandma Noer lived on the farm adjoining ours to the north. It was a productive farm on better-than-average Sand

Creek soils. Grandma, an erect, regal-looking lady with hair piled on top of her head, wore round gold-rimmed glasses. She was known for her wit and outspoken tongue. She kept house for her sons, my Uncles Arnold and Fritjof, who farmed together. Although they had noisy arguments, the three of them usually got along well. Both brothers were balding, stocky fellows with a good sense of humor. Fritjof, the elder son, was the more difficult and could be overly inquisitive of other people's personal affairs. Arnold, Ma's twin brother, was more conciliatory but loved to play jokes on other people. He, unlike his siblings, had bicycled to Chetek and boarded there to attend high school for two years and then dropped out. Grandma was always upset that he had never finished high school. Pa, who was fiscally very conservative, thought the brothers were big risk takers because they gambled by investing in the stock market. At Arnold's death, his financial wisdom was apparent as his widow Effie inherited a modest sum in stocks like General Motors, MGM, Coca Cola, and IBM, extremely profitable investments.

As a child I liked to hike across the fields to visit Grandma as she always had something good to eat in her pantry and also she was a good story teller. Grandma was an outspoken lady and was not one to be bossed around. She and my uncles frequently had lively loud arguments which included a few mild swear words in Norwegian. As a small child, I was intrigued by some of these words and repeated them when I got home. For this, I was scolded and told never to use them. Pa did not use swear words so they were not a part of our household vocabulary. Grandma was a good story teller and convinced me that we could see nisser (elves) and trolls around us if we learned how to look for them. She had a marvelous imagination. One time she was sitting in her rocker reading aloud from the newspaper while I stood behind her. I had learned to read English fairly well by then and felt I was mighty smart. As Grandma read a sentence, she inserted some different words so I foolishly challenged her, "Those words are not right, Grandma." She turned to me, "Pshaw, when I am reading, it's what I want it to say." It was a lesson in creativity for me.

Another time when I was there, there was a knock on the door and subsequently Pastor Ingel Hovland was invited in for a visit. Grandma didn't attend church much except for Ladies Aid and funerals, so he had come to talk about her absences. I sat in a corner quietly hearing him say in Norwegian, "Maren, you haven't been to church in a long time. Why?" "No, I haven't" she said. "Well, why not?" he asked again. Grandma looked at him and bluntly said, "I haven't been coming because you don't have anything to say in your sermons that I want to hear." I was scared, the way she answered the pastor who was a stern forbidding man to me. His face got red as he told her how serious it was for her to be absent from worship and went on and on berating her. As he continued, Grandma was getting more and more angry. Finally she had enough, and stood up. In a firm voice she said, "There is the door" and pointed to the door. Pastor Hovland looked at her, mumbled something, then picked up his hat and departed. Grandma won. I was awed at her courage in defying authority. She apparently was courageous as a young bride too. Soon after moving to this farm, a poor destitute Indian came to the door and asked for something to eat. Grandma was scared, but instead of taking the broom to him, she grabbed a loaf of bread she had just baked and gave it to him, earning his gratitude.

The matrimonial life of my two uncles was unusual. Uncle Fritjof married Cora Peterson in Colfax in 1933, but she did not move to the farm until 1940 when Grandma left to live with us for a year before her death in 1941. Fritjof would frequently spend a weekend night with Cora while Arnold did the milking and other chores. In the meantime, Arnold was courting Effie Gunderson in Colfax and married her in 1937. Their unusual honeymoon took them to Yellowstone Park in his Model A Ford car, a phenomenal trip for someone in our community. Both couples continued to enjoy alternate weekend connubial visits until Arnold and Effie bought the Wick farm in 1939. The Noer brothers' marital system elicited some good humored remarks and were often referred to as "trial marriages."

Northern Neighbors

Just north of Grandma's farm was that of John and Emma Harrington. He was a tall, gangly, good humored Irishman, and she was a short, sunny, hard-working German. They had five children. Gerald took over the farm and managed it well. He was one of just a few neighbors who owned a tractor in the 1930s. Hazel married Al Tietz, a butcher in Dallas. Dora became an elementary school teacher in Chetek. Ernest rambled around the country and finally went to Alaska and married a widow who owned a dairy farm near Palmer in the Matanuska Valley. Millie married Herb Ziebel, a policeman who eventually became police chief in the village of Colfax.

Across the road from Harringtons was the farm of Pa's Uncle George Hoveland and Aunt Ida. Uncle George was a patient man with a marvelous sense of humor. He needed to have these attributes as Aunt Ida was a born complainer and found fault with everything. In addition, she was always sick, but doctors usually could find nothing wrong with her, and she lived to a ripe old age. They had three children: Clarence who owned the Chetek Chevrolet-Buick garage and also the local ice business, Ruth, who married Gustave Johnson who had a successful insurance business in Chetek, and Viola who was mentally slow and lived with her sister.

Just across the county line was the farm of Julius and Inga Nelson with daughters, Irene and Ella, who were both elementary school teachers. When this wonderful couple retired to Chetek, their farm was bought in the mid 1930s by Ray and Bessie Foss and their four children. Bessie was a registered nurse and helped many people in the community. Next door was the farm of William and Clara Nelson and their son Wallace. The brothers Julius and William Nelson were from Denmark and had heavy gutteral accents in their spoken Norwegian.

Down the hill on the other side of the road lived brother and sister Gerhard and Edna Gregarson. They were warm hearted hard-working people, who were noted for their tidy farmyard and garden. They had a sister who married a Swede and lived in Chicago. Their son, Gerhard Osterberg, spent many summers working on his uncle's farm. He was a pleasant, gentle pudgy fellow about my age who enlarged my vistas a bit on city life. Across the road lived a bachelor, Lawrence Carlson, who operated a small dairy farm. As he aged, his health deteriorated and Edna brought him meals, but eventually they convinced him to move in with them where he lived for the last year of his life. When he moved, he insisted they bring along a suitcase, which was never opened in the Gregarson's presence but kept under his bed. At his death, without a will, they opened the suitcase and found stacks of US currency. Pastor Iver Olson was asked to assist them in counting the money, which took a long time. A total of over $10,000 was found and the judge handling the estate awarded the money to the Gregarsons. At that time, this was a sizeable amount of cash. The big question in the community was how this bachelor could have accumulated so much money with only a few cows on his tiny farm.

Rumors were widespread. One of the most exciting was that this man had been a Norwegian sailor on merchant ships who had made money illegally and then came to America to escape prosecution.

Neighbors South of Us

Across the road south of our farm on Lover's Lane was that of Uncle Sophus and Aunt Clara Noer and their daughter Swanhild. It was a tranquil setting with big maple and elm trees along the Red Cedar River, the farm on which Pa was born and raised. Their farm was fairly large with considerable river frontage and forest in addition to farmland. However, because they lacked electricity the barn was lit with kerosene lanterns that emitted about as much light as a tiny flashlight. Milking was a gloomy task. In the house a dim light was provided from wick flame kerosene lamps and brighter lights from gas lamps that one pumped up and then carefully lit a fragile cloth mantle over a gas jet inside a glass globe.

Uncle Sophus was a tall bony man with a good head of hair, who wore Oshkosh B/Gosh overalls. When dressed up, he wore high laced shoes, pants high on his ankles, and always had his necktie tucked into the shirt. This habit was probably acquired when he was drafted into the Army at the end of World War I and spent his time at a camp near Rockford, Illinois. He was a pleasant, garrulous man but a born pessimist. When good rains had crops looking good, he would remind one that it might not last and turn dry. He was highly opinionated, which generally resulted in noisy discussions when he and Pa, of similar temperament, got together.

When the three Noer brothers, Fritjof, Arnold, and Sophus got together, one could expect an exciting time; they were the best entertainment around Sand Creek. Fritjof and Arnold would pick on Sophus in a discussion, and the conversation would get louder and louder as they exchanged verbal blows. If Sophus or Fritjof picked on Ma in conversation, her twin Arnold would defend her. Aunt Clara was a short plump lady with glasses, who wore her hair coiled on top of her head. She had been a school teacher before settling on the farm with Uncle Sophus. I liked visiting their house as Aunt Clara was a good cook and in summer served fresh vegetables and strawberries from their spacious garden. The only drawback was that Uncle Sophus' table prayer was tediously long for a little kid as he rambled on, praying for lots of people, events, church, and the weather.

Cousin Swanhild was four years older than I but graciously played with me. I enjoyed many games like Rook, Old Maid, and checkers. However, one of her favorites was "playing house" where she was the mama and I the papa as we sat at a little table with little play dishes and some food or attended to her dolls in the carriage or doll bed. I hated it and wanted to do anything else! As I got older and learned to ride a bicycle, I looked forward to riding her bike when we visited there as I never owned one.

Another member of their family was Harvey Austin, an orphan who Uncle Sophus kindly took in as a boy to finish elementary school and become confirmed at church. He continued working on the farm for many years until he moved away and married. Harvey was a dedicated hardworking fellow who wisely would go ahead and finish a job while Uncle Sophus and his brothers were arguing about how it should be done. I enjoyed watching how Harvey with good humor handled these noisy sessions.

Across the road from Uncle Sophus was the farm of Leonard and Helen Toycen. They also milked cows by the pitiful light of kerosene lanterns even though electric power lines ran along one side of their farm. The power company, Wisconsin Hydro Electric, claimed it would not pay them to run a line to service the two farms but their policy changed in later years when the government-owned REA offered competition. Leonard was a short, patient man with one of the kindest dispositions imaginable. In contrast, Helen was a large plump lady who was domineering and always right. She would have her say, and Leonard would just smile and go about his work.

Helen was a self-styled nurse and often helped people during periods of illness. She appeared at our house on a number of occasions when some or all of us were down with a bad case of flu. Her choice remedy for most anything was the castor oil bottle because she believed that a sick person needed a good purging of the bowels. Since my digestive tract was quite sensitive, constipation was never a problem. When Helen came to me holding a spoonful of castor oil, I just groaned, knowing the misery I would suffer with diarrhea. It did no good to object as she shoved the spoon into my mouth, telling me I needed it to get well. Her well-meaning nursing care was not appreciated by me! Helen was also an ardent Pentecostal who held services in homes with some of her Olson relatives from the New Auburn area and a few other families. They had two children, Irene who married a Pentecostal preacher and Laverne who married Elaine Sparby. Laverne started out dickering in used cars and did well, eventually owning a large Buick-Pontiac-GMC dealership in Bloomer. He was a talented salesman and had plenty of practical business smarts, contributing to his success. He later bought our home farm when Pa retired.

Adjacent to Uncle Sophus' place was the farm of Uncle Oscar and Aunt Margaret Hoveland who had seven children: Kenneth, Aldred, Orville, Vernoid, Venonah, Algene, and Yvonne. The buildings included a pitiful house in need of paint and other repairs and a lawn area consisting of sand.

The unpainted side barn and hay mow with a wood stave silo did not indicate prosperity. Uncle Oscar was a large handsome man with black curly hair, witty, good humored who spent more time visiting with people in town than tending to farming. They were the poorest family near us. Aunt Margaret was a short skinny woman who always looked tired. It was no wonder as she had a big brood to feed, clean, and wash for every week, working in a house with no modern conveniences. The children did much of the farm work. They got a better price for their milk than other farmers as they bottled it and delivered door-to-door in Sand Creek with a horse-drawn van. They also grew cucumbers and string beans for the pickle and canning plants in Chetek.

Across the road from Uncle Oscar and Aunt Margaret's farm lived Henry and Amanda Hendrickson and their five children: Harvey, Corrine, Betty, Harriet, and Helen. Life was better at this farm, and the buildings showed it with a well painted large house and dairy barn. In addition, Henry did custom sawing of logs at his saw mill. He was also an expert at sharpening saws and had a good business.

North of the Hendrickson's on the road to New Auburn was the farm of Oscar Anderson who was widowed early in my childhood. Two spinster daughters lived with him; Evelyn who was the housekeeper, and Margaret who was an Augsburg College graduate and managed the Sand Creek bank. A son, Norman, farmed with his father. Oscar, a quiet, tall, gaunt man, contrasted with his brother, Albert, a cantankerous, short man who was locally known as "Stubben" or "Shorty." Stubben lived with them but also owned an 80-acre-farm with a house and barn across the road from Grandma Noer which he rented out for cropping.

Farther down the New Auburn road were the farms of Alfred Madison and Julius Johnson. Across the road from the Johnson's was a farm purchased in 1941 by Harold and

Evelyn Greenhill (Gronnhaug in Norway) who moved from near Colfax. Harold had emigrated in 1921 from Upland County in central Norway. They had four children: Gaylon, Thelma, Mary Ellen, and Arne. Gaylon, the eldest, and my sister Hannah were classmates at Sand Creek elementary school and later married. Hannah became an elementary school teacher while Gaylon had a distinguished academic career as a political science professor, department head, dean, and, chancellor of the University of Wisconsin-Whitewater.

Hanson Valley

The farm of Garfield and Mabel Ness and daughters Mae Arlene and Gertrude lay north of the Andersons and faced Hanson Valley Road which veered eastward from County Highway I. Garfield was a short, stocky man with a sunny disposition. Mabel was a spare woman with a more severe outlook on life. Both were good workers and always neat. It was a prosperous farm where buildings and grounds were well painted, trimmed, and neat. The girls were near my age, but since they attended school in Sand Creek, my only association with them was in Sunday School. Of course, my shyness around girls and lack of social skills didn't make me very appealing.

Across the road on a hill was the Casper Field farm. He was a warm-hearted bachelor who lived with his mother. He was said to be "well fixed" which meant that he may have had $10,000 or so stashed away in the bank or investments. That was a lot of money for local folks and meant that he had enough money to retire comfortably. After his mother died, he married a lovely local woman, Rena Svalestun, who had worked as a nurse in Minneapolis. She entered enthusiastically into farming with Casper, wearing striped overalls as she worked with Casper milking cows.

Nearly a mile down the road were three farmsteads clustered together, owned respectively by Gilbert Severson, and two brothers—John and Julius Hanson. Uncle John and Aunt Laura's farm was relatively large so they had quite a few cows. He did not marry until he was thirty when he married Ma's sister Laura who was sixteen. Her youngest son, Frederick, was curious and once asked her if it was a romantic courtship. Her curt reply was, "Pa had a big farm and needed someone in the house to take care of him." Although this did not seem like a romantic beginning, it was a highly productive one as they spawned seven sons: Andrew, Martin, Julian, Philip, Daniel, Aaron, and Frederick. Andrew and Julian bought nearby farms of their own, Philip took over the home farm, Martin became a high school principal, Daniel a loan official, Aaron a banker, and Frederick a research bacteriologist with Upjohn Pharmaceutical in Michigan.

Uncle John was a scrawny, balding man with a clever wit, who delighted in playing devil's advocate in discussions and getting the other conversationalist drawn into foolish positions. Since Pa was too literal and lacked a good sense of humor, he was often a victim of Uncle John's wit. It was always a joy to be at their house at a gathering when all the sons were home. They enjoyed each other and had a wonderful time of laughter and story telling amid clouds of cigar smoke. I also liked being there for two other reasons: a bathroom and special toys. Their indoor bathroom was a rarity in our community. It was such fun as a child to use and flush the toilet. One time in winter, Ma even let me use the bath tub, which was sheer luxury. Uncle John was a good businessman. He, his brother Julius, and Gilbert Severson negotiated a better price by contracting to install bathrooms on three farms at the same time. They often used this same technique when buying farm machinery. Another attraction for me was riding in cousin Frederick's rubber-tired cart that was harnessed to a big black Newfoundland dog. Frederick also built a small go cart powered by a gasoline washing machine engine, and he would give me rides in this wonderful machine. Frederick was seven years older than I but was unusually patient and kind with me.

Aunt Laura was a lean, dishwater-blonde lady who always looked tired. I suppose she was actually tired after all those years of raising seven boys in a big rambling house with an unusually inefficient kitchen. Fortunately, she had electricity, running water at the kitchen sink, a refrigerator, and electric wringer washing machine. When the boys were small, Ma used to come and help her sister for a week, but then she had to come home as the noise and distractions of all those rowdy boys was too upsetting. As the boys grew older, they helped with the washing but Aunt Laura still had plenty to do. With mountains of cooking, ironing, patching, and sock darning facing her, she was always busy. Even when all the boys except Philip had moved out, Aunt Laura still looked tired.

Next door was Julius and Hilda Hanson with six children: Raymond, Torphin, Helen, Esther, Doris, and Willie, who was mentally handicapped. The farm had a look of prosperity with well-painted buildings and neatly mown lawns. Across the road was Gilbert and Josie Severson. She was his third wife, as the first two had died. Gilbert was the choir director at Zion church and Josie the organist. Their hired man, Walter Borge, lived with them and sang in the choir. Quite often Walter would drift off to sleep in the choir area during the sermon, especially when he had too many beers on Saturday night in Chetek with neighbor Philip Hanson.

Northward

Just west of the Ness farm where County Highway I made a sharp turn was the "Ness corner." At this juncture, a dirt road ran northward. The first farm on the left was that of Fritz Nelson whose land adjoined our farm. Fritz lived with his aged father Peder, who had emigrated from Denmark. Peder was a dour man whom I had difficulty understanding as his Danish language was more gutteral than the Norwegian I knew. One time when I came to sell Christmas seals for letters, he bought ten cents worth, and as I was opening the door to exit, I turned to see him toss the seals on the fire in the wood heating stove. I was shocked to see him burn up those beautiful Christmas seals that could have been pasted on envelopes of Christmas cards. I suppose that he didn't send any cards.

Fritz was a jovial, lean, craggy fellow with large teeth stained by long years of snus. His striped overalls were always several sizes too big; the cuffs were rolled up, and hung loosely on his frame. He was a good farmer, and a good neighbor, but he never attended church except at Christmas and Easter or funerals. Lena Larson was the housekeeper, a short squatty lady, always cheerful, full of energy, and generous to a fault. She was a hard-working lady who adored Fritz and he appreciated her. It was commonly known that their relationship was more than employer-employee, but was accepted in the community. Lena drove a tan Model A Ford car and in summer would frequently stop at our back door, announce her arrival with the loud "ooga" horn and deliver fresh vegetables and cut flowers from her huge garden. She and Ma were good friends, having attended County Line School together. Lena was active in the church Ladies Aid and a friend to all.

A short distance along the road over two small hills was the 80-acre-farm of Roy and Nettie Rathbun. He had originally been the Sand Creek buttermaker but retired to eke out a living on his small farm where he raised two children, Joe and Helen. Joe never married and often worked out for other farmers. Helen, a portly lady, worked in an Eau Claire factory for some time. She was courted for awhile by Andrew Myran, who built a new house in anticipation of marriage, but Helen backed out of this potential union and married Adolph Swanson. Next door was the farm of Anton and Sadie Saastad and three boys: Clayton, Kenneth, and Ralph. Anton was not much of a farmer, but his greatest problem was booze. He abused Sadie and was known for commonly giving his boys severe whippings with a belt for any misdemeanor. It was not a pleasant household.

My Best Friend

In the late summer of 1932, a 1927 blue-green Buick brought Clarence and Theodora Wick with their children, Billy and Carol, from eastern Montana to the Helmer and Anna Anderson farm just southeast of us, which they bought (Wick, W. Q. 1991. *Tales of the Red Cedar*. Unpublished). Theodora, nicknamed Dody, was a small, attractive woman who had been raised in New Auburn, and was the daughter of C.P. Hansen who was retired and quite well off. He had trained as an accountant in Denmark and emigrated. He became president of the Farmer's Store Company, a chain of cooperative general stores in our area. Dody graduated from St. Olaf College as a teacher and ended up teaching school in Opheim in eastern Montana. There she met and married Clarence Wick, a handsome, ebullient man, who was manager of the local bank. Son of a Norwegian immigrant ships blacksmith from the Lofoten islands, Clarence grew up in eastern North Dakota. Banking was stessful for Clarence, and his health deteriorated. Doctors recommended that farm life might help him recover. Thus they decided to start dairy farming near her family in Wisconsin even though Clarence lacked farming experience.

Plenty of farm problems challenged their resolve during the Depression. The barn was run down, so the inside was gutted and rebuilt. The next year the barn burned from spontaneous combustion of hay that was stored too wet. A new Gothic style galvanized corrugated iron barn and steel silo replaced it. Later, a tornado ripped the silo out of its concrete foundation, lifted it over the barn and dropped it across the road in a field of Garfield Ness. The metal silo roof flew more than two miles and landed in a blueberry bluff. Some farmers would have given up, but Clarence Wick was determined to succeed and he did. In addition to working hard with the dairy herd, he sold gravel to the WPA government agency from a pit on the farm, and helped farmers with income tax preparation and other business matters.

It must have been a tough new life for Dody who had enjoyed the conveniences of growing up in a relatively affluent New Auburn home. It was a typical two-story wood siding farmhouse without conveniences except electric lights, a refrigerator, and a Speed Queen wringer washing machine. An outdoor pump provided water. The family enjoyed the delights of an outdoor toilet. A shanty out back was used for summer cooking and bread baking to keep the main house as cool as possible. Since there were no freezers, she canned massive amounts of vegetables from their garden plus blueberries and other fruit. Potatoes, rutabagas, and beets were stored in the cellar. Two more children arrived to join Billy and Carol: Ruth in 1934 and Dick in 1936. After they left Sand Creek, another child, Daniel, was born in California.

Dody was a busy lady even though she was spared having to work in the barn and fields, thanks to having a hired man most of the time.

Billy, blond and somewhat pudgy, was my age with our birthdays a day apart. He soon became my best friend. He was a gentle, patient, caring person with an inquisitive mind. We had much in common and enjoyed doing the same things during the limited time we spent together. Like me, Billy was also an important part of the farm labor. We fished in the Red Cedar River, tramped in the woods together imagining that we were explorers, watched bugs, birds, chipmunks, squirrels, and clouds. I soon discovered that even though we were the same age, he knew much more and had a wider knowledge of the world than I did. It did not take long to understand why.

Spending time in their home was an education for me. Table conversation encompassed world affairs, the economy, sports, and politics. They had many books and read them. Dody read poetry to the children and urged them to memorize it, and the family sang together around the piano. The family played games like dominoes, Anagrams, Rook, Flinch, and Monopoly. They subscribed to magazines like *Country Gentleman, The Saturday Evening Post,* and *Hoard's Dairyman.* Somehow, Billy's father found time to fish with him in the Red Cedar River and in Lake Chetek.

We did none of these things at home. We had few books and subscribed only to the *Wisconsin Agriculturist and Farmer.* I was the only one who read books. We didn't play games or sing together. Our conversations were mainly about neighbors, relatives, church, school, and farm work. Pa didn't have time to go fishing. It was a highlight for me when we went fishing together once on Prairie Lake even though we caught more mosquito bites than fish. Being at the Wick house was more fun, and they enjoyed life more even though both families suffered economically during the Depression.

Billy greatly enriched my life. Even though we attended different schools and Lutheran churches, he had a huge impact on my life. He made me realize there was a bigger world than Sand Creek and made me want to learn about it. I felt inadequate as he knew so much about things I had never thought about, but he never looked down on me. In third grade, both of us discovered stamp collecting and became entranced with stamps from all sorts of fascinating places like Azerbaijan, Liechtenstein, South Africa, Ecuador, China, and New Zealand. This encouraged us to learn more about these places as both of us loved geography. We had fun together.

In late 1938, when Clarence Wick's health began to fail, a decision was made to sell the farm and move to Long Beach, California, where Grandpa Hansen, two uncles, and two aunts had moved the previous year. A farm auction was held in April 1939, and the Wick family departed in their new 1939 Chevrolet purchased for $854. It was a sad day when Billy and I said our goodbyes. He gave me his much loved big black and white curly-haired dog, Cappy. We both cried, not knowing if we would ever see each other again.

I walked Cappy to our farm, pleased to have a dog again after the death of my previous pet. The next morning, Cappy was gone and we guessed where he had gone. I walked to the Wick farm where Cappy greeted me, wagging his tail. We walked around the farmyard together, the buildings empty and lonely. The wonderful people I loved who once lived here were gone. I had never felt so alone in my life. I sat down beside Cappy who seemed to understand my feelings. His eyes looked so sad. Our best friend, Billy was gone forever and we were suffering together. I burst into tears, one arm around the dog, and sobbed for a long time. My world seemed so empty. Finally, Cappy and I got up and started the walk home to our new life together.

Cows

Dairy Farming

Farming for us meant dairy farming because that was virtually all there was in a large part of northwestern Wisconsin. In school, I read about farmers who had no dairy cows but just grew crops of corn, wheat, rice, oranges, or cotton. I thought how easy it must be to raise crops, beef cows or sheep and not have to milk twice a day. Instead, our lives were scheduled around milking twice a day all year, growing and storing hay and silage in summer, feeding it back to the cows in winter, and hauling manure out to the fields. We joked about being tied to a cow's tail but accepted it as a normal way of life.

Most of the 80- and 120-acre-farms had 15 to 25 cows and were operated by a husband and wife plus the valuable labor of children. Farms of 160 or more acres with more cows generally had a hired man unless an older son was part of the operation. A lot of bachelors were glad to have a job as hired man during the 1930s Depression era. It didn't pay much, but one had substantial meals, a room, and some spending money. Even on our little farm, we had a hired man in the early 1930s who worked on the farm and helped Pa in the sawmill and with other custom work. Our man, Ed Austin, was a shy, quiet, muscular fellow who was a bit slow mentally and never quite met Pa's work expectations. From his small wages he managed to buy a bicycle from Sears Roebuck, using it to visit Sand Creek or his brother Harvey who worked for Uncle Sophus. Pa finally let him go, a combination of exasperation with Ed's work performance and our much reduced income during a long drought during the Depression.

Dairy cows were a part of my life as early as I can remember. We had a herd of Guernseys that were good milkers. Pa was a member of a milk testing association, so kept records on lactation levels and milk fat content as measured by a technician who visited our farm monthly to collect milk samples. Since our milk was used for manufacturing butter, we were paid on the basis of butterfat content. Abbotts was a Grade A dairy plant located in Cameron and had high sanitation standards, so field inspectors checked our barn, milkhouse, and even the outdoor toilet for cleanliness. Annually, the interior of our barn had to be whitewashed with lime by a local contractor, who had spray equipment for this nasty job. Armour's at Bloomer produced canned condensed milk and was a Grade B dairy; so sanitation inspection standards were lower. Our neighbors, the Myrans, sent their milk there where they received a lower price.

Pa kept Guernsey cows because the higher fat content of their milk, as compared to Holsteins, made it more valuable. As a child I thought fawn-colored Guernsey cows were prettier than black and white cows. They were friendly cows and one could pet their soft necks. Scratching the little dip at the top of their heads where dandruff accumulated was something they appreciated. In summer when the cows were on pasture, I enjoyed bringing them in for milking.

There were red winged-blackbirds, Baltimore orioles, bluebirds, butterflies, bees, and wild flowers to enjoy while walking in the pasture, where I was invariably accompanied by the dog. It was a pleasant task, but there were a few hazards. One needed to be observant to avoid stepping in a squishy new cow pie, especially when barefoot. When the cows had been put on a new pasture containing considerable clover or alfalfa, its laxative properties could result in a liquid eruption on the cow herder if following too closely behind a cow. Each cow was named and I regarded them as part of our family, which they actually were, as we lived with them so much of the time.

Manure

Our wood side-barn was attached to a large hay barn. In the side barn the cows put their heads through metal stanchions that were closed when they entered their own straw-covered stalls where they had access to a feed trough in front of them. In back of the cows was a concrete gutter where feces and urine accumulated and had to be scooped up with a shovel daily. The manure was then shoveled into a half-moon shaped bucket about the size of a bath tub which was hoisted via a chain pull up to a wheeled trolley on a cable and then pushed outside to be dumped into a manure spreader or on a pile for later transport to the field. Cleaning the barn was hard work, and one could work up a good sweat even in winter. One soon learned that a Guernsey cow excreted a lot of manure in a day. It was commonly said that we worked all summer hauling cow feed into the barn and worked all winter hauling it back out again as manure.

Two horses pulled each heavy load of manure to be spread on a pasture or crop field. Driving the horses, one sat at the front while a chain belt on the spreader floor slowly moved the manure back toward big beaters that flung the stuff into the air. Forgetting about wind direction could furnish a long remembered educational experience. One always drove into the wind, as a strong wind from the rear could plaster the driver with globs of sticky, stinky manure. In winter, there were new problems spreading manure. Sub-zero temperatures caused the cast iron links of the chain belt to become brittle so they could break, leaving the manure partially unloaded. This is why one carried a manure fork to shovel it off in an emergency. With a wind blowing, the manure quickly froze to the spreader chain and floor, so the shoveling job got progressively harder. This was a character-building experience for a farm boy. When the snow got too deep for a manure spreader, we moved the daily manure via a "stone boat" or flat bed on skids pulled by a team of horses and then spread it by hand using a fork. This was another fun job on a cold winter morning, especially with a biting wind. Pa insisted on doing it this way as we had more time in winter to spread manure than dumping it in a pile that had to be moved to the field in late spring when it had thawed. Admittedly, I had to agree that forking compacted manure from a pile into the manure spreader in late spring was hard, stinky work. Unfortunately, even with winter spreading by hand, we always had a substantial pile accumulated during periods of heavy snow in winter. Manure handling was one of the jobs I hated most on the farm.

Cow Feed

Cows were fed silage and hay plus a mixture of ground corn and oats with some flaxseed meal. Timothy-red clover (later we used alfalfa) hay was dug out of the hay mow in the hay barn and forked down the chute where we carried it to the feed troughs. It was a tough job digging tangled hay out with a pitchfork, but one stayed warm even on a cold winter day. Corn silage was dug out of the stave silo with a wide silage fork, pitched down a chute, and then carried in a steel bushel basket to each cow. This wasn't too bad a job until mid-winter when the silage was frozen solid. The only way to break it up was with a pick ax before forking the frozen pieces down the chute.With this beastly job, one could work up a good sweat even in sub-zero weather. The human caloric input for getting feed to the cows was high and easily utilized the energy from the many meals we ate each day.

In addition to roughage, the cows were fed a concentrate feed of ground oats and corn that we grew on the farm. We bagged this in our granary and took it to the feed mill to be ground into smaller particles for faster digestion by the cows. The local feed mill was just west of Sand Creek. A stream had been dammed to form a pond for water power to operate the grinding equipment. Farmers brought corn and oats in pickups, larger trucks, or horse-drawn wagons to be mixed and ground. Tom Pruzek, a native of Bohemia, operated the mill. His English was less than perfect, and he had not mastered Norwegian. Tom was temperamental and did not take kindly to orders or advice. When farmers pressured him to speed up to reduce waiting time, Tom's favorite exasperated reply was, "I grind, I grind!"

One chilly autumn day as a little kid, I accompanied Pa with his grain to the dusty feed mill, joining the queue of waiting pickups and wagons with grain sacks. It was an interesting place for a kid to be, watching the grinding process, or playing in the water, but best of all was watching and listening to the talk of farmers as they waited for Tom to grind their grain. A narrow wooden deck was on the mill side facing the pond. A door into the mill was always open in warm weather. Just inside was a toilet with a rough wooden door which ended about a foot from the floor. A sturdy hook inside could be fastened tightly to insure privacy for the occupant. A large wooden door pull was on the outside.

On this particular day, two little boys decided it would be fun to crawl under the toilet door and hook it from the inside. After they finished their task and disappeared, I figured that it would be interesting to watch at a distance what happened next. After awhile, Otto Madison, a big burly farmer, strode over to use the toilet but found the door fastened. He waited awhile but no one opened the door and came out. Finally, Otto shouted, "When're you gonna get off the throne?" No reply. Again, "I gotta take a shit—I gotta go!" No reply. He jiggled the door and found it firmly locked. "Damn it, no one's in there and it's hooked!"

Otto grabbed the door pull and yanked hard. The toilet door remained shut as the door pull came off in Otto's big hand. He lost his balance and tumbled backwards out on to the deck and finally into the mill pond. Then, a big splash as Otto hit the cold water and yelled, "Help, I'm gonna drown!" All this commotion attracted the attention of farmers talking nearby so one of them found a long pole and pulled Otto to the pond edge so he could crawl out. Otto was soaked, shivering, and mad, swearing that he was going to get the guy who hooked the toilet door. Of course, the two little boys were not to be seen anywhere, and Otto never found out who did it. I had a wonderful morning at the feed mill!

Milking

Cows were milked by hand twice a day. I started milking when I was five, but only for the 5:30 pm milking. The next year I graduated to milking twice a day and continued to increase the number of cows I milked as I got older.

Sitting on a wood stool with a shiny steel pail between one's legs, there is initially a metallic sound as streams of milk hit the metal surface. Later, there is a gentle "puff puff" sound as foam and milk rise in the pail. Squeezing cow teats to empty a full udder quickly tires the hands of inexperienced milkers. With experience, hand muscles strengthen and milking speed improves. Then, one can milk a cow while enjoying talking to a nearby milker or think about all sorts of interesting subjects. In nice weather it wasn't a bad job.

Most cows were gentle, but occasionally there was a pesky cow who waited until the milk pail was about full, then quickly lifted a foot to step in the milk and ruin it. Our cows were bred to freshen in late August and September as the milk price was highest in autumn and winter. By mid-summer, milk flow diminished, but many cows still had to be milked. On a 90+F evening it was beastly sitting by a steamy cow, especially when one was sweaty and hot from working in the hay field all day. Compounding the problem were flies and nasty coarse cow tail switch hairs swatting one in the face with a sharp sting. Even worse was when the switch hairs had accumulated hard globs of manure or cockleburs which could give one a painful whack on the head.

Milking in winter was different. It was rather nice to come into the warm barn for the evening milking, thinking about the good supper that Ma would have on the table for us. Pa and I would talk some about farming while milking. Ma didn't like to milk. She was always afraid a cow was going to kick her, even though they rarely tried. She left milking early to fix supper for us. Pa was a fast milker and I never matched him.

Morning milking in winter got the blood flowing fast. Pa was up first, usually before 5 A.M. After he was dressed and ready to go to the barn, he called upstairs to awaken me. Then I would lie in bed, listening to Pa closing the door and stepping onto the snow-covered back stoop. The sound of his feet on that surface gave me a relative temperature reading. If the snow squeaked as he walked, I could expect −10F or colder so I had better bundle up. Dressed for the morning, I ventured out, often greeted by a spectacular panorama of black sky studded with stars that sparkled like diamonds. Occasionally we would see the aurora borealis. It was breathtakingly beautiful and I wanted to savor it, but the penetrating cold dictated otherwise so I would run to the barn. Inside, Pa was feeding silage before we started to milk. It was a glorious feeling to sit down beside my first cow, push my head into the soft hair coat of her warm flank and put my cold hands on her warm teats. I always chose a patient, gentle cow for my cold hands, allowing me to warm up while emptying her full udder. I often thought that maybe heaven was like milking that first cow on a cold morning amid the pleasant aroma of corn silage in a warm barn. Our pleasures were simple.

After we filled a pail with milk, it was poured into a 12-gallon can, through a stainless steel strainer, fitted with a cotton pad to filter out any dirt, hair, or bits of hay or straw. Most creameries used 10-gallon milk cans, but Abbotts Dairies' butter factory in Cameron used 12-gallon cans which weighed 110 pounds when full of milk. We moved these cans from the barn to the milk house on a small low platform two-wheeled push cart where they were dropped into the concrete water tank.

Our milk hauler, Fern Schofield from Chetek, earned his wages lifting these gut-busting heavy cans out of the tank and up on to the truck platform. Fern, a cheerful, reliable man, drove a red Diamond-T truck with an enclosed platform to keep road dust off the cans. He took pride in his truck, keeping it clean and well polished. In addition to milk pickup and delivery of empty cans each day, he also brought monthly reports on milk sanitation with a cotton filter showing any dirt, butterfat content, and he also delivered butter we had ordered.

One of our little pleasures during milking was to occasionally squirt some milk toward our cats who would sit waiting for this treat. They slurped the milk as fast as they could and then licked off any surplus from their fur. After we finished milking and removed the used milk-sodden cotton strainer pads, they were tossed on the floor where cats pounced on them to suck out milk, often swallowing the entire pad. Because this created constipation problems, it was common to see a poor cat straining to excrete the remnants of this delicacy. People said that cats were smart, but I had my doubts as they never associated swallowing cotton strainer pads with constipation that caused them so much discomfort.

A New Barn

Our old side barn attached to a large hay barn was a dreadfully inefficient place to feed, remove manure, and milk the cows. Side barns with an attached hay storage and wood stave silos were common on smaller farms where farmers spent much of their time attending to chores. Our silo was constructed of cedar wood staves held together with steel hoops that were adjusted as the staves expanded with wet new silage or shrank in summer as silage was fed and the staves dried. These silos needed attention and if hoops were not adjusted as needed they could buckle or collapse. Many farmers had built silos of sandstone blocks or solid concrete. However, concrete stave silos with steel hoops soon dominated on farms as they were permanent and required less maintenance.

By 1938 our economic situation on the farm had improved enough so that Pa was able to build a new barn with a stone basement and a Gothic roof hay area above it. The stone came from piles of big granite quartz "hardheads" collected off fields at the farms of Nils Tiller in Souix Creek and Nils Traseth in Dovre. The 8-foot-high stone barn basement walls were built by a group of stone masons from Bloomer, headed by Charlie Revels, a good natured, dark-skinned man. These men were skilled masons who normally built fancy stone vacation houses on lakes of northern Wisconsin for affluent people from Chicago or Milwaukee. However, since this was the Depression era and expensive house building was limited, Revels took on this mundane barn-building job to keep his crew working.

Breaking rock was hard work. Each of the 6 to 18-inch diameter boulders used for facing had to be split. This was done with a small sharp-edged hammer that edged a line all around the rock. Then a huge steel mallet was swung by a big muscular German to split the rock, making a big boom. The flat split surface of these rocks was laid on the outside, creating a colorful pink, gray, black, violet, and red wall. Another layer of unsplit rocks faced the inside with rock chips filling voids in the center of the 18-inch thick wall. All this was held in place by concrete "mud." Black concrete mud was used to "point" between the outside split rocks to accent their color.

This backbreaking work went on for several weeks during hot early summer weather. Each day, our farmyard resonated with the boom, boom, boom of rock breaking. The men arrived from Bloomer early each morning with a big washtub full of Bloomer brewery beer bottles and ice that was placed in the center of the barn area to drink throughout the day as they labored on, sweating profusely in the hot sun. Pa was impressed with how hard these men worked. They did the entire job for only $150.

The Gothic-roof hay storage area atop the stone basement was built by Ludvig Larson and his crew of carpenters, who made the arching rafters on the ground, then lifted them into tall roof arches using rope and tackle as there were no big cranes available. Next, to complete the barn they added roof boards, shingles, and board walls which were painted red. It was a hard job in hot weather, but there was no tub of beer for them as they were not German but Norwegian carpenters. They didn't drink beer on the job.

Next to the new barn was a tall Madison concrete stave silo with a shiny metal globe roof erected by a crew from Chippewa Falls. A metal ladder was attached to the outside of the silo and removable wood doors faced a steel chute toward the barn for silage feeding. When the silo was completed, the old side barn was demolished along with the wood stave silo. The old concrete barn floor remained and was never removed during our time on the farm. Our old hay barn was put on skids and pulled around to the rear of the new barn for straw and machinery storage. Pa was proud of the new barn with a colorful stone basement and red board walls and our new silo. It was quite an accomplishment to put up these buildings during the Depression.

A year or two later came the biggest change in our dairy farm, a milking machine! Many farmers like Uncle Fritjof and Uncle John had Surge milkers where the enclosed bucket and teat cups hung by a strap under the cow's udder. Pa thought Surge was too expensive so purchased a machine where the milk bucket was placed on the straw between two cows with hoses and teat cups reaching their udders. Alternating air pressure to run the unit came via a permanent line from the pump. Our world changed and milking now was an easy task. All we needed now was an indoor bathroom, but Pa insisted that such an expenditure didn't improve farm income or make work easier. Major expenditures needed to go into the barn or field machinery.

With a milking machine, Pa and I had more time to carry on a conversation. We usually talked about farm activities or custom work that Pa did for other farmers. At the evening milking, occasionally we would have visitors who seemed to enjoy seeing us milk cows as we conversed with them. There was a hazard for them in that a cow might decide to defecate while the visitor was standing behind. If there was straw and firm feces in the gutter, there was no problem. However, if the feces fell into a urine puddle, there was a good chance that some of the brown juice would splash on the spectator. It was a special hazard when cows were grazing pasture containing abundant clover or alfalfa, with results similar to a heavy dose of ExLax. One summer evening at milking time, my three-year-old sister Hannah came to the barn to show off a new dress Ma had made for her. Standing immediately behind a big Brown Swiss cow, the animal belched heartily while defecating and sprayed the front of Hannah's dress with stinky liquid brown feces, testimony to the effects of alfalfa pasture. It was especially hard for a child as neat as Hannah to be in this condition; so the tears flowed as she ran off to the house.

Cow Care

Reproduction is an important part of farm life. However, Ma and Pa never explained the basics and I had no older siblings to educate me. My first real learning experience on this topic came at an early age when I happened into the horse barn one sunny afternoon and spotted one of our cats lying in a nest of hay in a horse manger. She seemed to be in some agony as I saw something coming out of her rear end. Slowly, a wet fuzzy tiny kitten appeared attached to a cord that the cat bit off. Soon another kitten popped out, then another, and another. It was awesome watching these kittens come out of the mama cat. I sat there watching the mother licking them off; then they somehow found their way to her teats and began to suck milk. Now I knew where kittens came from, but I still had not figured out why tom cats growled and jumped on the back of a mama cat. In my ignorance, I just thought they were mean so I continued chasing them away from their normal sexual activity.

Later, I noticed that when the herd was turned outside for exercise in winter, sometimes a cow would jump on the back of another cow, not realizing that this indicated they were coming into heat and needed to be bred. Then Pa would snap a sturdy wood staff into the nose ring of our bull and lead it into the cow yard where a cow was waiting to be bred. After smelling the cow, he would eagerly ride the cow's back to perform his work. At first, I had no idea what was going on, but I was afraid to ask what this strange business was all about. It took me awhile to figure out the purpose of the bull in the procreation process. I knew there was something secretive about it as Ma never watched the breeding process and always referred to the bull as a "gentleman cow." Watching the birth of a calf was interesting as the cow often moaned and struggled to expel her young along with the afterbirth. When birth occurred in a pasture, there was the added attraction of seeing the cow consume the afterbirth. Watching the new calf struggle to get up on its wobbly legs, one wondered how they were able to find a teat on the swollen udder of its mother. Eventually, I realized that the same reproduction process went on in dogs, horses, and pigs as well as cows and cats. It was much longer before I concluded human beings did the same thing. Sex was never discussed at home.

We didn't spend much on cow health care. The veterinarian was called only when Pa was unable to assist a cow in a difficult birth. Occasionally, a medication was applied to treat mastitis. Sometimes in summer, an insecticide was applied to the cows' backs for the purpose of controlling a fly that laid eggs, resulting in big gray grubs. The insecticide apparently was not too effective because in some years there was an abundance of large bumps on the cows' backs. Squeezing the sides of a bump caused the grub to pop into the air, providing considerable entertainment. Calves suckled their mothers for only a couple of days and then were fed milk replacer mixed with water. I fed the mixture to the calves, struggling to hold the bucket as the calf drank and frequently bunted its head as though it was trying to spill the liquid which sometimes happened. One of the worst experiences in feeding new calves was when they developed scours or diarrhea. Calf diarrhea is a yellow-tan thick liquid with a vile odor, and a little of it spattered on one's clothes lingered awhile. Whenever I see a car or woman sporting this color, it brings up memories of calf diarrhea.

Bull calves were sold to a dealer for veal when only a few weeks old. Heifer calves for herd replacements had to be dehorned as horns were undesirable. Originally, we used to saw or clip them off, but this was a bloody job. Later we learned that one could put tight rubber bands on them that squeezed off blood to this area and caused them to fall off. When mature cows with horns were purchased and added to the herd, dehorning was a major task but it had to be done. Bulls with horns were dangerous and dehorning was essential. Pa had a high respect for bulls based on his boyhood experience. He and Uncle Art were in a pasture and a bull with horns came after them. They ran and Uncle Art escaped, but the bull knocked Pa down at the fence and started goring his back. Fortunately, Pa was pulled under the fence by his brother, thus saving his life. Pa had deep gashes in his back for the rest of his life and a high respect for bulls, regardless of horns.

The Cycle of Dairy Farming

Dairy farming for us was an annual cycle. It involved planting, growing, and storing various crops for silage, hay, and grain. Next, we fed all these stored crops to the cows during the long winter to produce milk. Finally, we hauled the manure from the cows and applied it on the fields. It was a cycle that assured year around employment for the farmer and his family. Uncle Fritjof summed it up as, "Working all spring and summer putting up cow feed to shove it through the cows all winter so you can haul the shit back out to the fields."

Field Work

Tractors

Plowing for our feed crops of corn, oats, red clover, and timothy was done as much as possible in autumn, but sometimes it had to be done in spring. Most farmers used a horse-drawn one- or two-bottom moldboard sulky plow on which they could ride, which was an improvement over a single furrow walking plow. Few farmers had tractors in the early 1930s. Farmers owning tractors had small models of McCormick-Deering (International), John Deere, Allis Chalmers, Fordson, or Titan. Tricycle-type tractors were rare.

Pa owned a big tractor that pulled a three-bottom moldboard plow, and was also used to power the threshing machine. When I was very small, he had a green Rumley Oil Pull tractor that burned kerosene. It had a big platform where Pa allowed me to sit on a wooden box and enjoy the ride as he plowed. I liked the "poom, poom" sound of the tractor engine and felt so important high above the ground. Several years later Pa bought a big dark blue Mc-Cormick-Deering 22-36 tractor with steel lug wheels. This gasoline-powered tractor was better suited for powering the threshing machine and saw mill as well as pulling the breaking plow. Cranking the huge engine on this tractor was hard work and required a strong man to turn the crank. In cold weather the oil was stiff, which made the job even harder. Because of this, Pa housed the tractor in an insulated garage heated by a wood stove. Since this big tractor was unsuited to other field work, horses were also needed. It was not until about 1942 that Pa bought a new Ford-Ferguson small tractor to replace the horses for many farm jobs.

Horses

Horses were commonly used for farm work in the 1930s. Some farms had four to six horses. We only had two or three, but they were used for nearly all the farm work except plowing. Horses pulled harrows, grain drills, corn planters, cultivators, hay mowers, hay rakes, hay and grain wagons, grain binders, corn binders, manure spreaders, and sleighs. At one time we owned two huge red-brown dappled Belgians with spreading white-haired hocks. They were powerful animals and could pull heavy loads of hay or manure with ease. In Sand Creek, one could often see a team of horses and wagon tied up to a hitching rack along a side street while the owner was buying groceries in the Farmers Store or enjoying coffee and pie at the café. Horse-drawn farm implements or wagons hauling hay or grain were a common sight along farm roads. During the spring thaw when unpaved side roads were breaking up, cars would get stuck in the mud so the owner had to get a nearby farmer to extricate the car with his horses. Likewise, cars stuck in a snowdrift required horses to get them moving again., When winter snow storms blocked driveways, horse-drawn sleighs hauled milk cans to plowed main roads for pick up by the milk hauler. Horses skidded logs in pine forests. Horses were an essential part of our farm economy.

During winter, horses lived mainly on hay with a small amount of oats. When they were working hard, they ate more grain, and they also had to have access to plenty of drinking water. At noon, they needed time to eat hay and grain, as well as rest. Harnessing horses was the first job in preparing for a day in the field. A padded collar was buckled around the neck and shoulders. Then the leather harness was thrown over the back and buckled under the belly and neck. Thick leather traces on both sides of the horse connected the hames around the collar to the whiffletree and doubletree attached to the implement to be pulled. Some harnesses were quite elaborate and decorated with chrome buttons. During summer, many farmers also put a fly net of fine loose leather thongs over the harness to keep flies from biting the horses. A wire screen nose bag was attached around the horse's mouth to keep it from eating crops while working. Harnesses had to be kept in good repair; so there were plenty of customers at Harry McIntire's harness shop in Dallas. Horse feet needed to be in a good state of health for work. This required frequent trimming of hooves and shoeing that was often done by the farmer. Harness sores needed to be treated promptly or the animal would be unable to work. Pa and most farmers took good care of their horses, but a few folks had a reputation for poor feeding and mistreatment of these patient animals.

Planting

Spring field work began as soon as the ground dried sufficiently after the snow melted. This ranged from early to late-April when plowed ground was disked to break up the thick clods and sod from plow furrows. Then it was smoothed with three sections of a spike-tooth drag harrow with the horse driver walking behind. One soon learned not to turn the horses too sharply at the end of the field or one of the harrow sections would buckle and flip upward onto the rear end of the horses. This could easily cause a runaway of the horses with the driver left helplessly running behind. Oat seed, cleaned during winter in a fanning mill cranked by me on Saturdays, was bagged, and at planting was brought to the field and dumped into the grain drill box. A small seed box contained inoculated red clover seed and sometimes timothy that was planted at a shallower depth than oats. The driver stood on a narrow board platform on the drill holding the leather lines to guide two to three horses, depending on the drill size. In addition to the squeaking sound of the flexible metal seed tubes, "Whoa" and "Giddiap" were heard as they turned at the end of each round during grain planting.

If winter manure piles had thawed sufficiently to dig them out, we tried to get it spread on land to be planted to corn. "Gjodsel" or manure was highly prized by farmers as it was it was the key to our farming system. Uncle Fritjof always referred to manure as shit and said that it took lots of cowshit to make a good corn crop. Superphosphate was occasionally applied, but mixed commercial fertilizers were rarely used, probably because of the expense and poor growth response, a result of the low nutrient content. As a result, use of available manure and red clover for nitrogen fixation in the crop rotation maintained a reasonable productivity level at minimum cost.

Our neighbors, Andrew and Annie Myran, always had poor corn yields and overgrazed their pastures. Uncle Fritjof said the problem was that Myran's had too many cows that didn't get enough to eat so they milked less and produced less shit to put on their corn fields. He figured that if they sold off a batch of cows and fed the remaining ones better they would produce more milk and more shit for the corn fields, thus getting more and better corn silage for the cows. Knowing Uncle Fritjof, he likely told Andrew and Annie what to do but nothing ever changed on their farm. In his mind, plenty of cowshit was the key to good farming. His observation was correct.

Corn seed required warm soil for germination so planting was usually not done until early to mid-May. Corn was planted with two-row planters pulled by two horses. Open-pollinated seed planted in the early 1930s, gradually was replaced by higher-yielding hybrid seed in later years. The early planters planted seed in a continuous row, but a later innovation was check-row planting where seed was dropped in a hill, allowing the corn to be cultivated in two directions for better weed control. Weeds like pigweed, crabgrass, and quackgrass were serious pests, and no herbicides were available to control them. The problem with check-row planting was that it required a long wire with knots on it to trip the planter and drop seed at each hill. The wire stretched the length of the field had to be moved at each round and fitted back into the planter, greatly slowing down the planting operation. Occasionally the long wire would break, encouraging many farmers to use words not appropriate for church or home.

Cows were moved out of the barn to pasture as soon as there was sufficient growth in spring. Hopefully, cows could be kept on pasture from early May to mid-October if we had adequate rains. Pastures were mainly timothy with red and white clovers. Kentucky bluegrass, commonly called june-grass because that was its peak period of growth, was not highly regarded. It produced little or nothing during summer dry periods. Reed canarygrass was drought-tolerant and also productive in swampy areas, but cows weren't fond of it because it contained bitter alkaloids. Drought-tolerant smooth bromegrass did not come into use until the 1950s.

By the late 1930s, alfalfa became more commonly grown for hay and also was used for pasture. It was higher yielding than red clover and its deep roots allowed much better growth during dry summers; thus it eventually became the main hay crop. Unfortunately, alfalfa has a higher requirement for lime, so unlike red clover would not tolerate the acid soils of our area. We in the northeastern edge of Dunn County were neglected by the Extension Service and never saw a county agricultural agent, nor did we have a 4-H club. However, Pa went to a special meeting sponsored by a feed and fertilizer dealer where C. J. Chapman, an enthusiastic soils extension specialist from the University of Wisconsin, spoke about how to use lime for successful production of alfalfa on our acid soils. Pa was so impressed with this very persuasive speaker that he decided to invest in lime and grow alfalfa that would produce more than red clover in dry summers.

Pa had trucks bring ground limestone and dump it on the field to be planted. Then, we shoveled the limestone into a manure spreader and spread load after load on the field. It was a back-breaking job. As Pa and I were working one day, Uncle Fritjof next door stopped to find out what we were doing. Pa explained that the limestone was necessary to grow alfalfa. Uncle Fritjof laughed saying, "Herman, you're a damn fool spreading all that ground rock on the land. Red clover grows just fine without wasting money buying rock." Pa plowed his ground limestone into the soil, planted alfalfa, and it soon attracted attention. He was the first in our community to grow alfalfa successfully. It was deep rooted; so stayed green and made hay even in dry summer periods when red clover did poorly. Three years later, Uncle Fritjof was spreading "rock" on his land and planting alfalfa. Pa was no longer a damn fool.

Haying

I grew up during the loose hay era. There were no mobile field balers. Putting up the hay crop was hard work, and it often occurred during hot humid weather. The first cutting of hay was the biggest one which usually came in early to mid-June. Hay was cut with a sickle-bar mower with a seated driver pulled by two horses which made a clackety-clack noise as it moved across the field, cutting a six-foot swath. A reciprocating bar with v-shaped, serrated blades moved past stationary blades. These blades had to be sharpened at intervals, a job that was done on a grindstone turned by me while Pa held the bar with the blades. I cranked and also periodically poured some water on the grindstone. It was a boring job. The v-blades were attached to the bar with rivets to allow replacement of worn blades. When I was old enough to do the job, cutting hay was a pleasant task as one could watch birds, gophers, and field mice scurry around. Occasionally, a bird nest would be hit or a snake cut apart. Sometimes one could be unlucky when rivets in a serrated blade snapped to jam the cutting mechanism, requiring a trip to the shop.

The cut swaths of hay were allowed to dry for a day or two and then raked. Some small farmers still used a dump rake pulled by horses to leave the hay in bunches that were then forked by hand to make a rounded haycock that was built to shed rain and cure in the field. It was tedious work and could result in considerable loss in hay quality. We used the most up-to-date method of raking the swaths with a side delivery rake that left the hay in fluffy windrows to cure. When it was sufficiently dry, we picked it up with a hay loader pulled behind a hay wagon drawn by two horses. The loader had a big drum with wire teeth that picked up the windrow and put the hay on a conveyer belt, moving it upward where it dropped the loose hay on the hay rack. There, Pa moved the incoming hay around with a pitchfork and built a stack. This job required experience as sometimes the moving wagon would hit a bump, and a man could lose his balance. I had the task of driving the horses and guiding them over the center of the hay swath. As the hay built higher, it soon covered me until I was wedged tightly between the front of the hay rack frame and hay. When fully loaded, the wagon was unhooked from the hay loader, and moved to the barn.

The wagon stopped in the driveway at the end of the barn, the wheels blocked, and the hay was lifted through an open door near the roof top. Putting hay in the barn required three people. A long rope extended from the hayfork through pulleys at the top of the barn and along a track attached to the roof, then to the other end of the barn and down to the ground where it was connected to a harnessed horse. The clam-like hayfork had four hinged pointed arms which a person on the hay load stomped into the hay, then moved to the other end of the load and hollered, "Go ahead." Then the driver (usually me) started the horse, tightening the rope, with the hayfork at the other end. A clump of loose hay rose into the air until it reached the rail, where it was locked into a wheeled carriage that moved into the barn and was dropped at a desired place by a trip rope operated by the person on the hay load. The horse was then turned around and trotted back to the barn, pulling the rope, part of which had to be dragged back by hand to make it easier for the load person to pull the hayfork back again. Pa had the worst job of being in a steamy hot hay mow and spreading the loose hay. If hay was simply left where the hayfork dumped it, a compacted, tangled mess resulted which was difficult to dig out for winter feeding.

Sometimes things went wrong when unloading hay. If the boy driving the horse on the hayfork started too soon, the hayfork person on the wagon didn't have time to scurry out of the way before it lifted. One time, when Ma was on the load I thought I heard her say, "Go ahead," and I started the horse. Ma was still setting the hayfork in the hay and as the area she was standing on rose, she lost her balance and nearly rolled off the wagon, but she did end up in a pile of hay. Pa and I thought it was funny as no one got hurt, but Ma was mad. Another time when I was working on the hay wagon, we had a hired boy drive the horse on the hayfork and he didn't stop when Pa yelled from the hay mow. The carriage with the hayfork load of hay jammed into the end of the barn and broke some parts, ending haying for the day. Pa was not happy.

Haying was sometimes interrupted by thunderstorms. If we saw big black thunderstorm clouds developing, we worked even faster to get as much hay as possible into the barn before a downpour. Sometimes it was a race to get a wagonload of hay moved to the barn and under cover before the rain came down. Our new barn had a covered driveway where a load of hay could be parked to escape an incoming shower. Haying left us hot, sweaty, and dirty at the end of the day. Then we had to bring the cows in from a pasture and do the milking. Sitting down beside a hot cow in a hot barn after a day of haying was a bum way to end the day. Fortunately, by summer the milk flow was down as cows were late in their lactation.

Swimming in the Red Cedar River was an option to get clean, but it was often too cold in early June for the first cutting of hay. With no shower or bathtub, all one could do was wash off some sweat and dirt from the upper part of the body. It was then that I really longed for a bathroom. However, if the river water was warm enough, our reward for the day was to put on our swim suits and drive down to the nearby Red Cedar and wash off our day's sweat and dirt. It was such a glorious feeling to come out clean, dry off, and then come home for supper. After milking, trips to the river for swimming were a frequent event later in the summer. Pa had learned to swim as a boy and could do the side stroke while I dog paddled. Ma couldn't swim, but enjoyed being there although she was frightened of "water snakes," which were actually harmless eels. With the sun low in the sky, it was pleasant to relax and enjoy the slow flowing river bordered by maple, oak, and willow trees.

Cultivating Corn

A continuing task in summer was cultivating corn. Annual weed pests like pigweed, crabgrass, and lambsquarters were problems, but quackgrass, a perennial, was by far the worst. This grass has thick underground stems filled with stored food to develop new shoots and roots as it spreads under the soil surface. Farmers rode horse-drawn, two-row riding cultivators with wide shovels that glided about an inch below ground to loosen the soil and hopefully kill the weeds. It was fairly effective on the annual weeds and delayed the quackgrass, especially if there was no rain for a few days afterward. In long periods of rainy weather, quackgrass would grow fast between the corn rows so it soon looked like a hayfield. In a bad quackgrass year, corn silage yields could be reduced. Pa rode the cultivator as it took someone expert at using his feet to steer the foot pedals for the cultivator wheels to prevent the shovels veering into the rows and digging out corn plants.

As the corn grew taller, one could not use the riding 2-row cultivator as it damaged the corn plants. Some people just quit cultivating at that stage, but Pa wanted to keep after the weeds so he used a one-horse walking cultivator between the rows. As soon as I was old enough, that became one of my summer tasks. By then, we had only two old horses, Nig, a black stallion, and Maid, a white mare. Maid was a patient horse who was ideal for cultivating corn as she plodded between the rows, then automatically turned into the next row at the ends of the field and started off again with no instructions. I walked behind the cultivator, guiding it as I held the wood handles. It was a boring job, tramping hour after hour in the loose soil with corn leaves on either side brushing my arms and making them itch. On a steamy hot day, the interior of a tall corn field was even hotter as there was no breeze at all; so both horse and driver did a lot of sweating. Since wildlife in the corn field was nil, there was nothing to enjoy, and one had to keep the cultivator exactly between the rows or one could injure some corn plants. The job required too much attention to do any daydreaming. I was always glad when cultivating season was over.

At the beginning of World War II, our new Ford-Ferguson tractor took over the corn cultivating as well as other field jobs that the horses did. By then we had only one horse, Maid. She was kept around mainly to use on the hayfork and a few other small jobs. She had been a good, faithful worker and Pa hated to see her go, but she couldn't work any more because of arthritis and other ailments. Finally, he phoned the man that bought old horses for feeding the mink on his fur farm. I recall the day he came to the farm with his big truck. Pa led Maid out near the truck where a bag was put over her head. I hid behind the granary where I heard a rifle shot and the thud of Maid's body falling on the ground. I hurt all over and hated to look at the scene. Sadly, I looked toward the truck and saw Maid's body being pulled with a cable winch up a ramp to the platform. It just wasn't right to kill someone who had served us faithfully so well over the years. It was a sunny day but it seemed dark. Maid was thirty-four, an old age for a draft horse.

Jobs

Pa was always good at finding jobs to do between major chores like plowing, planting, and haying. Fence repair or building a new fence was one of them. Digging holes with the post hole digger for large corner posts was hard work. Smaller sharpened wood posts were driven into the ground with a big steel mallet into holes enlarged with a steel crowbar. This job was done after a good rain when the soil was soft. Hammering staples into posts to hold barbed wire was another of my non-skilled jobs. Pa was a good mechanic and kept our machinery in excellent repair but there always seemed to be something that needed fixing. I had no aptitude or interest in mechanics. He loved all sorts of machinery and thought I should do the same. Pa never understood how a boy could be so devoid of mechanical ability; unfortunately, I was just like Ma in this respect. In spite of this, he often used me to hold things, push bolts through holes, or tighten nuts on them. I held pieces of hot iron from our forge for him as he hammered them on the anvil, held parts as he was assembling machinery, hammered nails into lumber when building something, sawed lumber where he marked it with his pencil and square, nailed cedar shingles on a roof, and cranked the sandstone grinder as he sharpened cutting blades and knives. One of my continuing jobs was to fill grease guns and grease the fittings on tractors and machinery. I found it all boring; work with the cows was much more interesting.

When we were caught up on regular jobs, there was the never-ending task of clearing bits of land on which big pine trees had been cut. A narrow strip of cut-over land lay next to the highway facing the Myran farm. Old stumps there had partially rotted roots so they could be pulled out by the tractor and a cable, then laboriously pushed or dragged into piles for burning. Next, the land had to be turned with a breaking plow pulled by the tractor. Then the rough furrows were disked to break them up, leaving lots of old tree roots to pick or pull up and put on the burn pile. One soon discovers that big pines have a lot of roots. This soil was also full of small stones which had to be picked up. The stones were placed on a stone boat, a platform on skids, pulled by the horses. Each load of stones was hauled to a depression at the end of the field and deposited there. After many days of stone picking, it appeared that our tiny strip of new land was ready to till and plant. After another couple of diskings, the soil surface was again littered with more stones. It was discouraging to see this ground sprouting more stones. It took a number of diskings and many hours of stone picking before we were able to plant anything on this new land. Pa always planted rutabagas as the first crop because they grew well on new land. Pine land soils were acid, and rutabagas grew well in this unkind environment. The travail of preparing land for rutabagas may have contributed to my dislike of eating this root crop.

Every few years the pines would be logged off from another narrow strip so we could repeat this conversion from forest to crop land. I gained a high regard for my immigrant ancestors who had struggled for years at this miserable backbreaking job. Pa had one advantage over the immigrants in being able to put dynamite under large new pine stumps and blow them up. However, it was an agonizing job pulling one's guts out on pine roots, finally chopping off the biggest ones. Of course, stone picking continued as usual. Years of practice at this miserable job furnished a valuable education as nothing else I did later in life matched the rigors of root and stone picking.

Threshing, Silo Filling, and Custom Work

Grain Harvest

Nearly all the small grain grown in the Sand Creek area was oats, utilized for feeding dairy cows and draft horses. It was normally harvested in late July when it ripened to a bright gold or pale yellow. Ripe fields of grain contrasted beautifully with rich green hayfields of red clover or alfalfa. Harvesting was done with a grain binder drawn by horses and late in the decade by tractors. The operator sat on a high seat overseeing on his left a reciprocating sickle cutting the grain while slow-turning wood reel blades pushed the cut grain stalks onto a canvas conveyor belt that moved it to the right and up an incline belt to the binder mechanism. Here, long metal fingers formed a bundle, and twine looped around the center of it where a knotter mechanism tied a knot, cut the twine, and dropped the bound sheave into a bundle carrier. When a number of bundles had accumulated, the operator would then use a foot pedal to dump them into long rows on the ground. Power for all the moving belts, chains, and sickle was supplied by a big lugged bull wheel as horses pulled the grain binder forward.

The grain binder was a remarkable machine, with the reaper or cutting part invented by Cyrus McCormick, a Virginia blacksmith, in 1831. The knotter device for binding the sheaf with twine was not perfected until 1878 by John Appleby in southern Wisconsin. It saved an enormous amount of labor and made grain harvesting relatively simple. However, the machine had to be kept in good repair with attention to canvas conveyor belts, sickle blades, chain belts, and sprockets. Most of all, the knotter had to be in good condition and properly adjusted, or bundles would not be tied adequately. A cranky knotter could ruin a day of grain harvest.

Once the oats were cut, the rows of bundles had to be picked up and assembled into a shock that would await threshing at a later date. Grain shocking was done by adults and children in the family. Ma sometimes worked with Pa and me in the field to get the grain shocked before a summer rain shower. The shocker grabbed two bundles and set them upright on the ground with the grain heads touching to form an A-shape. Two or three more sets were placed next to them in a row to form the shock. Then, a single bundle was placed on top with part of the straw pulled down on both sides to form a cap, remaining in place to shed water in case of a rain. A fast shocker like Pa could cover quite a few acres in a day, depending on the crop yield. It was wise to have one's arms covered with long shirt sleeves to protect against sunburn and irritation from the grain and straw.

Threshing

A threshing machine was a sizeable investment; so threshing was done on a custom basis by someone who owned one along with a large steam engine or gasoline tractor. Since Grandpa Hoveland had operated a custom thresher and steam engine, it was not surprising that Pa should do the same. Pa owned a thresher and steam engine for custom threshing of wheat in western Saskatchewan. Then when he moved back to Wisconsin he purchased a McCormick-Deering thresher to serve neighbors. By the 1930s there were few steam engines used for threshing as they were cumbersome to handle and consumed a lot of fuel from old fenceposts and other wood. Uncle John Hanson, Julius Hanson, and Gilbert Severson threshed their own grain and that of the Myrans, powered by the steam engine they owned. It was exciting as a little boy to greet Uncle John as he tooted the whistle while driving this smoking monster by our house enroute to Myrans.

For a month or more each year Pa threshed for farmers over a large area extending from south of Sand Creek and north into Souix Creek and Dovre. Uncle Oscar was hired to help him as grease monkey, setting up the machine, and general maintenance work. While Pa drove the tractor and thresher from farm to farm, Uncle Oscar drove our Chevy truck and later the Ford pickup that carried gasoline, tools, and other supplies. At each farm the thresher had to be leveled, blocked, and the tractor lined up with the drive belt in place for operation. The blower pipe had to be cranked out and raised as needed to direct the threshed straw either to an outside stack or into a barn.

Threshing was a community effort at each farm with farmers in an area bringing a horse-drawn wagon with hayrack to haul oat sheaves from the field to the thresher. Some men worked in the field as "pitchers" with 3-tined forks, tossing bundles from shocks up into the wagon where the wagon man stacked them into a load. Occasionally, someone would find a harmless snake in a bundle and scare the wagon man with it. Working as a pitcher was not a hard job and one could learn a lot of local gossip and hear some good stories. When I got old enough to be a pitcher, I earned some money working for various farmers on this job during threshing season.

When the load was complete, it was driven to the thresher where both teamsters pitched in bundles from each side of the conveyor belt. The thresher made a steady loud drone, punctuated by grunts as bundles entered the machine. This sometimes frightened a team of horses, and the owner had to settle them down. Sharp serrated knives on rotating arms slashed the twine, and the loose oat stalks moved to cylindrical steel concaves with bolted teeth that rotated against stationary teeth to beat the grain from the straw. This mixture was then blown by a fan over a shaker and sieves to separate the grain, which fell into a grain augur while the straw and chaff blew into the straw rack and then out the blower pipe. The grain was augured to an elevator with small buckets on a circulating chain that deposited it into a weighing box on top of the machine, which automatically dumped each time it measured one bushel on the scale. At the end of threshing at each farm, Pa would record the number of bushels threshed, which was used to assess charges for the job. From the weighing box the grain moved down a metal pipe to the bagger with two outlets where canvas bags were attached and filled by the bagger man., The bags were then picked up and carried on the shoulders of men carrying them to the nearby granary to be dumped into a bin.

Probably the best job around the thresher was the bag-german, who didn't do much heavy lifting. At our farm, Grandpa Hoveland liked to do this job. Carrying grain bags to the granary took strength, but it allowed time for jokes and pranks like tying up a bag in the middle to irritate the baggerman. It was also close to drinking water. The worst job was held by the man stacking straw either outside or in a barn. Amid heavy dust and chaff which he breathed, his face, arms, and clothes took on a gray appearance. If the oat crop had a bad infection of smut or rust, the stacker man might be mostly black or red. Working in the strawstack earned extra pay, but it was not an enviable job. Uncle Oscar enjoyed visiting with people, but Pa stayed near the thresher, watching and listening for any problems, then stopping the tractor belt power to fix it. Lubrication and minor repairs were made after shutting down for the evening or the next morning. During threshing season Pa's work days were long, and he often came home late dirty as a pig. Still, he loved threshing season and the excitement that went with it. He had a good reputation for running a dependable threshing outfit, and farmers wanted him to thresh their grain.

Threshing was a busy day for the farmer's wife. Since she had to prepare food for this big crew of men, she started on this task several days in advance. Help was provided by daughters, neighbor women, or relatives who would come to help on threshing day. At our house, Grandma Noer and sometimes Grandma Hoveland came to help. The threshing machine did not shut down for morning and afternoon coffee (with sandwiches, cookies, and cake), so team drivers and others working around the thresher would just come in the house for a quick bite. A child would bring food and coffee in a thermos to pitchers in the field in the morning and afternoon. The big meal was dinner at noon when the thresher was shut down so everyone could come in to eat. Horse teams were watered, then tied up in the shade and given hay and oats. Most men did not use the outdoor toilet unless they had to take a dump, so they peed behind the barn or granary. Outside the house under the trees, pails of water, enamel wash basins, soap, and towels were available to wash off dirt and sweat on their faces and arms.

Inside the house, tables put together and a mixture of chairs and wood benches would provide seating. Everyday table china and table utensils from several farm homes were set on oil cloth or print cotton. There were no napkins. It was a noisy, talkative, good-natured bunch that sat down to help themselves to ample portions of potatoes, gravy, meat loaf, roast beef or pork, bread, butter, pickles and fresh sweet corn or other vegetables from the garden served in dishes that were passed around. With plates heaped, conversation ebbed and the room became quieter. Women rushed around, refilling serving dishes and water glasses as men shoveled food into their mouths. Next, came fresh blackberry, blueberry, or rhubarb pies for dessert along with coffee.

After they had eaten, the crew would lie down on the grass under a shade tree to rest, smoke or enjoy some snus or chewing tobacco. Pa and Uncle Oscar couldn't eat with the crew as they worked during the dinner break, greasing, filling up the tractor with gasoline, checking belts and sometimes doing minor repairs. They took turns coming in later to eat. Pa also had to predict if they would finish threshing today or be there for dinner the next day. The farm wife needed to know if she would be feeding them dinner the next day or if another farm would have that obligation. Farmers rarely stayed for supper as they had to get home to do their milking. Cows weren't milking much by late summer, which was fortunate for Ma and me as Pa often did not get home in time to help us.

Farmers would tease Pa that he tried to make a threshing job last longer at farms with a reputation for good meals and move on faster to avoid eating at a few households with poor cooking. There was a kernel of truth in this as the crew expected poor eating at a few places. One of the worst farms Pa threshed at was Olai and Jenny Roseland's south of Sand Creek. Jenny Roseland was a domineering woman who treated her husband shamefully and was tight as bark on a tree. Farmers didn't expect much when eating a threshing dinner on this farm. Pa said one time she served boiled weiners for the meat along with potatoes, and several of the crew put two or three weiners on their plates so the serving bowl was empty by the time it came to the last few men at the table. She had made an approximate count of the crew and apportioned only one weiner for each hungry farmer. Pa said that Jenny Roseland deserved her reputation as a skinflint.

Pa's big tractor had steel lugs on the rear wheels that provided excellent traction when pulling a big breaking plow on new land. It gave a bumpy ride when moving the threshing machine from farm to farm on the gravel or dirt roads in the countryside. However, by 1937 County Trunk I past our house was paved with asphalt, which meant that steel lug tractors could not travel on it. The tractor had to be equipped with rubber tires, so he bought another set of old steel lug tractor wheels and had a welding shop cut the outer rims off and weld the spokes to rims for big tires. Since times were hard, he bought used heavy construction equipment tires and mounted them on his rims. The threshing machine was also equipped with rubber tires so there would be no damage to the new asphalt road. It was a big expense at a difficult time, but necessary to enjoy the advantages of dust- and mud-free main highways.

Corn Cutting

Silo filling with chopped green corn was done when the corn was well dented, but before frost. This operation usually occurred during mid- to late-September in our area. Weather was usually cool and sunny, but occasionally a chilly drizzle made it unpleasant. Each farmer owned a horse-drawn one-row binder to cut the corn when the ears were nicely dented. When the binder moved forward, corn stalks were held in place as knives cut them off near the ground, then were carried in an upright position by rotating chains to the binder and knotter that tied twine around the center. The corn bundle then fell onto a bundle carrier that collected a number of bundles that at intervals were transported by a moving belt and then dropped in long rows on the ground. A few farmers owned binders without bundle carriers so the corn bundles were scattered all over the field, making it a big task to drive all over the field to pick up bundles. Sitting on a corn binder was an easy job compared to filling the silo.

Silo Filling

Silo filling was hard work. Unlike oat threshing, corn bundles were eight-foot long, heavy, wet, green corn stalks with large ears. These heavy beasts had to be lifted from the ground and thrown up on the wagon platform with corn tassels all on one side. One soon learned how to handle the bundle to avoid having stalks going in different directions since they were held together only at the center. It was arduous work and got worse as the load got higher. Each team owner loaded his own wagon, assisted by several hired workers. As I got older, I worked at this job on Saturdays and sometimes stayed home from high school on weekdays to help.

It was hard work, but there were some moments of fun. During one unusually warm day, a thunderstorm threatened just before loading Uncle George Hoveland's wagon in the field at his farm. He was peeing behind the wagon when a loud boom of thunder scared his horses so they tore off with the wagon toward the barn, leaving him standing in an embarrassing position. "By goodness," yelled Uncle George, "those damned horses won't even let a man pee in private." No damage was done but we all got a good laugh that day.

Chopping the green corn bundles required a silo filler to put the chopped material into the tall upright silo. A silo filling machine, either a Gehl or Papec, was owned by several farmers who helped each other at all the farms. Pa shared ownership of a Gehl silo filler with John Harrington and Uncle George Hoveland. A big job was hoisting the silo filler pipe sections up the side of the silo with block and tackle, then bolting them together. The silo filler consisted of a steel-slat conveyor belt that carried the corn bundles at a right angle into whirling blades of the chopper. Four long knives on the rotating drum cut a corn bundle into 1/2-inch pieces like a giant scissors. Steel paddles whirling at high speed swept the chopped corn along and blew it up the long vertical metal pipe to the top of the silo and through flexible pipes directed to distribute it. Because a silo filler required a lot of belt power, a good size tractor engine like Pa's big McCor-mick-Deering was needed.

At the silo, a wagon loaded with corn bundles stopped at the end of the silo filler conveyor belt. The man on the load tossed each bundle straight on the belt to move into the chopper. It was important that bundles be well spaced or they would plug the filler pipe, requiring taking pipes apart to empty them. Another man stood on the ground to guide the bundle into a deep-ribbed rotating cylinder that squeezed it into the whirling knives. He had to pull unruly stalks down on the bundle so they would enter properly. This was a very dangerous job and one could easily end up with a finger or even an arm being pulled into the machine and severed by the knives. There was good testimony to the dangers of silo filling as many farmers were missing a finger or part of one.

Gerald, John Harrington's son, was a good farmer and willing to try new things. One year he planted sunflowers in his corn as this crop was supposed to yield more than corn alone. The sunflowers did fine and looked like a winner.

However, trouble came when we started to pick up the bundles in the field. The huge sunflower heads, loaded with seeds, made the top of the bundle extra heavy as we strained to lift them up on the wagons. A worse problem awaited us at the silo filler as the big wide sunflower heads dropped over the edge of the load and made pulling the bundles off a gut-wrenching ordeal. Then as each heavy seed-filled sunflower head hit the silo filler knives, there was an awful garoomph sound as the machine nearly ground to a halt. It was a slow, backbreaking job finishing Gerald's mixed sunflower-corn silo filling. He was told that if he planted sunflowers next year he would be filling his silo alone.

One man was in the silo, moving sections of removable distributor pipe to spread the chopped corn stalks over the surface and not end up with a cone that resulted in all the grain rolling to the edge of the silo. The silo man added new silo doors as the chopped material rose in the silo, and it was also supposed that his trampling the chopper material would pack it to aid fermentation for better silage. As a little kid, I enjoyed helping John Harrington who was the usual silo man. It was fun to be with him because this Irishman had a big supply of stories to keep me entertained. I also wondered how a cow would regard a bite of silage containing a big wad of used chewing tobacco that John disposed of before he replenished his mouth with a fresh chew.

The silo man had the easiest job, but it was still important. Once when filling silo at Uncle John Hanson, his mentally handicapped nephew Willie who lived on the adjacent farm, was the silo man. In late afternoon the silo filler ground to a halt, plugged up. Uncle John shouted up the silo chute to Willie. No reply, and climbing up the chute, he found the silo empty. Finally, someone spotted Willie hurrying across the field toward his father's barn. Everyone knew Willie had a pocket watch in his overall pocket and checked it frequently as he always did his chores on time. Since it was time to get the cows from the pasture for milking, Willie climbed out of the silo without telling anyone and headed home, leaving the silo filler pipe to become plugged.

Custom Work

Our 80-acre-dairy farm was too small to furnish more than a modest income, so Pa bought machinery to do custom work for other farmers. Since he loved working with machinery and he gained a reputation for good work, this added substantially to our income, which was limited during the Depression. In addition to threshing grain, he had four other enterprises: plowing, breaking new land, a saw mill, and sale of lumber.

Plowing

In the early to mid 1930s, not many farmers had tractors, so they sometimes got behind on their plowing. Horse-drawn moldboard plows had only one or two bottoms while Pa had a 3-bottom plow for his big tractor and could travel faster than horses. Pa could plow more land in a day, so many farmers were willing to pay him to get their land ready in time for planting. Plowing was not big income, but it helped. Most of his custom plowing was done in autumn until it got too cold to crank the stiff tractor engine in the morning. This could be a bone-chilling job sitting in the cold wind without the comfort of a tractor cab. Spring plowing was more limited because of wet soil conditions.

Land Breaking

Most land around us had been developed long ago from cut-over forest land. However, just north of us in the hills of Souix Creek and Dovre townships there were areas that still had land that needed to be broken and developed into useful farmland. Pa owned a big single-bottom breaking plow that was pulled behind the steel lug wheel tractor. This plow was raised and lowered to maintain proper plowing depth via a long lever operated by a man standing on the platform just behind the tractor driver. Pa drove the tractor, and a number of people were hired as lever man. Orville Hoveland enjoyed working with Pa on this job. As I got older and able to do this tough job, I would do it on Saturdays during school and then again in summer.

The land we broke was rough, generally covered with grass sod that had been grazed while pine stumps rotted. Many of these rough fields in Dovre and Sioux Creek also contained stones, some of them a foot or more in diameter. Several of the farms we worked at had long stone fences, bearing testimony to a lot of tired backs. Standing on the tractor platform as it swayed up and down while moving over uneven ground, the lever man tried his best to hang on and adjust the plow depth. Occasionally the plow point would hit a big boulder, and if one had just unlocked the lever while adjusting it, the lever could fly up and clobber the man in his gut. For a kid, it was about enough to knock him off the tractor so one held on to the lever for dear life. After a couple of hours of this torture one was ready for morning coffee and then dinner at noon.

At most farms, a good meal would be on the table. However, Nils Traaseth was a bachelor farmer with no cooking skills so dinner there was poor eating. He also did not have a refrigerator or even an ice box, so the milk I drank at his

121

farm was sometimes sour. By late afternoon, coming home to cow milking was a relief after a day on the breaking plow. In contrast, Pa enjoyed the challenge of developing new farm-land and liked to talk about how much land we broke that day.

Logging

Many farms in our area had some pine or hardwood forest, mainly on land not well suited for farming. We had about 10 acres of fairly large white pines; second growth forest that had grown up since it was logged off in the mid-1850's. Our electric power line ran through a corridor cleared of trees to the transformer near our buildings. We were lucky to have power even though we were at the end of the line. Unfortunately, hard spring or winter winds, heavy snow, or ice storms sometimes would fell some big limbs or even a tree across the line and leave us without power. Wisconsin Hydro Electric made a lot of emergency calls to repair our broken line and restore power, so it is doubtful they made money selling power to our farm.

Logging of fallen trees and others chosen to be cut down was a Saturday or a Christmas vacation job as soon as I got old enough to handle a two-man cross-cut saw with Pa. If a tree was to be cut down, Pa sized up where to fell it, then notched it on that side with an axe. Next, we used a cross-cut saw to cut the tree close to the ground. Leaning over and holding on to the wood handles each man had to pull the saw toward himself on each stroke. Two strong experienced sawyers could cut down a tree fairly fast, although it was a tiring job. Things were a good bit more difficult when the sawing was done by a strong experienced woodsman like Pa paired with a small kid like me. I strained to keep up, but tired and did not always pull it back fast enough so the saw buckled on the other side where Pa was pushing. I discovered early on that sawing trees was hard work and that Pa was a strong man. He was only of average height but was well muscled and could lift heavy objects with ease and do it for a long time. I just couldn't keep up with a man who had worked in logging camps.

Most logging was done in winter when there was snow on the ground. Often in cutting down a tree one had to saw while kneeling in the snow. In addition, the temperatures could be bitter cold. Even with wool mittens inside of leather ones, my fingers would get so cold they would ache. I would complain about it to Pa, but his usual reply was to saw faster and I would stay warm. It didn't work for me as my fingers continued to ache. Pa never seemed to get cold and couldn't understand why I did. Pine pitch could make a saw stick while it was in the cut so kerosene from a bottle was applied to make it pull easier. Sometimes the tree would bend back on the saw when it was nearly cut through, pinching it. That required pounding a steel wedge in to clear the saw so it could be pulled out after one handle was removed. A tree nearly cut through that refused to fall was dangerous, particularly if there was some wind. Pa was clever at sawing from the other side and eventually getting it to fall, but he had to jump at the right time to avoid getting hit.

Pa was good at felling a tree where he wanted it to go and avoid getting it hung up in other trees. Once a tree had crashed to the ground we used axes to trim off the limbs, then carried them to a brush pile that would be burned later. Next, Pa used his wood measuring stick to notch where to cut the trunk into appropriate length logs. Sawing them into logs was easier than cutting trees down as the sawyers were in a standing position. Cut logs were rolled by hand into small piles to be picked up later by a team of horses and a log skid which pulled the load to our saw mill. A cold day in the woods cutting down trees was hard work, so a warm barn at milking time was a pleasant experience.

Saw Mill

Pa had built a small saw mill in the woods near our barnyard. We used it for our small output of logs, but it was mainly intended for custom work sawing logs of neighboring farmers. Logs would be unloaded from trucks or horse-drawn wagons or sleighs into piles scattered near the mill and sawed during the main season in early spring and sometimes in autumn. Most of the logs were white pine with a very small amount of oak or maple. Logs of each owner were marked and instructions on size of lumber desired noted by Pa. Sawed lumber had to be placed in separate piles for each customer to pick up.

Logs were piled high on heavy round timbers, allowing them to be rolled with a canthook to the carriage where they were held in place against steel posts by two sharp daggers that were moved up and down on steel posts, depending on size of the log. A man or boy standing on the carriage pulled a lever to move the log out the width of slab or board to be cut. Then Pa, who was the sawman, slowly pulled a lever that caused a cable to pull the carriage along a track toward the large whirling circular saw to cut a slice off the log. The cut slab (waste) and board dropped on a flat surface with several rollers to where the lumber man moved the newly cut wood either to the slab pile or lumber piles. Slabs were placed in a separate pile and used for firewood. In the meantime, Pa sent the carriage swiftly back toward the log pile so the carriage man could pull his lever to move the log toward the saw for another slice. This was done rapidly with the carriage zipping swiftly back and forth. The carriage man had an easy but boring job riding all day. It was a job I did as soon as Pa thought I was old enough to do it. The mill was powered via a belt to a pulley on the big International tractor. We also had a planing machine that would skim off rough sawn lumber to produce smooth boards for finished surfaces to be painted. The waste from this machine was wood shavings which were used for building insulation and sometimes as cow bedding.

It took a minimum of three people to run the saw mill, but four or five allowed more logs to be sawed in a day. It was easy to spot persons who had been working in the sawmill as they accumulated a lot of pine pitch on their overalls, jackets, and leather gloves. Pa had to hire day labor to help saw lumber, local younger men who were glad to get a temporary job to earn a few dollars during the Depression. When I was little, Pa's Uncle Dave Bonkrude sometimes came from Dallas and stayed with us several weeks to saw lumber. I enjoyed having him as he had such a good sense of humor, thus entertaining me, and sometimes he would carve simple wooden toys in the evening. Favorite items carved from single pieces of wood were linked chains and a moving ball within a frame.

When we employed labor for the saw mill, it made more work for Ma as she had to feed the crew dinner plus morning coffee and afternoon lunch. Pa enjoyed running the sawmill, but as I grew older it became just another place for hard work. In addition to riding the carriage, there were plenty of other jobs for me like moving logs, crawling under the saw to clean out sawdust, greasing the machinery, piling slabs, and helping Pa make repairs. It was not a fun place. Later, Bennie Myran decided to start a saw mill so now there was nearby competition. To power the sawmill, Bennie had bought an old Case steam engine that attracted a lot of attention from customers. Our business dropped off, so Pa decided to sell the saw mill. It was a good day for me when the buyer came with trucks to move the saw mill away.

Lumber

Sawing our own logs produced lumber for sale. Also, some log owners left the lumber with Pa so we grouped it by size and located the piles just beyond the clothes line where buyers could back their trucks in to load. Piling lumber was another boring, extra job to do when we were not busy at other farm work. Lumber was piled on rows of concrete blocks that were leveled to avoid twisting the wood and each layer was separated by strips of wood edging. Lumber would lie in piles to dry, and would remain there until sold. Several of the more prosperous farmers used lumber from their piles to build rental houses in Eau Claire as an investment for additional income. Uncle Fritjof built such a house and rented it for a number of years, then lived there during his retirement. Pa never risked such an investment but just sold our lumber.

Church

Our Lutheran Church

When we spoke of church it meant the Lutheran (pronounced "Lutran") church, as that was all we had in Sand Creek. In addition to the two churches in Sand Creek and other nearby towns, there were a number of Norwegian Lutheran churches scattered in the countryside such as Running Valley, Dovre, Maple Grove, Hay Creek, and others. Bloomer had a big German Catholic (pronounced "Catlick") parish and there was a mainly Polish parish in Chetek and a tiny one in New Auburn. There were small Protestant churches in other towns, but they had no impact on us. We were Norwegian Lutherans, and they were the most important part of Christianity. There were some German Lutheran churches south of Sand Creek, but they didn't count with us. It was a small world.

Our Saviour's Lutheran just west of town was a member of the Norwegian Synod. They used a formal liturgy and clerical vestments during worship, similar to the state Church of Norway. We were members of Zion Lutheran in Sand Creek, which was a member of the Lutheran Free Church, a breakaway denomination with pietistic leanings. In Running Valley south of Sand Creek there was a similar situation where the Synod church was just across the road from the Free church. The liturgy in the Free church was less formal, and the clergy wore gray striped pants and long black Prince

Albert swallowtail coats. Some of the members were devout followers of Hans Nielson Hauge, a pietist layman in the Church of Norway, who believed Christians needed a special "experience" of salvation as an adult like that of John Wesley. In Norway, these people met in a "bedehus" (prayer house) for special prayer meetings apart from the state church and stressed personal piety, rejecting worldly evils such as alcohol, playing cards, dancing, and theaters. Tobacco was not mentioned. Warnings on these evils were frequently mentioned in sermons at our church. Every word in the Bible was taken literally with interpretation done as needed by the pastor. Infant baptism, confirmation, marriage, and burial were important rites of the church.

Ecumenism was not part of our culture. We had no relationship with Catholic churches or their priests, and our pastors sometimes spoke out in sermons on the evils existing in the competing denomination. I grew up in total ignorance of the Catholic church, wondering if they were true Christians. We were told that Catholic churches had statues in them to which people prayed instead of to God. The priest at the Bloomer Catholic church was known to enjoy his beer, and we suspected other sinful things must go in the rectory where the priest and a number of teaching nuns lived. Marriage between Catholics and Lutherans was regarded as a dreadful blot on the family and strongly discouraged. Many cemeteries used by both denominations were divided with Catholics on one side and Lutherans on the other side. Minor dissenting groups such as Methodists were buried amid the Lutherans. As a child, I did not personally know any practicing Catholics although George Pfeiffer, creamery manager, was an active member of that communion. I never dared enter a Catholic church until at university when I attended mass one Sunday out of curiosity. Relations between Lutheran sects were cordial, although there did not appear to be any substantial cooperation. We enjoyed attending weddings, funerals, and lutefisk dinners at each other's Lutheran churches.

Only essential work like milking, feeding, and barn cleaning was done on Sunday in Norwegian Lutheran households. This contrasted with German Catholics who often put up hay on Sunday if rain threatened. We also differed in attitudes toward alcohol. Catholics openly drank beer, but Norwegian Lutherans were officially teetotalers although some enjoyed their beer when away from home. Good Lutherans used Luther Hospital in Eau Claire and avoided being hospitalized at Catholic hospitals, cared for by nuns, amid statues of saints, and crucifixes instead of empty crosses. In addition to never attending a Catholic mass, I do not recall my parents ever attending a Catholic wedding. Our religion separated us and the break was total.

I knew nothing about the few people in other Protestant groups. There were tiny Methodist churches in Colfax and Dallas. New Auburn had a Seventh Day Baptist church where they worshiped on Saturday. Bloomer had Congregational and Methodist churches. Chetek was the most ecumenical town with Methodist, Presbyterian, Advent Christian, Pentecostal, and Mormon churches in addition to the dominant Lutherans and Catholics. Our neighbors, Helen and Leonard Toycen, worshiped in homes with a few other Pentecostal folks. They were always talking about being "saved" and didn't seem to observe any of our Lutheran liturgy or sacraments except for adult baptism, which was done by dunking in the river during summer. One of their farmer members would tediously insert the phrase, "Praise the Lord", after every few sentences in a conversation. He was commonly known as "Praise the Lord Olson" by us Lutherans who were more restrained in conversation about our faith.

Sunday morning worship was held every other week at 11 am in Sand Creek during my early childhood since the pastor also served the Running Valley parish, and poor roads, especially in winter, did not allow him time to dependably conduct two services in one morning. Later, better roads permitted a service each Sunday at both churches. Services could not be held too early in the morning as dairy farmers would not have their chores completed in time. This problem was solved at the Catholic church in Bloomer by having a 5 am mass for farmers to attend before they did their milking. We Lutherans were not that dedicated. Services were held in Norwegian and English on alternate Sundays, and by the late 1930's Norwegian services had declined to once monthly. Pastors were poorly paid, but even so it was difficult to maintain even a small church budget during the Depression years. The annual giving by each member was published in a church bulletin and always was read with great interest. I suppose that it was hoped that members would be shamed into giving more, but in many households during some of these awful years, there was little extra money to share with the church.

Nearly everyone in our community was Lutheran and a member of one of the two Sand Creek churches. However, there were a number of people that rarely attended worship except for Christmas, Easter, weddings, and funerals. Fritz Nelson, a next door neighbor, was one of them. Uncle Art was likewise not a church goer. Most of these men never wore a suit except for these special church occasions. When Bennie Myran bought a new suit, I recall the size and price tag on one sleeve remained there for several years, indicating that it wasn't worn much and never had been sent to the cleaners. As a child, I was taught that church attendance was important, but it was puzzling to me that the non-church goers did not seem to be bad people, rather they were just as nice as everyone else.

Morning Worship

Our white board church with a tall steeple was typical of most rural Lutheran churches. At worship one walked up many concrete steps to enter a small anteroom where overshoes and large coats could be dropped off. The high-ceilinged long sanctuary was filled with pews on both sides of an aisle that led to the altar, which was surrounded by a circular kneeling pad for worshippers to receive communion at infrequent intervals. Above the altar was a tall canvas oil painting of Christ leading a flock of sheep. On the left side of the church was the choir area and organ. On the right was a wood pulpit located high above the congregation so people sitting near the front would find their neck getting sore as a result of being cocked at such a sharp angle during the long sermon. In later years the pulpit was lowered, putting the pastor closer to the people but possibly a bit farther from God.

Families arrived in their cars unless they lived in Sand Creek and walked to church. Before men went up the steps, it was common to see them spit or take a finger and scrape a wad of chewing tobacco or snus out of their mouth and flip it on the ground, then wipe their mouth and finger on a handkerchief. A kid learned early to avoid walking on the grass near the church entrance. In winter, these wastes discolored the snow and ice. In pleasant weather, early arrivals often visited with each other outside before entering. Inside, people generally sat in the same place each Sunday. When a rare visitor came, parishioners would change their seating to accommodate them. However, Julius Field was insistent on sitting in exactly the same pew location each time. One Sunday when Julius arrived, a visiting couple was sitting in his place. He gruffly told them that was his seat and they must move as he needed it to have the correct angle for his neck during the sermon. Surprised, these people graciously moved for this arrogant bachelor.

Pa made sure we always arrived in plenty of time for the service; so I enjoyed watching these mostly farm people walking up the aisle to their pews. My parents sat together, but there were a number who still observed the old custom of men sitting on the right and women on the left side of the church. There was no question this was a Norwegian community as indicated by parishioner surnames such as Anderson, Johnson, Eyk, Olson, Ness, Severson, Swanson, Svalestun, Noer, Hoveland, Nelson, Thompson, Madison, Gregarson, Hanson, and Paulson. The Seph Petersons, a poor family with seven kids, were always there and the children were well behaved in church. Uncle Sophus, a tall man, always arrived well after the service started, rushing up the aisle with short-legged Aunt Clara and little Swanhild struggling to keep up. It was not a style show, as money for new clothes was limited during the Depression. However, men wore wool suits, white shirts, and neckties while women had a "church dress," coat, and a hat. Children were clean and wore their best clothes.

The worship service was long, usually lasting an hour and a half, although as a child it seemed much longer. I had been trained from an early age to sit quietly in church as Ma did not tolerate "uskikkelig" or naughty children. I was not allowed to read a book in church other than the hymnal, which was not particularly exciting for a pre-school child. Consequently, sitting beside Ma at the end of the pew, I did a lot of people watching, something I continued to enjoy throughout my life.

Henry Anderson and family sat in front of us. He was a friendly bear of a man with a lush handlebar mustache and gold capped teeth that sparkled as he laughed or talked. His big shoulders and head insulated me from a direct view of the pulpit. However, on my left I had a great view of people across the aisle, the altar, and the choir. It was exciting watching Josie Severson pumping the organ bellows with great enthusiasm as she played for congregational and choir singing. Pa had a good voice and sang lustily, but Ma generally did little singing. Gilbert Severson led the choir in one anthem each Sunday, waving his arms to keep time. Because the choir of farmers and their wives were not musically trained, the anthems were simple, and I was never exposed to anything like Bach, Haydn, or Mozart chorales. Sometimes there was a solo singing of an old Norwegian hymn, many of which were based on lovely folk tunes. Handel's oratorio "The Messiah" was unknown to me until many years later when a university coed invited me to a concert. I had never heard anything so beautiful in my life and was immediately smitten by such glorious music.

Sermon time was the longest period for me as a child, because I had absolutely nothing to do except look around from my restricted position in the pew. One did not move around, period! The sermon was beyond me, and it always lasted a long time. I have no recollection of what Pastors Ingel Hovland or Alfred Knutson preached. Looking at them in the pulpit, they were stern, never looked very happy, and seemed to talk a lot about sin. Watching people, I soon discovered that many listened intently, while some farmers drifted off to sleep during the sermon. A few even snored. Women remained awake. In summer a fly might light on the pew in front of me and walk around, providing entomological interest. Colorful ladybugs also entertained me. Feeling under the pew, one discovered all sorts of hard chewing gum blobs that previous pew sitters had deposited. If I was in view of another child, we could wink or make faces at one another. Sometimes I day dreamed and traveled to various places. After such a session of enjoyment, one might be rudely poked and reminded to stand up for another portion of the service. I never figured out why one of our pastors always pulled out his pocket watch and placed it on the pulpit; he never seemed to look at it during his lengthy sermons.

One of the most interesting sermon times I had was on a warm summer Sunday with windows open to the breezes. As usual, Clifford Nelson in the back row of the choir drifted off for a nap during the sermon. With head slumped backward against the wall, his jaw opened wide as he snored. I was enjoying watching an extra big fly buzzing around from place to place. After awhile it headed over to the choir where several members brushed it away. Finally, the fly was attracted to Clifford's open mouth and eventually entered this cavernous opening. Apparently, the fly walking about on his tongue while enjoying the saliva must have triggered a response. Clifford's mouth snapped shut on the fly as he swallowed. I had been intrigued with this drama and burst out laughing. Ma had missed out on this exciting event, so simply swatted me and said "Shhh!" as I couldn't contain my laughter. To me it was excruciatingly funny that Clifford had swallowed a big fly during the sermon. It was the best sermon time I ever had as a small child.

As I grew older during Pastor Iver Olson's tenure, I took more interest in the sermon. He was a farmer's son, who was better able than his predecessors to relate Bible texts to our lives on the farm. Best of all, he was a warm, humble man who genuinely liked people. He had a friendly face and often smiled as he preached. The sermons were simple and generally concerned with applying Christian faith to everyday life. Pastor Olson was faithful in visiting parishioners, contributing to his popularity. With him, sermon time didn't seem as long for me.

Communion was celebrated quarterly. Many members like Grandpa and Grandma Hoveland always communed while others like my parents seldom did. I never knew the reason for the difference. I never communed until I was confirmed. Those communing walked up to kneel on a pad at a railing in a half-circle around the altar. There, the pastor gave out white wafers first, followed by tiny cups of grape juice. I never figured out why they served grape juice when the Bible said Jesus and his disciples drank wine at the Last Supper.

Sunday School

At Zion church our Sunday School classes were held in the hour before morning worship from about April until Christmas. There was no Sunday School during the winter months because it was harder to travel. Classes were taught mostly by women, although older children generally had a male teacher. There was also an adult class, but few attended. Pa would take me to Sunday School and then go home to get Ma for worship service. If there was no service that Sunday, he would stop and visit with Grandpa and Grandma or spend some time talking with farmers and milk haulers at Gilberts service station or Uncle Art's garage until my class was over.

Everyone met together in the church sanctuary where Margaret Anderson, the tall spinster bank manager who was also Sunday School superintendent, would lead us in a prayer and singing of a number of simple hymns. Then we would go to our respective classes that clustered in groups scattered about in the church pews or in the basement parish hall. The teacher would talk about the lesson for the day and ask questions that often didn't generate much discussion except for a few who just liked to talk. As a small child, I have little recollection of what was said in these classes that were taught by women. I do recall that there was plenty of conversation after class when we talked about more interesting things. At the end of our class period, we each received a four-page story paper, "The Child's Friend." It contained a Bible lesson, a poem or two, and several short inspirational stories. I always read them, but they seemed syrupy. They didn't relate very well to my life on the farm nor hold my attention.

As I got older, I was in classes taught by men. Farmers such as Norman Anderson tried very hard to teach us, but it was difficult to hold the attention of older kids, especially boys, as there was no fear of failing as in the public school. Lively, inquisitive boys like Edsel Peterson and Virgil van Gilder made these classes especially interesting. Boys would pinch someone while looking innocently in the other direction, pull a pigtail or untie the bow in the back of a girl's dress, untie a shoelace, or slide someone's cap along the pew behind another person's back. All these tricks were effective ways to waste time and have fun but created difficulties for the poor teacher who was trying to maintain decorum during the lesson.

Sometimes the poor teacher was tormented with impossible questions such as in Jesus' parable of the sower when a kid asked, "Why would a man be dumb enough to sow seeds on a path, on rocks, or in thorns as any farmer knows it won't grow?" When we had the story of Joshua stopping the sun at mid-day so it didn't set for 24 hours, one kid asked, "Why didn't it fry everything as it must have been awful hot?" Once the lesson was about Noah's ark, and a kid inquired, "What did Noah feed the hungry lions in the ark, and why didn't the lions eat the cows and sheep?" When we discussed the parable about a shepherd with 100 sheep and leaving 99 of them in the wilderness to go rescue one that is lost, one kid said, "That farmer sure was foolish to leave all his sheep in the wilderness where wild dogs and coyotes can kill 'em. My Pa would never have done that." Another gem was a kid's question, "Why is it bad to drink wine when

Jesus made wine from water in a miracle and had it served to the wedding guests?" The teacher creatively explained that the wine in the Bible didn't contain alcohol. Questions and comments like these enlivened the class lessons.

The annual Sunday School program occurred on an evening following Christmas. Margaret Anderson planned and supervised it all. The program was composed of group singing of Christmas hymns and carols, songs by duets and trios, a skit acting out the nativity story with children in costumes, kids of various ages standing up and "speaking pieces," and a message by the pastor. Wood planks were placed on blocks to make seats in front of the altar for the children. Because she believed in giving the parents their money's worth it was a lengthy program, much too long for little kids who often would fall asleep, sitting slumped over on the plank. Many adults also fell asleep in the pews. The pine planks got harder as the evening wore on, and we wriggled uncomfortably on our sore bottoms. It was a tough experience both for the children and the parents as they suffered through the long program. Margaret meant well but never realized that her program would have been far more effective if it had been shorter. What should have been a joyous occasion turned out to be an event that I dreaded each year.

Ladies Aid

Women of the church generally met weekly in the church basement. It was a social occasion for hard working farm women to enjoy time with each other. The afternoon program had a speaker, but the main feature was visiting and lunch with a charge which was contributed for missions or some other worthy cause. Two women provided coffee and food. It was usually a good spread with sandwiches, cookies, and cake; so it was frequented by men who lived in town as well as farmers who happened to be in town. Ma was not a regular attendee as she could not drive a car but occasionally came to Ladies Aid riding with Lena Larson.

Special Meetings

The Lutheran Free Church encouraged, "special meetings" that in other denominations were called revivals. The Norwegian Synod Churches didn't host such meetings. Special meetings were conducted by Lutheran Free Church evangelists who traveled around to various congregations and tried to awaken people from their lethargy and be reborn to a more active Christian life. People gave testimonies of how God was working in their lives and had changed them. There were prayers for sinners and an altar call for renewal. It seemed that the same people always responded. Some, like my parents, never walked forward or gave testimonies. Of course, there were many like Grandma Noer, Uncles Arnold, Fritjof, and John who never came to special meetings.

One summer early in the Depression we had tent meetings. Ardent Haugeans in the parish rented a tent that was erected on the Sand Creek school grounds for special meetings with a Lutheran evangelist from Duluth. People sat on chairs and benches. People sang from gospel song books and were led by someone waving his arms around up front while a pianist played. I didn't understand much of what the animated preacher was saying except that he talked a lot about sin and repentance. Some people got all excited and made long testimonies to the group. Pa insisted we attend many of the meetings and also hosted an evening home meeting of a few people where the leader tried to make us feel guilty about something. It didn't make much sense to me as I was baptized and knew Jesus loved me. I didn't know what I was supposed to feel guilty about. I was tired of special meetings.

Confirmation

Confirmation was our entrance into the church as adults, affirming our baptismal covenant. Prospective confirmands, usually in eighth grade of school, would spend much of a year meeting each Saturday morning with the pastor. This was referred to as "reading for the minister" which was derived from the Norwegian "lese for presten" where the confirmand would be expected to memorize and repeat to the pastor the answers to questions in Luther's Small Catechism. Pa said that in his confirmation class at Our Saviour's Church, Pastor Waage was strict and required every word in the answers to be memorized. Pastor Iver Olson was more reasonable in our class and just wanted us to know the meaning of what was being asked and answer the questions in our words.

We had six boys in our class: Duard Dalhoe, Wesley Paulson, Edsel Peterson, Clayton Saastad, Virgil van Gilder, and me. Duard and Clayton were in County Line School with me, and Wesley Paulson was a second cousin, who lived on a farm across the river from us. Virgil was the only one who lived in town. We boys got on well and enjoyed some fun before our class session each week. Edsel, the smartest one in the class, and Virgil, a prankster, provided the best laughs.

Pastor Olson had a warm friendly disposition and injected some humor into teaching subjects that were not very exciting to thirteen- and fourteen-year-old boys. During the week we were expected to learn the answers to a set of questions in the catechism and read a portion from the Bible history book. In the catechism we covered topics like the Ten

Commandments, the Apostles Creed, and communion. I looked forward to the commandment on adultery, thinking we would learn something about sex but was sorely disappointed. In spite of my interest in history, the Bible history book must have been badly written, and I found it deadly dull as it plodded through the creation, flood, prophets, life of Jesus, and the apostles. Amazingly, it contained nothing on Judaism or the long history of the Catholic church prior to Luther's Reformation. We were fortunate that Pastor Olson enlivened it with stories and made application to events in our life. He was a kind, patient man, and we respected him as he worked with us.

Confirmation Day came on a sunny Sunday in June, 1941. Each of us had acquired a new wool suit for this important event in our life when we were to stand in front of the congregation and answer questions that Pastor Olson would put to each one. Each of us was afraid that we might fail and have to repeat the class next year which would be disgraceful. As it turned out all went well, although poor Clayton had trouble remembering a number of answers and needed help from Pastor Olson. Clayton was a bit slow mentally, and memorization was not one of his strong attributes. At the end, each of us got our confirmation certificates and all was well. Ma and Pa were so proud that I had done well. Other relatives crowded around me afterward with congratulations. I felt so important on this day. In my honor, Uncle Sewell and Aunt Mabel from Chippewa Falls, were there and joined us for dinner at our house after church. As a special treat, Pa bought my favorite Gustafson black raspberry ice cream for dessert. For me, that was the most memorable part of getting confirmed.

Weddings

Some couples got married in the pastor's home, but most elected to have a church wedding. Weddings were usually held during good weather after spring planting was done and before haying started. No one with any sense chanced a winter wedding when one might get snowed in. At church weddings, the bride wore a long white dress and veil, and the groom a dark wool suit. Often, one or two solos were sung by a lady with a strong voice. In addition to the nuptial ceremony, one could count on a sermon that usually lasted too long for the eager couple. A reception at the bride's home followed afterward. Usually, it was a big buffet spread on the dining room table with whipped cream-apple-raisin-walnut salad, various baked hot dishes of noodles-meat-vegetables, potatoes, ham or roast beef, several kinds of home-made pickles, home-made yeast buns, and butter. On another table would be a big decorated wedding cake made by a local lady, and nearby there might be ice cream. There was no champagne or other alcoholic beverage, as this was a Norwegian Lutheran Free Church wedding, and our members officially did not drink. Some people had attended German Catholic weddings where they had keg beer at their receptions. Even German Lutherans did that. Polish Catholic wedding receptions were even better as they partied much longer, enjoying lots of food, beer, dancing, and polka music.

One of the most memorable wedding receptions I attended as a child was that of cousin Julian Hanson and Ione Wall, held at the bride's home in Dallas. It was a joyous event with all the Hanson brothers and others laughing together amid big clouds of blue smoke from cigars furnished to everyone by the bridegroom. Her parents were wonderful hosts and spread a good table of food that I enjoyed heartily. I wasn't interested in the wedding cake, but they had big tubs of Gustafson's vanilla ice cream and bowls of garden-fresh mashed strawberries. It was the opportunity of a lifetime as I never got enough ice cream, my favorite dessert! I indulged myself with one dish after another as the evening progressed. It was so good. By the time Pa said it was time to go home, I was feeling uncomfortable and a bit nauseated. Riding home in the back seat of the car, I got sicker by the mile. As the car stopped in our garage, I flung open the door and dashed around to the north wall where Pa and I usually peed. There, I gladly deposited a lot of my delicious ice cream and strawberries as I broke out in a cold sweat. It was awful. It was quite awhile before I wanted to eat ice cream and strawberries again.

The real entertainment came when the newlyweds got into their car to leave on their honeymoon. It was a rare wedding car that escaped getting the full decorative treatment by local young men, who were specialists in this activity. Banners were tied to the car, comical messages were daubed on the car body and windows, and tin cans were tied with strings on the rear bumper to provide music for the couple as they rode. Additional car treatment depended on how much they wanted to torment the couple and who was ringleader of the decorating group.

Orville and Toddy Hoveland were especially talented in thinking up imaginative pranks on wedding cars. Stones were inserted into wheel hub caps to entertain the couple as they drove along. Sometimes small prank bombs were attached to the starter and exploded when the ignition was turned on, emitting a big cloud of smoke from the engine hood. Another trick was to disconnect one or more spark plugs to cause the engine to run rough. One time someone slipped a cat into the trunk after the suit cases were loaded. One of the worst tricks, reserved only for special people who were wed during chilly late autumn weather, was to smear soft, smelly limberger cheese on the heater coils so the couple could enjoy the aroma as the heater kept them warm. Having survived the car treatment, the newlyweds often had another hurdle before enjoying nuptial bliss the first night of their honeymoon. The car tormentors worked hard to discover where the first night would be spent and somehow managed to secure access to the room. The bed would be short sheeted to greet the couple. Grape Nuts breakfast cereal, pepper, or salt would be sprinkled on the sheets. Curtains might be taken down and hidden under the bed, or thick wood clothes hangers were placed under the mattress. This fine welcome helped make it a memorable event in the lives of the newlyweds.

After the newly married couple returned from their honeymoon trip and settled into their farm home, there remained one final wedding event called a shivaree. This was a late evening party conducted mainly by younger men in the community a week or two after the newlyweds returned from the honeymoon. As the group gathered around the house, they would pound on pans, ring cowbells, and blow horns to make a dreadful noise that was certain to wake the couple if they were asleep. Normally, the couple would come out on the porch to be greeted with more noise, singing, and stories. The object was to get the couple to provide treats for the group. Sometimes it was just a big lunch provided by the couple. More often, they demanded a treat such as ice cream, which had to be purchased in town. In Catholic areas, the usual treat was beer. Normally, a couple yielded in good spirits and met their request. If the couple resisted, the noise got louder and continued until they finally met the demands of the noisemakers.

Occasionally, a tight-fisted groom would refuse to cough up anything for a treat, and the shivaree celebrants would eventually give up and go home. In one celebrated case this did not work. When Julius Johnson, a strong-willed tight-fisted old widower, got re-married it was a splendid opportunity for an exciting shivaree. It was a cold moonlit evening in autumn when a big delegation of noisemakers appeared at the farmhouse. The noisy concert continued for a long time before Julius appeared to the crowd and told them to go home as he wasn't going to buy them any treats, then slammed the door. All that did was make the noise louder, but as they kept on for quite awhile it was apparent that Julius was not going to give up. Finally, Julian Hanson said to the crowd, "Let's smoke 'em out tonight!" They found a ladder and crawled up on the house roof to cover the chimney, which had a good volume of smoke coming from wood heating stoves inside. After awhile the door opened, and Julius came out yelling at them for smoking up his house. He wasn't about to buy treats for a gang like this, and slammed the door. Julian, on top of the house yelled, "Let's give 'em some more and smoke 'em out this time." Sure enough, finally the bride and groom came out coughing and yelling at these fellows who were trying to burn their house down. Julius was mad, but having no choice he paid for plenty of ice cream to treat the shivaree gang. Worst of all, he had a smoke-filled house that night. Julian said this was the best shivaree he had ever been to at Sand Creek.

Funerals

Departure from this world was celebrated in a big way by old neighbors at Sand Creek. Most people died at home among those they loved. The corpse was picked up in the hearse by the Halvorson brothers who had a funeral home in Dallas. Neighbors got together and dug the grave for the deceased either at Zion cemetery or the little Myran cemetery adjacent to our farm. Several times I helped with grave digging, which offered an opportunity to chat with friends and exchange a bit of humor about the deceased. Digging in deep sand was easy, but since it lacked structure, the entire side of a dug grave might slip and collapse. This required shoveling a lot more sand out of the bottom again. We worked in shifts as we dug deeper, with usually two of us in the grave. It was hard work. One time at the Myran cemetery, Joe Rathbun was alone in the bottom when the sand collapsed, and Joe was buried up to his chest. As expected, Fritz Nelson said we might as well fill in the rest of the grave pit and save having a funeral for Joe later. Joe didn't see much humor in it as we dug him out. The worst time for grave digging was winter, especially winters when the ground was frozen three or more feet deep. That meant chopping the frozen soil with a pick axe which was hard work. One could develop a sweat chopping on a winter day. With a stiff cold wind blowing, the best job was pit man down in the hole out of the wind. Grave digging was done in love, a tribute to a deceased neighbor.

A funeral was a lengthy affair. The coffin was brought to the farm the day before the funeral, usually by the Halvorson Bros. who had a funeral home in Dallas, and the deceased was exhibited in the living room of the farmhouse. That evening there would be visitation by neighbors where people would evaluate the corpse and comment on, "How natural he looks," or sometimes "The skin color just doesn't look like him," or "I believe she would look better in a blue dress than in that black one." I detested looking at dead people and avoided it as much as possible. I felt very uncomfortable around corpses. The night that Grandma Noer's corpse was in our living room, I didn't like to walk through the room alone. Why, I don't know, unless it brought back scares from Grandpa Hoveland's burial stories.

The day of the funeral was a long one with three separate services. In the morning, neighbor ladies would start preparations for the late afternoon lunch at the home of the deceased. Food would be furnished by them, and they would bring in additional dishes and silverware. Around noon, we would get dressed in our church clothes in preparation for the home funeral service conducted by the pastor. Close neighbors would be there to pay their respects. A hymn or two would be sung, and the pastor would read some Scripture and give a short homily. Sometimes there were unplanned attractions. The day before Grandma Noer's funeral we had a whopper of a March snow storm. A big county Oshkosh truck snow plow was busy the next morning clearing parking areas in our farmyard for cars during the home service and the big coffee party after the burial. Another time on a hot, steamy July day we were at a home service where the pall bearers in heavy wool suits (men owned only one suit and it needed to be warm for winter) sat on a newly varnished wood bench. When it was time to stand, the pall bearers got up together and the bench stuck to their hot, sweaty bottoms, then dropped to the floor with a loud thud. It was a nice salute to the departed.

After the home service the coffin would be loaded into the Packard hearse, and we would all drive to the church for the main service. At the church, the pall bearers had to lug the coffin up many steps to the church door, a tough job in winter when there was ice and a cold wind. Then the coffin was wheeled down the aisle on a collapsible carriage accompanied by Henry Halvorson, a skinny man with a left leg that locked into a bent position so that when he walked he bobbed up and down. This amiable man also drove the hearse as his brother Alfred had eyesight problems.

To allow friends to view the corpse, the open coffin stood in the front of the church for nearly an hour before the service. Flowers were laid on the coffin and arranged around it on wire stands. Funerals were generally well attended as it was a last tribute to the departed. One would see church members at funerals that rarely attended regular services. This may be the reason that during the long service the pastor would have a lengthy sermon that often seemed directed at those people. A number of hymns and solos were sung, and at funerals of elderly members they included Norwegian ones like "De stor hvit flokk" (The great white flock). At the end of the service, mourners filed out and stood visiting in good weather until the coffin came out and was loaded into the hearse. If it was bitter cold, they huddled in their cars with the engines running.

The pastor, family, and close friends gathered at the cemetery for another service. Most others drove directly to the house for coffee. All the flower arrangements were taken to the cemetery and laid on the coffin and around the grave site. It was sad to see the flowers wasted as they dried up or were frozen rather than distributed in homes. The cemetery service consisted of a final liturgy, Scripture readings, some short remarks by the pastor, prayers, and occasionally a solo. This was a cold service in winter if a bitter wind swept across the snow covered fields. It was no wonder that the warm house, hot coffee, an abundance of good sandwiches, cookies, and cakes were welcome. Regardless of weather, the atmosphere was not dreary, but warm and supportive, often jovial. Most important, the house was filled with neighbors, relatives, and friends who visited with the bereaved and told stories about the deceased. It was a wonderful experience for the bereaved family to have this warm experience of love from neighbors who cared. In retrospect, this social time was probably the best service of the day.

Christian Love

As a child I believed that God was concerned about me and that I could talk to Him. I was confused about where He resided. In church, God was "out there" or "up there" on a throne. Looking up in the sky at all the stars, I wondered how high this might be. Did God live in a big house, what kept Heaven from falling to Earth, and how did my prayers get to God?" I didn't dare ask anyone such questions as they might be considered sinful. At church they seemed to have trite answers for all sorts of things, but they didn't answer many of my questions.

It was much later in life that I began to learn that the spirit of God is within each person, and we meet Him through other people. At a later date I had the awesome thought that God resides within me and that my actions affect other people. When I wrestled with Jesus' summary of the commandments as an admonition to love God and love one's neighbor as oneself (Mark 12:30-31), I began to understand the richness of Christian love for another as practiced by the people of Sand Creek. It had nothing to do with church dogma, confessions, or piety, but genuine love for their neighbors which meant everyone to them. The interesting thing was that this love was practiced by both active church goers and those who were errant. There was no expectation of payback for good deeds; people loved their neighbors and looked after one another as needed. They truly loved one another in their daily lives. I was blessed abundantly by having the opportunity to grow up in such a community of loving relatives and neighbors. They taught me what love is all about.

County Line School

The School Building

We lived in a joint school district spreading across the county line; so I attended elementary school just inside Barron county even though we lived in Dunn county. It was the same school that my mother attended for eight years around the turn of the century. Not much had changed since then. There were no electric lights or telephone, water was obtained from an iron hand pump outside, outdoor toilets took care of our necessary needs, and one teacher taught eight grades in one room. The school was a tan wood-sided building with a bell tower, surrounded by a number of large maple and elm trees under which was "junegrass" (bluegrasss) that was cut several times a year with a hay mower. It was built on a high concrete foundation providing windows for a basement used as a crowded play area in inclement weather. The entry room had hooks on the walls to hang mackinaws, jackets, and caps, beneath which winter overshoes were dumped. Lunch containers from old syrup pails to various-shaped metal lunch boxes were stored on shelves along the side walls.

The classroom had six rows of different sized desks with seats. At the front of the room the teacher's wooden desk was next to the large circular floor heat vent from the basement furnace. Blackboards covered part of the front wall above which were large framed pictures of George Washington and Abraham Lincoln. A large pendulum clock hung on a side wall over the pull down maps. Large windows were located along both sides of the classroom. In my earliest school years, a table at the rear of the room had a pail of water and dipper used for drinking. Later, we used a more sanitary covered earthenware jug with a press button bubbler for water. On the other side were large cabinets for old textbooks as well as the pitiful library available for student reading. Some of the books may have dated back to Ma's years there. The school board composed of local farmers probably didn't have a high priority for library books, and they also faced the constraints of limited school tax money for their budget during the Depression.

Teaching

Teaching a one-room country school was not an attractive job. Paid about $50 a month, teachers boarded with a nearby family unless they lived with their parents. My first teacher, Louie Repaal, a blacksmith's son from Dallas, was unusual in having a four-year degree. He had graduated with a degree as a vocational agriculture teacher but was unable to find a job in 1932 so he ended up at County Line School teaching eight grades. He stuck it out for two years before departing for California to work as a restaurant waiter. All the rest of my teachers, Ella Nelson, Agnes Baaken, Ione Hanson, and Ruth Harelstad had only two-year normal school training. All except one were good teachers and one, Ruth Harelstad, was outstanding. She later married my cousin, Aaron Hanson, got two college degrees, had a fine teaching career, and became a principal.

Life as a country school teacher must have been grim. On bitter cold mornings he or she had to build a fire in the furnace and attempt to warm up this uninsulated building.

The teacher was responsible for keeping the schoolhouse clean. None could afford a car. Using the communal outdoor toilet must not have been a pleasant experience, especially for a woman. It must not have been easy for a young woman to teach classes and maintain discipline over fifteen to thirty children ranging in age from six to seventeen. Some husky grown farm boys had no interest in learning anything and enjoyed tormenting the teacher. Somehow, most of these teachers succeeded although several times they had to contact the president of the school board to administer some discipline.

The school year was from early September to mid-May, with a week or two off at Christmas. The only holidays with no school were Thanksgiving and Good Friday. Classes were held for 15-minute intervals from 9 am to 4 pm with 15-minute recess morning and afternoon. At noon an hour provided time to eat and play games or ski during winter. In some cases, two grades were combined for teaching a class. Since one heard each class session during the day, over a period of eight years a student had repeated the classes many times, which probably helped in the learning process. Teachers taught from a standard curriculum developed by the state board of education. At the end of eight years, graduating students had to pass a state exam in all subjects before getting a diploma.

Starting School

One was supposed to be six before starting school, but since my birthday was in October, I was allowed to enter at age five. Thus, in September 1933 I started my education at County Line School. It was over two miles to the school from our house, which was a long, lonely walk for a little kid. As

151

a result, Pa found time to transport me in the car each morning and most of the time in the afternoon for the first autumn and winter. By spring when Pa got busy in the field, I started walking to and from school.

My first day of school was an exciting one. Because Ma wanted me to look my best, she had worked hard sewing a little jacket and short pants made of tiny red- and black-checked cloth and had also made a white shirt. Ma was so proud of me all dressed for school. Pa dropped me off at school with my lunch box and drove away. A large group of children I did not know were milling about outside the schoolhouse. As I walked toward them, they started to point at me, laughing and making funny remarks about my attire. I looked around and soon realized why. All the other little boys were wearing denim bib overalls and chambray shirts. I was the only boy wearing this silly little suit with short pants! I was crushed, and tears came to my eyes as I entered the school. I just wanted to run home and hide. Somehow I made it through the day and was so glad when Pa picked me up that afternoon. Ma was saddened with my story of what happened as she had worked hard to give me her best. I never wore that suit again. I think she used it in making a bed quilt.

Things went better after that when I attended school in bib overalls like other boys. Girls wore dresses or skirts and sweaters with long cotton stockings. I didn't know any of the other children except my cousin Frederick, who was in eighth grade, but he didn't have much interest in a little first grader. The other children chattered away in English often mixed with some Norwegian words. Unlike most of the other children except older ones like cousin Frederick, Norwegian was my home language and I was far from fluent in English. I also had trouble pronouncing English words with a "w" as it ended up as "v." Words beginning with "th" were impossible as I pronounced them as "da." I was a peculiar first grader and didn't fit in. It took some time before I developed any friendships and felt comfortable in English. It is doubtful that I learned anything at school the first few weeks. Louie Repaal, the teacher, had no training in educating first graders and didn't quite know what to do; so he mostly left us alone while he concentrated on teaching the older children. To keep us busy, he handed out sheets of paper with outlines of various animals hectographed on them for us to color. I colored pigs, cows, horses, chickens, bison, and turkeys, then handed them in to await his approval. He simply gave us another sheet of animals to color. We got tired of coloring the same stuff hour after hour. School was boring.

Finally, Louie started teaching us our A, B, C's. That, too, was boring as I had already learned that plus several extra Norwegian alphabet letters at home. However, some of the other kids didn't know their A, B, C's; so we were drilled until they mastered them. Finally, one day we each received a thin reading book with stories about Jack and Jane running up a hill and similar exciting events. Since there was no challenge in this book it was tiresome as other kids plodded through their reading class recitations. I had already learned on my own at home to read simple English although sometimes my Norwegian handicapped me. Fortunately, Louie's home language was Danish and was able to help when I confused my languages. Reading turned out to be my favorite class in first grade and thereafter. In penmanship class we were supposed to write long lines of big ovals with a pencil on the paper while moving our entire hand. I never mastered that as my hand always rested on the paper so just my fingers moved to make the ovals. Overall, first and second grades were easy, and as my English fluency improved I began to read books from our tiny library that were well above my grade level. This was fun and gave me something to do when my class assignments were completed.

Arithmetic was my nemesis throughout elementary school. To improve our skills at addition and subtraction, the teacher would sit and hold up white cards with problems like 8 + 3 and the first one in class to shout out the correct answer was given the card to hold. I was always slow to give the answer to number problems so rarely ended up getting any cards. It was discouraging and a forecast of my continuing struggle with mathematics and dislike of it. Ella Nelson struggled trying to teach me fractions, but I made little progress. Finally, she said maybe my father could help me. He tried, then asked his cousin, Ovida Bonkrude (who later married my cousin Daniel Hanson), to help me. Ovida, a talented teacher from Dallas, tried her best with this blockhead boy and somehow managed to help me understand fractions that others found so easy.

It was soon obvious that I was grossly lacking in social skills with other children as I had grown up as an only child and had associated mainly with adults. This was forcefully demonstrated one day when I was out in the schoolyard at recess. I was wearing a little cap that Lloyd Jorgenson, an older boy, grabbed from my head and tossed high in the air where it hung on a maple tree branch. As Lloyd laughed, I was seized with anger, "How could anyone do this to me, Carl Hoveland!" Lloyd, a big fat slob, stood not far from me. I tightened my little fist and ran toward him, punching it into the squishy soft belly of his tight bib overalls as a number of other children watched. He didn't expect I would be so dumb as to attack him but he quickly retaliated by throwing me to the ground and pounding my face with his big fists, causing blood to flow. It hurt my face and especially my pride as I cried in front of the gathering crowd. Soon, two older sisters, Elaine and Doreen Sparby rescued me. They escorted me to the school house and washed the blood off my face. Most of all, they comforted me when I needed it most. I never forgot their kindness. I also learned a valuable lesson: never pick on someone a lot bigger than oneself as they might counterattack. From then on, I avoided fights and became a pacifist.

Traveling to School

Walking to school in early autumn or late spring was usually enjoyable unless it was raining. There were so many interesting things to see as the seasons changed: goldenrod, milkweed, wild roses, cocklebur, fleabane, mayweed, asters, black-eyed Susan, coneflower, columbine, smartweed, bluets, and violets. Birds such as blue jays, swallows, hawks, orioles, sparrows, crows, wrens, robins, blackbirds, and others entertained me. In warm weather, large bugs and caterpillars left wavy tracks in the sand. Farmers with their horses working in the field provided more sights. Probably the worst time for walking was early spring when snow melted from high snow banks that channeled water on the thawing road and became a sea of mud. Sometimes in early morning the mud would be frozen into rough tracks interspersed with water, which was difficult to traverse. In early winter the road was dry with some snow, which made walking easy. That changed later as the big truck plow pushed snow to form high banks with heavy clumps of packed snow rolling down into the road.

As snow got deeper, skiing was a much faster and easier way of going to school. I could cut across the fields and reduce the distance considerably. It was a glorious feeling of freedom as one raced across the fields on skis. Even though it was bitterly cold at times, cross country skiing used a lot of energy and kept a person warm. This was a popular way to travel, judging by the number of skis leaned against the south wall of the school. It also offered a noon hour opportunity to ski down small hills near the school. On one wooded hill, we adventurously skied down a curving trail between trees. Luckily, no one ever hit a tree. Two of our teachers, Ella Nelson and Ruth Harelstad, wearing colorful wool ski pants and jackets, skied to school from their parents' farms where they lived. I thought them very daring as I did not know any other women who skied.

Duties

Older students were assigned jobs, called "duties," which were usually done during recess or after school. Erasers were dusted by pounding them outside on the concrete foundation wall. Blackboards had to be washed daily with water and a stinky rag. The schoolroom, basement, and entry hall had to be swept and windows cleaned occasionally. Wood had to be carried from the woodshed to the basement and fed to the furnace at intervals.

The worst job, often not handled well, was cleaning up the boys' and the girls' toilets. It involved picking up waste paper from the floor and washing down the seats. The toilets were normally in a wretched stinky condition since the school board removed excrement far less often than needed. One of the nastiest pranks was normally performed in the girls toilet each winter. On a below zero day, a boy would sneak into the girls' toilet and pee on the wood seats where it would immediately freeze a coating of ice. The girls were rightly furious. The teacher then would lecture the classroom and attempt to get a confession from the miscreant. Of course, no one ever knew who had done it. I do not recall that anyone was ever punished.

Another duty was considered desirable as it allowed two boys to go outside and pump water into a pail and carry it inside for drinking purposes. This was especially attractive when the water needed to be replenished during class time as it allowed some play around the pump and always took more time than needed. At one time, our water took on a foul taste and could not be used for drinking. Water was then procured by sending two boys to the Dalhoe farm about a quarter mile from the school house, making this an especially good way of getting out of school on a nice day. When a school board member finally crawled down into the well, he found a dead squirrel lying in the water. They pumped out as much water as they could, but it took quite awhile before the water became drinkable again. No one thought about getting laboratory tests on drinking water in those days.

Everyone participated in an afternoon spring clean up of the school grounds that involved raking leaves and burning them, cutting weeds, and picking up any trash. Most kids worked well because on completion of the work we roasted "weenies" (wieners) and "mushmellows" (marshmallows) on sticks over a little fire. This was a highly popular event.

Class Time

I liked attending school. My attitude was not shared by a number of the other boys who could always think of some excuse to stay home and work on the farm or do as little as possible when at school. Consequently, several boys had been held back to repeat a grade. This resulted in a few big husky fellows with no interest in learning who posed a challenge for the teacher. In contrast, I liked school because it was far more interesting and a lot easier than working on the farm. I was thrilled with learning new things, especially in history and geography classes. I was fascinated with maps and soon knew more names and locations of countries, cities, rivers, oceans, and mountains than anyone else. Ione Hanson, my sixth grade teacher, was furious with me when I once arrogantly pointed out that she had made an error in identifying a location on a map. History opened up a new world of knowledge for me as I learned about famous people and events. I liked language and literature classes as I loved to read and write. Poetry was not a favorite although I memorized classics like "The Midnight Ride of Paul Revere" and "Hiawiatha." Arithmetic and civics bored me. Once, I complained in civics class how useless it was for me to learn the names of the Barron County government officials since we lived in Dunn County. I lost that argument. I loved to write, and when teachers gave me essay assignments, I would write more than most others on a particular topic. This did not make me popular with some of the boys who teased me because I had more in common with some of the girls who enjoyed studying and writing.

It was a big event for me when teacher Ella Nelson was authorized to purchase a set of World Book Encyclopedias for our pitiful library. As I opened these volumes filled with information and photos, it opened up a new world. I would rush to complete my assignments and spend free time soaking up the riches of this fabulous set of books. It was Ella's greatest contribution to my education. The other big event for me was when Ruth Harelstad started teaching me in seventh grade because she ordered books from the Wisconsin traveling library. A box would arrive once a month with a wide array of books. This is where I was introduced to the fascinating world travel books of Richard Halliburton and those of Osa and Martin Johnson's stories and photos of their African wildlife trips, which gave me the desire to visit many of these places. I also read fine biographies and novels that gripped my attention. By the time I reached high school, reading was my passion. Again, this did not endear me to many of the other boys who viewed reading as drudgery only done under duress.

Lunch

Each child carried a lunch box to school. A few had fancy metal ones that included a small thermos bottle for hot food or homemade soup. Most used a flat-top metal elongated box, while the poorest ones carried a gallon syrup pail. Ma tried her best to fix me sandwiches I liked such as peanut butter, canned salmon, or cheese (Swiss or limburger but not cheddar as I disliked the strong aged stuff Pa bought) along with a cookie or a piece of cake. A real treat in winter was Grandma's lefsa and butter. I rarely had fruit unless it might be an apple in autumn or early winter. A few lucky children like Robert and Dorlan Carlson sometimes had a banana or grapes in their lunches. The McDonald kids, from a family of six, were the poorest ones in school. Their lunches in the depths of the Depression consisted of homemade bread with lard as they could not afford butter. In addition, they carried an old Vaseline bottle filled with homemade sorghum syrup that they poured on their bread. The McDonald boys wore home-sewn overalls and shirts, attesting to the hard work of their mother. Since their poor hill farm supported only a few milk cows, the milk checks must have been small. They were unusual in being Pentecostal in a Lutheran community.

On sub-zero winter mornings our lunches froze solid on our trek to school. If we left the lunch boxes in the entry room with our mackinaws, caps, and overshoes, the food would still be frozen at lunch time. So, in cold weather we set them on a table at the rear of the schoolroom. On bitter cold, windy days they often did not completely thaw out as the furnace heat at the front of the room did not circulate well and a cold draft would flow in under the doors. If one was unlucky enough to be sitting at a desk near the rear of the room, it was common to pull one's legs up and sit on them to keep warm and avoid the cold draft. On those extreme days, we would place our lunch boxes on the floor around the furnace register and have our food thawed by noon. During such weather, hot food from a thermos was especially appreciated.

Play Time

Morning and afternoon recesses were only 15 minutes, but it was common to engage in short games. At the noon hour in good weather we would gulp down our lunches and rush out to play longer games. When there was no snow on the ground, popular games included "anti-I-over," "pump pump pull away," "red rover," "keep away," "cops and robbers," "hide and seek," and "run sheep run." Kitten ball (softball) games were popular in good weather. Team leaders would alternately choose kids for their team, obviously avoiding the poorest players until the end. I was always one of the last kids chosen as I had no athletic skills, and an incoming ball would normally drop right through my hands. I was dreadful at throwing a ball and admired kids like Orley Larson, Kermit McDonald, or Myrtle Foss who could expertly throw a ball where it was supposed to go and who would also effortlessly catch a ball in the air. A favorite winter game after a fresh snowfall was "fox and geese." In winter, noon hour provided time to take our sleds and go sliding on the nearby hill. This offered the option of sliding down an open area or a more exciting route curving between trees down a hill. In bad weather, we played indoor games like hide the chalk and musical chairs.

Snowball fights were popular in winter. Teams would build forts and then throw snowballs at each other, hoping to smash the opponents' fort and then batter their team. All would usually go well unless snowballs were packed ahead of time and iced so they were extremely hard as they clobbered someone on the head. In warmer weather, there were occasional fights between two boys, attracting spectators. A rare bully might pick on a smaller kid. This was not smart as Myrtle Foss, a strong, muscular, kind-hearted girl, would enter the fray and soon knock the guy to the ground. They soon learned not to attack her younger siblings. Myrtle was tough and could handle any boy in school. As a different diversion, several of the older boys constructed a hideaway in a brushy area that was off limits except for a few chosen members. It was here that older boys like Elias and Lowell Grendahl would smoke their pipes and share with some of the others. I was never invited to this exclusive club.

Shared Misery

Infectious diseases of many kinds were common among school children during my years at County Line. When a kid came down with some bug, one could easily predict a lot more would catch it, too, unless they had developed immunity. As a group, most of the time we had no choice but to share our misery with each other.

Colds were common throughout the winter season with a chorus of kids sneezing, coughing, or blowing noses loudly at times in the classroom. Runny noses and coughing up sputum required cloth handkerchiefs. Kleenex tissues had not yet been invented. We often used cotton cloth pieces cut or torn from old bed sheets for blowing and coughing snot out of our noses and mouths. As globs of yellow snot accumulated on these rags, they hardened and were appropriately called "snot rags." Since we didn't wash clothes often in winter, snot rags were used longer than they should have been. They were not a pretty sight when pulled out of an overall or dress pocket, but they served our purpose. Sometimes one did not have time to reach for the snot rag to catch an involuntary cough or sneeze. Then the snot would be simply wiped on a shirt, sweater, coat sleeve, or mitten if outside.

Teacher advised us to cover our mouths when we sneezed or coughed so the germs would not be spread, but that was often ignored, resulting in a generous distribution of spray that infected other kids. Since there was no place to wash our hands, we had ample opportunity to pass bugs from one child's dirty hands to another. Before we had a bubbler fountain, drinking water from a common dipper and pail added another chance to pick up more germs. Cod liver oil was supposed to help build resistance to catching colds; so Ma dosed me daily with a tablespoon of this slimy, vile-tasting stuff. It didn't seem to help me as I was particularly susceptible to colds and flu. A commonly used remedy for a chest cold or flu was to pin a piece of wool cloth smeared with Mentholatum over the chest. I am not sure how valuable this was, but it warmed the chest and smelled like cough medicine. It seemed like a good remedy.

Flu was particularly nasty as one ended up with exhaustion, chills, fever, aches, sore throat, coughs, and stopped-up nasal passages. We suffered through it all as there were no effective medications like antihistamines to alleviate some of our symptoms. Some kids dragged to school part of the time they had flu, but most stayed home in bed. I was one of them, as flu hit me hard. School attendance dropped off sharply when a flu epidemic was in progress, leaving only a few hardy souls that had a light case. Amazingly, our teachers always seemed to evade the worst sieges and were able to remain on the job during these episodes.

There were a number of infectious diseases we endured that today are controlled with vaccinations. For us, our only vaccination was for smallpox, especially during my early school years. Diptheria was feared, as people died during epidemics of this malady. Fortunately, we never had a case of it. However, we had a number of highly infectious diseases during our school years. Whooping cough was not a serious problem, but many endured a few days of it as part of their education. German measles caused a red rash and a fever but only lasted about a week. Red measles was much more serious and could cause lasting problems. I experienced it toward the end of my seventh grade school year and thus missed my final exams. I was quarantined for two weeks, spending it in bed with a fever, a strong red rash, and eyes filled with pus that formed hard crusts. Because the room was kept dark to protect my eyes, I could not read during my miserable days convalescing. Mumps were commonplace, causing severe swelling of salivary glands in one's jaws, making swallowing difficult and painful. Kids who had mumps when they were little were lucky as this malady was much more painful as one grew older and could cause infertility in adults. Scarlet fever was one of the worst childhood diseases and persons unlucky enough to have it were quarantined for many weeks at home. I was lucky enough never to catch this bug, which had the potential to be fatal.

Several skin infections spread nicely among us because of poor sanitation. Ringworm caused itching and spread over hands and fingers. Pinkeye caused pain and redness of the eyelid for a week or two. A few kids had bites from lice, which inhabited bed clothes at home. It was usually associated with a low level of cleanliness. The treatment for lice was painful: application of kerosene, which burned the skin. Ma was proud that we did not have lice at home, and I never caught them from another kid. Goiter was common among many older people, a result of iodine deficiency in the diet as our northern Wisconsin water and soils were very low in this element. This caused the thyroid gland in the neck to swell, sometimes causing severe gland enlargement. To prevent this problem, our teachers had us take iodine pills as table salt was not iodized.

With all of our shared misery from infections, it is impressive that we kids managed to survive and get an education. No one died, but we had to cope with a number of bugs and gain natural immunity rather than through vaccination. It was just another facet in our training to survive hardship.

Basket Social

In November it was popular in country schools to host a basket social, which was an event to raise money for candy, nuts, and fruit for the Christmas program. The schoolroom desks were pushed to the side to give room for games such as fish pond in which one paid for a chance to hold a fish pole with a string flipped to the other side of a curtain where someone attached a small prize. One could also pay to bob for apples floating in a wash tub of water, hoping to grab an apple with one's teeth. It was far from sanitary as all the participants had their mouths and noses in the same tub of water. Along with a few other games of chance, one could buy homemade candied apples on a stick, fudge, cookies, cake, pie, and hot coffee.

The highlight of the evening was auctioning of large, attractively decorated cardboard boxes, each containing a fancy lunch, to the highest bidder. Most of the boxes had been decorated with bright colored paper to look like a red barn, fancy house, steamboat, church, or flower garden. Each of the boxes and the lunch in them was made by a single eligible young woman in the community whose identity was a secret. Bidding was done mostly by single young men who tried to guess who had made each box. Occasionally, the secret was out on a particular box that a young man was especially eager to buy; so bidding was brisk to see how high he would go to prevent another guy from eating lunch with his girl. In contrast, fellows hoped they would not get stuck eating lunch with an undesirable girl. Basket socials attracted a lot of young people from other school districts as they were a source of community entertainment.

Christmas Program

The Christmas program was the highlight of the year, an evening event on the last day of class before vacation. Proud parents were there to see their children perform, and young people who had graduated from elementary grades at nearby school districts would often come for the entertainment. A month before the program, the teacher assigned each of us several roles and gave out the parts to be memorized. Practice sessions of the program were done for a week or more and decreased class time considerably. A couple of days before the program we erected the stage and curtain, moved desks aside, and brought in extra chairs. The Christmas tree had been erected and trimmed a week earlier. Since the school had no electric lights, large gas lamps were hung from the ceiling to provide moderate lighting. A big snowplow came and pushed snow aside to provide parking space. During the evening program, most kids dressed in church clothes while parents and others were more casual.

The little schoolroom was stuffed with people, causing the air to become hot and clammy, but the floor had a cold draft. On an especially cold night, car radiators were wrapped with heavy horse blankets, but they quickly cooled so car owners would often slip out to run the engine a bit to be sure they would start after the program.

The program usually started with Christmas carols sung by the entire school. Our group singing was pretty bad, and words were commonly mispronounced. Gilman Anderson, with his strong Norwegian accent, always sang "wit" instead of "with," "da" instead of "the," and "mudder" for "mother." We had several short comedy "dialogues" or skits with several persons performing. I normally played parts in several of them each year. I had no acting talent, I was scared on the stage before all those people, and I had trouble remembering my lines so I improvised, which got some laughs. We performed on an elevated stage of wood planks set on several low sawhorses. Two black curtains attached to a wire stretched across the front of the stage and were pulled back and forth by two boys between acts. Occasionally the curtain got stuck on the old bent wire and one year the wire broke. The curtain fell on the actors, embarrassing the teacher but giving the audience some laughs.

There were usually several duets or small groups of girls who sang Christmas music. The Sparby sisters had musical talent and performed well while others could only be appreciated by their parents. Smaller kids would "speak a piece," generally some Christmas poem that they were supposed to have memorized. But sometimes they got scared on the stage and forgot everything. Proud parents in the audience clapped loudly when their kid remembered his/her lines. One time a little boy who was probably coming down with flu forgot everything as he was to speak his piece and then puked on the stage. It was a memorable occasion as the mama rescued her child and other women helped clean up the stinky mess.

We eagerly awaited the end of our program when Santa Claus entered, dragging a big gunny sack of treats. A local farmer, sometimes Anton Saastad but usually Vernon Madison, wore a decrepit old Santa costume with a ragged beard. He gave each child a brown paper bag that contained sticky hard candy, waxy chocolate cones with a sickening sweet center, yellow foam candy covered with dark chocolate, peanuts in the shell, a few almonds and walnuts, an orange, and an apple. Apples and peanuts were passed out to adults. The treats were paid for with money raised at the November Basket Social. School students had drawn names to purchase a gift costing 25 to 50 cents that were wrapped and placed under the Christmas tree, then handed out to each child. Also, parents often had a gift under the tree for their child or children. I was lucky as Ma and Pa always had a gift for me, but poor kids like the McDonalds got nothing extra. After this, we bundled up and put mittens over fingers sticky from candy (there was no place to wash and no paper napkins) to go out in the bitter cold and sit on the ice block car seat to drive home. Christmas programs were a big event each year and provided entertainment for the community.

Excitement

The biggest event in my life at County Line School happened when I was in fifth grade. One spring afternoon a severe thunderstorm blackened the sky, and the schoolroom became quite dark during the final class period of the day. I was standing near the teacher's desk holding a social studies book and reading aloud when a ball of fire appeared to come through a window, hit my left hand, and then rolled behind the desk. From there it traveled to a storage room in the southwest corner of the basement, setting some old maps on fire and then exploded outside, leaving a mass of wood splinters in the right front tire of the 1934 Ford car where Pa was waiting to give me a ride home in the stormy weather. Following this, there was a dreadful crash of thunder that shook the schoolhouse.

Meanwhile, the book fell from my fist as my left hand became quite numb. The lightning left me with a distinct black mark on the palm of my hand. I was shaking as frightened children crowded around to see my hand. Ella Nelson, the teacher, was examining me when Pa came in the room and learned of my experience. Smelling smoke, Pa went downstairs and found old maps burning in a store room so he got boys to help carry pails of water from the pump and quenched the fire. I was scared and felt weak as several girls escorted me to the car where I sat while Pa and Ella checked the school for other possible fires. Sitting in the car, I realized I could have been killed by the lightning and how fortunate I was to have survived. I was truly blessed and thought I was a special person. My hand was numb for a few days, but it gradually recovered, and I suffered no permanent damage.

News of the lightning strike at the school and me as a victim traveled fast via telephone party lines. I even got mentioned in a tiny news item of the Chetek Alert weekly newspaper. It was my first experience as a celebrity, and lots of people wanted to see my hand. When Vernon Madison, head of the school board, heard about it, he couldn't understand how lightning could strike as it did since the school was protected by tall lightning rods atop the roof ridge. A heavy woven wire cable was connected from the lightning rods down the side of the building to a heavy steel post driven into the soil. When the school board examined it, they found that the cable had been broken, apparently by children ~~ing on a loose loop of cable. Since we didn't have any sw~~ on the school ground, the cable provided substitute entertainment. No one had ever checked to see if the lightning protection equipment was operational. I suspect that our school didn't receive any reimbursement from the insurance company for lightning damage.

Our Education

Eight years in this one-room rural school provided us with a good basic education. I could competently read and write English. I had been exposed to English and American literature and poetry. My struggles with arithmetic had taught me how to add, subtract, multiply, divide, and use fractions or decimals. I gained a fair knowledge of American history, government, and had a good basic understanding of world geography. Training in art was limited as our teachers had only one book with color photos to show us some great paintings of world art. One that I recall was Rembrandt's "Night Watch" which I was privileged to see thirty years later at the Rijksmuseum in Amsterdam. One of the richest contributions to my education came from reading widely in the World Book Encyclopedia. In addition, I learned a lot about getting along with other children. Overall, this one-room school gave me a good elementary education at low cost to the community.

Hard Times

I was born during an era of good economic times on the farm. The year of my birth, 1927, featured the first non-stop transatlantic flight from New York to Paris by Charles Lindbergh in 33½ hours. The stock market crash in October, 1929 marked the end of prosperity and the beginning of the Great Depression. By 1932 unemployment exceeded 12 million people in the USA out of a total population of just over 123 million. Unfortunately, the Hoover administration and Congress were clueless and actually made things worse by hiking tariffs on foreign goods, which resulted in retaliation by other countries and a precipitous drop in world trade. Farm prices plummeted and hard times hit the previously prosperous Sand Creek community. Dairy farmers with substantial debt were in trouble and had insufficient income to make loan payments, so many lost their farms to banks. Many banks with an abundance of bad loans went bankrupt, resulting in losses by depositors as there was no Federal Deposit Insurance at that time. Fortunately, the local bank survived this disaster.

Early Recollections of Depression Era

As a small child, I had no recollection of any hardship at that time. I was well fed and clothed, I had my dog and toys, and was loved by parents, relatives, and neighbors. It was not until I was in first grade during 1933 that I [...] not all was well in the world. Poorly dressed, sad-faced [...] walking through the countryside would come to our door looking for a farm job or ask to work just for food. Ma usually gave them something to eat and sent them on their way as we didn't need anyone on the farm. We had Ed Austin as a hired man at that time. Others asked to sleep in our hay barn overnight, but Pa was afraid they would smoke and start a fire in the hay so he usually sent them away.

Traveling vendors such as the Watkins salesman would visit our farm once or twice a year in hopes of selling spices, liniments, and toiletries but about all Ma bought was a few spices. As the Depression progressed, more peddlers appeared trying to sell a wide range of products such as Bibles, clothing, tools, and a variety of household items, most of which we didn't need or couldn't afford. Some had a pathetic tale to tell, hoping to elicit sympathy and a sale. One time Ma stood by the open screen door while a skinny man in a wrinkly suit and tie offered for sale thread and sewing needles while quoting Bible verses from the Book of James on how it said she should show charity to the poor. Ma told him she didn't have any money but he just moved closer to her and she quickly stepped inside, hooked the screen door, and told him to leave. Ma ran out of charity just then.

The election of Franklin Roosevelt as president in 1932 was regarded as a major calamity in our family and by the Republican voters of the Sand Creek community. His promises to use government funds and deficit financing for public works and relief, and especially to repeal Prohibition laws, were regarded with horror by our family and generally in the community. Listening to adults speak of Roosevelt, I imagined that he must be the devil with horns and a forked tail. Nothing good could come from this president and our nation must be in great danger.

d dropped to pitiful levels as demand for
cities where closed factories had greatly
ower. Even so, farmers without debt sur-
ot-free and had some bank savings; so we
for the time being with food from the farm
side enterprises. However, it became harder
to collect ... y owed to Pa for threshing grain, as debt-
laden farmers often had little to offer except promises. I recall
travelling with Pa to collect threshing bills and hearing honest, hard-working farmers in heavily patched overalls say,
sometimes with tears, that they had no money as the tiny
milk check was used to pay a little on their mortgage and
buy a few groceries. These collection trips with Pa were some
of my most poignant recollections of the Great Depression.
In contrast, we were still managing well at home.

Drought

The year 1934 brought hard times to our household.
The winter had been relatively dry with only small amounts
of snow to melt in the spring. Spring rainfall was sparse, just
enough to get oat and corn crops planted. Then it stopped,
interrupted only by a few small showers that did little good
as strong winds blew day after day, sucking the moisture out
of plants and soil. That spring, normally lush pastures could
not grow. There was little for the dairy cows to graze. Hay
fields had poor prospects for a first cutting in June. Most
farmers at this time of year had little hay left in their barns.
Some concerned farmers learned that rainfall was much better farther north and were able to rent pastureland on vacant
dairy farms owned by banks that had foreclosed on their
owners. Our cows, together with those of Leonard Toycen
and Uncle Oscar, were trucked to a farm near Ladysmith

where the older boys stayed and milked cows throughout the summer. The Hansons and Gilbert Severson sent their cows to a farm near Birchwood. Uncles Arnold and Fritjof, on heavier soils with better water holding capacity, had more pasture and hay than on our deep sand; so they kept their cows at home and purchased additional hay to cope with the drought.

It was a tough summer for us. Our single cow at home had enough pasture to keep us in house milk and to make butter. We managed to harvest some hay, but it was far less than needed to feed the cows in winter, especially since there was no corn to harvest for silage. I recall Pa and I standing in a corn field with twisted drying stalks two to three feet tall. It was depressing. Day after day the wind blew as the summer grew hotter, occasionally reaching 100F or higher. By mid-summer we noticed something else; the skies often darkened with dust blown by winds from the desolate drought-stricken wheat farms of the Dakotas and Montana. Ma would keep the house closed up much of the time to keep out dust, but then it would get so stuffy and hot that she would have to open windows and allow the dust to enter. Housecleaning and drying clothes on the outside lines were a challenge to her.

With the cows gone, we didn't have much to do on the farm that summer but somehow, Pa found jobs for me to do. We repaired machinery, painted, and cleaned around buildings. I had time to do some fishing, but with the water level low in the river and temperatures high, fish were not biting. It was often just a chance to sit in the shade, daydream, and listen to tree leaves flutter in the hot wind. One source of pleasure was the frequent trips we made to the farm near Ladysmith to look at our cows and visit with Laverne Toycen, Kenneth, and Orville Hoveland who did the milking. Pa soon learned that our cows were not milking as well there since the rundown weedy pastures on this farm didn't match those at home. Threshing grain for other farmers didn't bring in much income that year as oat yields were low. There was no land-breaking work this year as it was dry, and people didn't have money for new land development.

With little to do a home, Pa and Ma accepted the invitation of Uncle Sam and Aunt Ona to stay at their home in Chicago to visit the World's Fair Century of Progress. They made the long drive squeezed into our old Buick car with Uncle Oscar and Aunt Margaret, Grandpa and Grandma Hoveland, and cousin Vernoid. Grandma Noer stayed with me during the week they were gone so I had a good time. Chicago was hot, but they enjoyed tramping around the fairgrounds gawking at all the wonderful sights that most people in Sand Creek only read about in the newspaper. It was a big trip for those days, and they enjoyed telling neighbors about it.

Loss of Our Cows

In autumn we got rain, and pastures produced some grass so the cattle came home to graze for a few weeks. With little hay on hand, Pa had to buy more hay from out of state. Big trucks brought us baled hay to fill our hay barn. Fortunately, Pa had money in the bank to buy hay. We needed a bull, and Pa felt he was lucky that a cattle buyer friend allowed him to use a good Guernsey bull this winter. This turned out to be a costly mistake. During breeding season in winter, the bull started getting thinner and didn't look good. In the spring of 1935, all the cows in Wisconsin were required to be tested for tuberculosis. The results were disastrous for us as all except one cow and one heifer were found to have tuberculosis, caused by the cattle buyer's infected bull. Many of the carcasses could be used only for tankage and were worth virtually nothing.

The year 1935 was a relatively good year as rainfall provided good production of pasture, hay, and corn silage. We had plenty of feed but no cows and no milk check. Fortunately, Pa still had money in the bank so he started buying milk cows. Instead of our previous all-Guernsey herd, now we ended up with a colorful array of Jersey, Brown Swiss, Guernsey, Milking Shorthorn, and Ayrshire cows. My favorites were the big gentle Brown Swiss with their beautiful fawn and white hair coats. We were starting over with new cows and plenty of winter feed, although milk prices were still low. Desperate farmers in many areas organized protests against low prices by dumping milk, hoping this would drive up prices. Few local farmers participated. Newspaper photos and stories put farmers in a bad image since thousands of city families could not afford milk for their children. Milk prices remained at the same low levels.

More Drought and Really Hard Times

After a relatively dry winter, spring drought started early in 1936 and continued all summer. Scorching heat accompanied strong winds and blistered the landscape to a crisp brown, an extension of the devastating drought that covered the Great Plains. Pa liked to know the temperature so he would check our thermometer several times a day, often announcing to us that it was another day above 100F. It was one of the worst years in history, causing a huge exodus of people from Dakota and Montana wheat farms where winds scooped up the soil and dumped it in drifts along fences. Again, winds brought dust to Sand Creek. We trucked our new cows up to the farm at Ladysmith for another summer.

Little hay and no silage was produced on our farm that year, resulting in Pa having to buy hay again for the next winter. The problem this time was that his bank savings were running low and milk checks were small. Other enterprises brought in little income. The droughts had ground us down to the same level as most other farmers around us. It was an awful feeling for Pa who previously could solve a problem by working harder. He felt helpless when it didn't rain. The Federal WPA program of Roosevelt hired farmers with teams of horses to work on rebuilding roads. Pa thought about it a long time and finally hired on for a day to get some money. He came home that night, ashamed that he had taken government money to labor on a make-work project. He didn't want charity; he wanted to earn money honestly. Pa never went back again. Somehow we survived.

That year there was no money for new clothes. We carried water for the garden to grow potatoes and a few vegetables in the heat. We couldn't afford much at the grocery store. Ma had canned pork and beef, fish balls from ground sucker fish, also chickens, eggs, and we ate lots of bread, oatmeal, milk, and homemade butter. Lena Larson had a big garden that she watered, and shared fresh produce with us. I was poor in terms of money but didn't realize how well off I was in having sufficient food, clothing, and housing compared to so many people in cities who were inadequately nourished, poorly clothed, and ill housed.

A Bright Spot During Hard Times

On June 23, Ma said she needed to go the hospital as she was going to have a baby. Amazingly, I had not observed any changes in Ma's shape or figured out that there was going to be an addition to the family. Pa got Ma into the car, and they drove off to Luther Hospital in Eau Claire while I stayed home and tried to figure out how this was going to affect life in our household. Pa got home at supper time after I had finished milking our sole cow, excitedly telling me that I now had a sister who was going to be named Hannah Marie. As we ate, all we could talk about was this wonderful new person who arrived nearly nine years after me. In those days, new mothers were kept in bed for many days; so it was nearly a week before Pa brought Ma and Hannah home from the hospital.

I had expected to see a pretty little girl with beautiful white skin. Instead, Hannah was all red and wrinkly. She cried a lot as she suffered in the oven-like temperatures of our house. At this point, I was not sure Hannah was a desirable addition to our family. However, looking at it from her viewpoint, life in the outside world was not pleasant as the hospital rooms were beastly without air conditioning and cross ventilation, the ride home in the car was hot, and now she would be living in a miserably hot house. Nights were awful as the air was still, the house interior hotter than the outside air, and we lacked a big fan to make it more bearable.

Since my bedroom upstairs was unlivable at night, I took my bedclothes and slept on the floor downstairs near the front door of the living room to catch any air movement. Ma kept Hannah's crib in the living room near me to give her a little relief. She would try to cool her with wet towels, then dry her off. Still, Hannah developed heat rashes that added to her woes. I felt so sorry for her, but could do nothing about the heat that kept on week after week, with no rain to bring any temporary cooling. In spite of the heat, relatives and neighbors came to admire the new baby and wish the mother well. There wasn't much to do at home on the farms. People had plenty of time to visit and drink coffee in the heat. Aside from comments about the beautiful baby, the main topic was the heat and how this drought was worse than anything anyone could remember. There wasn't much else to talk about; the atmosphere was like a sad funeral.

Adding to our woes that summer was dust from dump trucks and road graders working to improve the highway past our house which was to be paved with asphalt. Whenever they were working in front of our house, clouds of dust rolled up from the machinery causing us to temporarily close the house and put up with the stifling heat. Somehow, Hannah survived the heat and the dust. As time went on, Hannah's red face disappeared, replaced by chubby cheeks and beautiful white skin which showed off her pretty blue eyes. I was proud of my new sister! She was a good baby and no problem in our household. Our main pleasure that summer was a trip to the emaciated river each evening to swim in the shallow water and wash off the day's sweat. Other neighbors would often join us at the river to share our little pleasure of the day. Occasionally, we made trips to the Ladysmith farm to see our cows and some green grass. Somehow, they seemed to get rain showers when we got only tiny showers or no rain at all.

In late August that year, another event brightened our lives. Life was especially hard for the Oscar Hoveland family so Pa invited my cousin Orville to stay with us to finish eighth grade and work on the farm. Orville was delighted to come as he loved working with Pa. We weren't living high but it was better than the poverty he shared with his six siblings. I was delighted to have Orville as the older brother I never had. Welcome rains arrived for pastures and our cows were brought home for grazing that autumn. Orville had no interest in attending school and was able to convince Pa that he was needed for the additional farm work this year, delaying completion of eighth grade until the following year. Orville added a lot to our lives. He worked hard on the farm, helped in the house, looked after baby Hannah, and was a good playmate for me. Unfortunately, Orville never finished eighth grade.

Finances

Our financial status was bleaker than in previous years since the bank savings were about exhausted. There was little income since summer pasture rental ate up part of the small milk check and custom work was almost nil except that Pa was able to sell some lumber. A few people with money were buying lumber to build houses cheaply in Eau Claire to be rented out for a few years until they were ready to retire from farming and move to the city. Uncle Fritjof was one of these people who bought lumber, and he also hired Pa to work with him to construct a house on the west side of Eau Claire. He later retired there. This gave Pa a little income when he desperately needed money. The birth of Hannah during this awful year resulted in hospital and physician bills that were probably small but added to his financial woes. There was also the looming cost of buying hay and grain to feed our cows during the coming winter. Fortunately, he had no other debts, but milk checks remained small. Pa was worried and showed it. Autumn rains and plenty of snow that winter gave good prospects that were borne out with abundant harvests the following year.

Pa continued to struggle with finances. One day in late autumn he came home from Sand Creek where he had been to the bank to get a loan. Telling us about it, he had tears in his eyes. For him, borrowing money was a sin as he had always paid cash. He equated debt with personal failure. Now, he had descended to the level of being in debt and had committed a grave sin. It was a lesson I learned well from Pa as throughout life I mostly avoided debt, even when it would have been to my advantage.

End of a Hard Times Year

I knew it would be a lean Christmas that year. We had always bought a lovely spruce Christmas tree for the house, but to save money this year Pa and I cut a small white pine in the woods. It was a floppy open tree, which I dressed up the best I could with our old electric lights, ornaments, and tinsel. I didn't expect much of a gift, but Pa had bought me an electric wood-burning pen to etch wood for various ornaments and other items that I carved. It meant a lot to me and I appreciated it.

For our Christmas Eve dinner Pa had splurged by buying a piece of frozen salmon in the Farmers Store and stored it outside under a wash tub on our back door stoop. The day before Christmas he lifted the wash tub and found the fish gone. Looking around outside, the gnawed remnants were lying in the snow, eaten by our dog. It was a crushing blow for Pa as he had spent precious money for a Christmas eve feast. We changed our menu for the evening. I headed for the chicken house, grabbed a hen, chopped off its head, soaked it in hot water and plucked the feathers so Ma could clean it and fix roast chicken. It was a memorable Hard Times Christmas as we had plenty to eat, a warm house, a Christmas tree, gifts, baby Hannah Marie, and our usual reading of the Christmas story from the Book of Luke. Somehow, we rejoiced in managing thus far in surviving hard times. We didn't know it, but we had survived the worst year of hard times, and the years ahead would be better with rains and more prosperity.

Spring

Mud Season

My childhood memories of spring in Sand Creek varied from bad to good, depending on the month. Early spring in March was usually a wretched time of year with highly variable weather. Snow might still be present on frozen ground, or the snow might be gone and the tilled soil and unpaved roads a sea of liquid sand. We called this "mud season" when tramping to and from school in our overshoes was an ordeal with water standing or flowing in the rutted partially frozen road. The ugly brown landscape, bare trees, piles of ice from unmelted snowdrifts, gray skies, and cold wind had nothing to recommend northern Wisconsin at that season of the year. Unpaved roads often developed "frost boils" where ice lenses formed, pushing a crust of soil up and then melted and created holes where cars and trucks sometimes got stuck. The only good thing was that occasionally farmers earned money getting a car unstuck with a team of horses.

Farmers, eager to start tilling the soil, were unable to do any field work at this time when the soil was thawing and leaving puddles of water everywhere. Even manure spreaders were unable to operate on the soggy ground. It was a time to stay inside, eat hot soup, and get ready for the busy planting season ahead. At school, ski and sledding season was over, and the schoolyard was too wet for outdoor games. At recess and noon hour we played indoor games in the cramped basement or in the schoolroom. Children were impatient with the mud season between winter and spring that could last for several weeks. A cruel cold wind reminded one that winter was not over. Late snowstorms and rains added to the water-laden mud atop frozen soil. It was a rotten environment for human beings. For me, it was the worst time of the year.

Spring Work

Usually things improved in early to mid-April when the soil had thawed and the ground dried up, hastened by strong cold winds and some sun. It was time to get moldboard plows into the field and get sod turned if it had not already been done in the autumn. Land already plowed could be disked and harrowed for planting oats, timothy, and red clover or alfalfa in mid- to late April. It was a busy time for farmers clad in heavy mackinaws and wool caps who endured the cold wind while driving teams of horses on field work all day in addition to the usual feeding, cleaning barns, and milking cows. By late April, pastures were beginning to grow, and farmers anticipated getting their cows out of the barn to graze and save the labor of indoor feeding. That didn't usually happen until early to mid-May when corn planting season started. The first day of cows being on pasture was a time for rejoicing. By then, it was warmer, trees were leafing out, and some early flowers appeared. Drier roads, greening of the landscape, song birds returning from their southern winter migration, and field activities of farmers provided wonderful diversions when walking to school. It was a different world now, and one began to feel alive again. Nevertheless, spring weather could be changeable. Reminders of this were chilly blasts out of Canada for a day or two, cold rains, and even light snowstorms. I recall one day in early June when snow flakes pelted down on us, causing no damage, but making us aware that days with beautiful weather should be appreciated.

Late May was normally a beautiful time of year. Trees were leafed out in various shades of green, lavender lilac blooms oozed their fragrant perfume, bees were busy with nectar collection duties, while pink and white peony flowers covered with ants brightened farmyards. We read in school books about early spring bulbs like tulips and daffodils, but no one in our area planted any such flowers. Nature provided us with a few wild flowers like violets, dandelions, and a few others for color. The ugliness of winter was gone and replaced with a fresh new landscape. Fortunately, spring planting was over and farm work had lessened with cows on pasture. There was more time to enjoy the beauty around us. Some farmers took time for fishing, visiting relatives, shopping, or working in the vegetable garden.

It was different at our farm because Pa always had plenty of jobs waiting to be tackled. Fence repair to replace rotted posts and rusted broken wire was high on the list. It was a tough job, opening a hole in the wet ground with a crowbar, pounding sharpened wood posts into the ground with a heavy steel mallet, stringing new barbed-wire from heavy rolls, and stapling wire to the posts. Other inspiring tasks included planting rutabagas on a strip of stony, root-laden new land we had cleared, cleaning a heavy layer of litter from the chicken house floor, forking semi-solid accumulated winter cow manure from the big pile behind the barn into the spreader and hauling it to a pasture, sweeping down cobwebs in the barn prior to the whitewash contractor spraying the interior, cleaning out the remnants of rotted silage in the silo pit, and cleaning out the winter accumulation of feces and catalogue paper in our outdoor toilet.

Ma's Vegetable Garden

Each spring Ma always was highly motivated to plant a vegetable garden, something not high on Pa's priority list. After many reminders, Pa would spread cow manure on the area below our plum trees, plow it with a horse-drawn moldboard plow, and disk it so I could rake it smoothly. This was not an easy task as the area was mostly covered with quack grass, a nasty perennial weed with deep runners that spread and took root easily and quickly. After a lot of raking and pulling, one could get it reasonably smooth so Ma could string out rows and Pa and I would plant seed of various vegetables from Northrup King packets with colorful pictures on them. After we finished planting, with seed packets staked on each row, the garden looked the neatest it would look all season. We usually got stands on most of the various vegetables, but the quack grass had a big advantage with all its heavy rooted runners. It didn't take more than a few weeks before Ma's garden, well fertilized with cow manure, looked like a lush green pasture, and later a hayfield. Pa tried to control it with a horse-drawn cultivator while I had the unenviable and hopeless task of trying to hoe and pull out quackgrass next to the vegetable rows. As the summer progressed, it was obvious that it was a futile task, and we would harvest few vegetables except some early onions, peas, and carrots. It was the same each year. Most fresh vegetables we ate came as gifts from Uncle Sophus or Lena Larson instead of from Ma's quack grass patch.

Pa apparently liked certain flowers better than fresh vegetables from the garden as shown by his special care for a bed of red cannas. This circular flower bed about 8 feet in diameter was located in the lawn by the driveway near the back door of our house. Each spring we spread rotted cow manure, then set out canna bulbs that had been stored in our basement during the winter. Fortunately, quack grass was absent in this soil. If it was dry, the cannas were watered so Pa always had magnificent red cannas blooming during summer to show visitors. Other than showy and fragrant spring blooms of the big honeysuckle bushes near the toilet, the red canna bed was our only horticultural success.

Memorial Day

Memorial Day was a special holiday as we toured each of the local cemeteries to see the graves of departed friends and relatives, and visited with neighbors. We usually visited Zion, Our Saviour's, and Running Valley cemeteries with family graves. Occasionally, we stopped at the little cemetery adjacent to our farm that contained mostly graves of Myran family members. Cemeteries were especially colorful as many of the graves would have flowers on them, and the American Legion placed an American flag on the grave of each military veteran of the Civil, Spanish-American, and First World Wars.

In Running Valley, the red brick Lutheran Free church usually had an 11 am special service with a visiting pastor giving the sermon, plus messages from previous pastors. The attraction for me was a big pot luck lunch served in the church basement by the Ladies Aid with a tempting array of hot dishes, sandwiches, home-canned pickles, cookies, cakes, and pies. There was always a big crowd of local parishioners and visitors, including many from Minneapolis, Eau Claire, Menomonie, and elsewhere. It was a very festive occasion as adults visited with many of our Noer and Isakson city relatives. This was a dress up occasion when men wore suits and women wore Sunday dresses and hats. People wandered around grave sites to pay their respects, examine gravestone dates, and talk about the departed. Even as a child I developed a love for cemeteries and the history they contained, something that has remained with me as an adult. I looked forward to our Memorial Day outing, which usually had sunny pleasant weather.

Late Spring

Early June started the corn cultivating season. School out now, I was a full-time farm worker. Pa always had plenty of jobs for me in addition to cow chores. Even so, I occasionally did some fishing in the Red Cedar, sometimes with Billy Wick. In addition to rock bass and sunfish, we also got our share of mosquito bites as June was a horrendous month for these bloodthirsty pests for which we lacked effective insecticides. The still air along the river would be thick with skeeters which would hum in our ears as we slapped at our faces and ears. At home we rarely sat on our open front porch to enjoy the long evening twilight as the mosquitos were so voracious. These tormentors of northern Wisconsin were always with us unless a strong wind was blowing. The only good thing was that their numbers and ferocity declined by late summer and autumn.

Officially on the calendar, spring ended about June 21. Haying season started during the last weeks of spring, but unfortunately the weather seemed like summer. Often, we had summer-like temperatures while harvesting the first cutting of hay. This back-breaking job was often done during temperatures in the upper 80's accompanied by high humidity. It was a sweaty job where a hot shower would have been a great relief each day. Lacking a hot shower after a day putting up loose hay, followed by hand milking in a hot barn, a good alternative would have been a swim in the Red Cedar, but the river water was usually too cold at that time. Instead, we rinsed off some sweat from our upper bodies and talked about the joys of having an indoor bathroom. It is no wonder that we were glad when the first hay cutting, the largest one of the year, was in the barn as we welcomed summer.

Visiting

The advent of fine weather during spring, summer, and early autumn offered opportunities to pay social calls on neighbors and relatives on Sunday afternoons. This was called "visiting" where a family drove to another farm to spend several hours in conversation followed by "coffee" which generally meant cookies, cake, and sometimes sandwiches along with the beverage. Neighbors often dropped in unannounced but were always greeted as welcome guests. It was a time for adults to exchange community news and gossip, talk about politics, and tell some funny stories. For children, it was an opportunity to play outside. Pa and Ma often visited older people with no children; so I would enjoy investigating the different things to be found in their farmyard and its surroundings. I could always find interesting things to see and do in these situations. Since most of these homes were devoid of books, there wasn't much for me to do inside except listen to the old folks talk. In addition to nearby neighbors and many relatives, Ma had many relatives to visit farther away in Trout Creek on farms of Uncles Henry, Otto and Paul Isakson, and Ole Rognstad. They were great fun and wonderful hosts as we visited, conversing in Norwegian. Sometimes we visited Pa's Uncle Dave and Aunt Helma Bonkrude on their farm near Dallas, Uncle John and Aunt Gurine Hoveland in Bloomer, or Uncle Paul and Aunt Kristine Gehler near Sand Creek.

Once or twice a year we would be invited to Sunday dinner at the home of Uncle Sewell and Aunt Mabel Hoveland in Chippewa Falls. This was special as both were wonderful hosts, and she laid on a really great meal. She would prepare good steaks from the nearby Gutnecht market along with potatoes, a vegetable, and freshly made pie. Uncle Sewell entertained us with humorous tales about people he met while supervising crews working on Chippewa County roads where he was assistant highway commissioner. The northern part of the county had land populated by some recent immigrants from eastern Europe that provided humorous incidents for him to describe. He had the most infectious laugh and enjoyed life to the fullest. After dinner, Uncle Sewell and Pa would light up big cigars in the living room while Ma and Aunt Mabel would clean up the dishes and talk in another room. I would head upstairs to plod away happily, trying to make words on their Underwood typewriter, a magical machine for me. After a late afternoon coffee lunch, it was time to leave after a happy day and return to the cows again.

Once in a great while there were memorable visits to other urban relatives. It was a big event to drive all the way to Eau Claire and visit Ma's dour Uncle Rasmus Shaker and delightful cousins Ralph and Joy Shaker who lived high on the bluff overlooking the city. Ma's childless Uncle Olaf and Aunt Ida Noer lived in Menomonie where he operated his own pharmacy. He was a charming short man with a big white handlebar moustache, which showed off sparkling gold teeth when he laughed. Their elegant old house was furnished with dark Victorian furniture and many bookcases filled with all sorts of fascinating books, some of which contained lots of photos on travel in foreign countries and wars. During our visits when the adults conversed, I would be lost in fantasy as I leafed through these rich book treasures. Best of all, Uncle Olaf would always present me with several of these books when we departed or on visits to our farm. I think he was pleased that a young kid would show interest in books that he enjoyed. Another place I liked to visit was Ma's cousin Victor Noer and wife Selma who lived in a big house on the banks of the Red Cedar in Colfax. Victor, who owned Noer's drug store in Colfax, was a short, pleasant man, with a big family of five girls and one boy. A special attraction for me was the pool table they had in a playroom of the house. Several of the children taught me how to play pool, which provided wonderful entertainment on our visits. One thing I soon learned on these town visits was that their life was very different from ours. They lived better, had luxuries like indoor bathrooms, and were not tied to the routines of cows and the land.

Samona

A highlight of late spring and early summer was Uncle Sam and Aunt Ona driving from Chicago to stay for several weeks to a month at their cottage on Prairie Lake near Chetek. Most cottages had names and their sign proclaimed "Samona." This couple were favorites of mine and added a lot to my life. Aunt Ona was Pa's only sister, an elegant, lean lady with a great deal of style. Amazingly, my sister Hannah is like a clone of Aunt Ona, both in appearance and attitudes. Aunt Ona worked as a bookkeeper at the Farmer's Store in Sand Creek and later in Chetek. It was at the latter place that she met Uncle Sam. Sam Corbin was born in Sicily and came as a child with his parents to Chicago. He had worked driving new cars from the Chevrolet factory in Janesville, WI for delivery to dealers, a system that preceded truck-trailer deliveries. At the time of their meeting, he worked for a biological supply company that sold plant and animal specimens to high schools and colleges for use in their science laboratories. Sam was self-trained, getting his biology education by reading voraciously in evenings at the Chicago Public Library.

Sam liked to fish, and spent his vacation each year in the Chetek area. Here he was attracted to the beautiful bookkeeper at the Chetek Farmers Store. She was charmed by this exciting olive-skinned Sicilian with a great smile, twinkling eyes, good humor, and unusual accent. He was so different from the farm boys in the area. However, there was a problem; Sam was Catholic! He soon solved that by volunteering to take instruction and become Lutheran. Initially, this mixed marriage was not well received by some members of the family, but over time they came to love Sam. Chicago became their home, where eventually they started their own biological supply company which developed into a highly successful and profitable business. I thought they were rich as every other year they bought a new Chevrolet two-door coupe car with a big trunk that Sam used to transport boxes of biological supplies to the post office. Aunt Ona wore fancy dresses and hats purchased at posh stores like Marshall Field and Carson Pirie Scott in Chicago. At the lake, she wore striped coveralls for fishing and working around the cottage.

Once or twice each spring or summer they would host a pot-luck Sunday dinner for family members. It was a treat for me as I got to go for rides in Sam's boat, sometimes fish, and play with cousins. Occasionally, Sam and Ona would come to Sand Creek for visits, and a few times Pa let me return to the cottage with them for an overnight stay. It was a big treat for me as I could ride in their fairly new Chevrolet car, eat fresh fish at the lake, and especially escape evening and morning milking. Sam was a good cook and prepared tasty Italian dishes that we never experienced at Sand Creek. Uncle Sam had a home movie camera. It was fun for us to view on his projector photos of us on the farm and at the lake. A real treat was to spend time in the boat with Uncle Sam and do some fishing. I learned from him that fishing was enjoyable even when we didn't catch any fish.

Spring started miserably and was a busy time on the farm with planting, but with the blessing of getting the cows on pasture and greatly reducing barn work. By late spring the weather was generally beautiful and nature was alive with excitement. Unfortunately, harvesting the first cutting of hay interfered with fully enjoying the song birds, flowers, and scenery in late spring. However, we did seize some opportunities to escape the farm for visits. Best of all, we had time to look forward to better things in summer.

Summer

Temperature extremes characterized the continental climate of northern Wisconsin. Winters were long and cold with a short summer season that could be pleasant but often had periods of high temperatures that often exceeded ninety. This, combined with high humidity, made life unpleasant in the days before air conditioning. Heat would build up during the many hours of daylight in summer, often resulting in hot, steamy, still air at night. Perspiration would cover the skin of a sleeper often completely uncovered and subjected to the whine and attacks of vicious big mosquitos that somehow found their way into the bedroom. Occasionally, on a hot humid day a thunderstorm would break out in late afternoon with colorful lightning and loud crashes of thunder, followed by a short, heavy downpour of rain. These welcome events cooled off the air as well as furnishing needed water. At our northern latitude, cool fronts would sometimes push down from Canada in summer to bring thunderstorms followed by dry cool air which furnished perfect weather for a week or so. Summer weather was changeable.

Eau Claire

The beginning of summer was a quieter time as haying the big first cutting was over. This was the time Pa carefully checked the threshing machine to determine what repairs

192

needed to be made. I hated working on machinery, but I was glad when Pa had his threshing machine parts list made out as this meant a trip to Eau Claire to buy parts at the big McCormick-Deering regional distribution center. On that big day, Ma would go along, and we would spend much of the day in the big city. In the morning, Ma spent her time downtown while Pa was on his business. They met again around noon when we drove out to Carson Park to eat a picnic lunch Ma had packed. In the afternoon we would all be together for additional shopping downtown. Sometimes Grandma Noer would accompany us on this big annual trip.

The 50-mile, 1½-hour trip to Eau Claire in the early 1930s involved driving on gravel roads from Sand Creek to New Auburn, then on narrow two-lane concrete Highway 53, passing through the downtown areas of Bloomer and Chippewa Falls to Eau Claire. All main highways passed through the center of every small and large city, greatly slowing progress on a trip.

The main shopping area of Eau Claire was clustered downtown as malls were unknown. Both sides of Barstow Street downtown were lined with offices, thriving shops, movies, and the big Farmers Store with an adjoining parking lot located along the river. Ma's Uncle Rasmus Shaker had a photo studio downtown and lived in a house at the top of a steep hill overlooking the city. Eau Claire, originally a sawmill city, had a large area across the river with the old Victorian mansions of wealthy timber and sawmill barons. With the demise of lumbering, it had become a commercial trade and industrial center with a large Gilette tire factory and Armour meat packing plant. It was also a medical center with the highly regarded Middlefort Clinic doctors who utilized Luther and Sacred Heart Hospitals. A small four-year teachers college was also located along Minnie Creek. Several large

old Lutheran and Catholic churches were scattered downtown, attesting to the Norwegian and German ancestry of
most residents, as compared to smaller Methodist, Episcopal,
Congregational, and Presbyterian churches of the "Yan-
kee" people.

Walking around downtown with Ma was exciting.
There were so many cars, some of them unlike anything in
Sand Creek where they were mostly Ford, Chevrolet, or
Plymouth. In Eau Claire one could see unusual cars like Packard, Cadillac, Pierce-Arrow, Hudson, Hupmobile, Stude-
baker, Reo, Graham-Paige, Essex, and others. One of the
strangest sights for me was an older lady driving an electric
car, moving quietly along the street. Ma usually spent most
of her time browsing in the dry goods sections of the Farmers
Store. They had a huge selection of fabrics and dress patterns,
as most women sewed their own clothes. Needless to say,
this didn't interest me so I wandered around the store where
people watching was my main entertainment.

My favorite store had a big red and gold sign with the
letters "F.W. Woolworth" and mentioned that articles were
5, 10, and 25 cents. Based on their advertising, this chain
store was popularly referred to as the "dime store" or "ten
cent store." They carried a huge range of items from toiletries
and clothing accessories to housewares, tools, and candy, but
especially of interest to me were toys and games. Hardware
and department stores carried toys only at Christmas time,
but Woolworth had them year around. I would normally buy
some small treasure with 10 or 25 cents from my savings
bank. It was especially nice to have Grandma Noer along as
she would buy me a highly desired toy, which was an unlikely
gift from my parents during the Depression.

One of my most treasures memories on Eau Claire trips
occurred on a hot summer day when we entered the Walgreen

drug store along Barstow Street, the first time I ever experienced air conditioning. Sweating profusely in the hot humid air outside, I reveled in the cool dry air, and Ma had difficulty getting me to leave. I was convinced then that I wanted air conditioning in my future! In later years I discovered Eau Claire Book and Stationery where I could browse through all sorts of wonderful books. I couldn't afford them, but it was tempting to just spend time paging through some, particularly those with photos of other parts of the world.

As I grew older, Pa wanted me along when he visited the McCormick-Deering distribution center to purchase threshing machine parts. Since he found it such an interesting place to visit with a huge parts department, displays of the latest tractors, farm machinery used for both horses and tractors, and International trucks, he assumed that I would share his enthusiasm. Pa always enjoyed looking at new machinery. Unfortunately, with no mechanical skills or interest in machinery I quickly became bored wandering in this huge multi-story building looking at farm machinery. I was glad when it was time to leave and Pa paid the bill on his parts order which would be shipped to the Farmers Store in Bloomer which sold McCormick-Deering products.

Around noon, Pa would meet Ma, and we would drive out to Carson Park for our picnic lunch. Ma always fixed a good lunch of sandwiches, usually with egg salad, ham, canned salmon, or cheese; cake; thermos bottles of coffee for the adults and milk for me. We had plenty to eat, but my desire was to eat in a restaurant when we were in the big city. Eating in a restaurant was unusual for our family and probably was looked upon as a waste of money during the hard times of the Depression. One time Pa relented, and we planned to eat at a restaurant in Eau Claire. Pa saw a little restaurant near the Farmers Store with a sign advertising a complete lunch for 25 cents and figured that was a good bargain. Ma didn't like the looks of the restaurant, but Pa said they had good business so it must be a fine place to eat. The 25-cent price included soup and a plate lunch. I was excited and looking forward to this treat in a restaurant. Our first course was supposed to be chicken vegetable soup, but mine looked like water with a few bits of carrot, potato and onion floating in it. There was no trace of chicken meat. The plate held a small piece of gray hamburger covered with a floury gravy, tasteless mashed potatoes, and some canned green peas. Water was included but coffee was extra. As expected, Ma told Pa she knew this would be an awful place. Pa retorted that one can't expect much eating at restaurants but that we did get a bargain today. I don't recall that we ever ate at a restaurant again except to have a hamburger and root beer at an A&W stand.

Minneapolis

Early in the Depression before the really hard times arrived, Ma decided we needed to buy some new living room furniture, and Pa agreed we could afford it. Ma had a relative in Minneapolis who ran a furniture store and had offered to sell them furniture at nearly wholesale; so it was decided to make the long journey of around 100 miles to the Twin Cities in a one-day trip. Back then, this was a long trip which probably most people in Sand Creek had never made. We started early in the morning, driving on gravel roads to Menomonie where we followed a concrete highway to "the cities" as they were called. For me, it was exciting, sitting in the back seat watching all these new scenes, crossing the wide Mississippi river bridge, and passing the state capitol in St. Paul before we reached our destination in Minneapolis. It was all so big with huge buildings, lots of cars, noisy yellow street cars, and power wires draped over the streets.

At the store, we looked at furniture; then the owner took us to visit a furniture factory so we could see how it was made. It was my first visit to a factory where men and women sawed and screwed wood frames together, sewed up fabrics, stuffed them, and assembled finished pieces. At noon, our store owner took us to dinner at a cafeteria where he told me to just pick out whatever I wanted as we walked down the line with our trays. I had never eaten at a place like this. I was awed with all the choices and probably took more than I could eat. The most amazing to me was seeing beautiful red watermelon slices in early summer! At Sand Creek, farmers growing watermelon did not have them ripe until late August or September. I recall that it was the best thing I ate for dinner that day. Back at the furniture store, Ma picked out a sofa and matching chair in a rust color design. In addition she got a fancy arm chair with carved wood arms and main body with the seat and back in a green brocade cloth. All this was shipped to us later. Then we departed for our trip back to Sand Creek. It was a long trip. I probably slept on the way home.

Fourth of July

By mid-June, most of our stores had fireworks for sale. They were all imported from China, wrapped in bright colored tissue paper, and cheap. Fireworks consisted of various sized firecrackers that made loud noises, silver bombs that detonated on impact when thrown against concrete or stone, Roman candles, sparklers, and rockets that shot high in the air to burst with a glorious shower of colored stars. Since Pa liked fireworks, he made sure we bought a supply. Days ahead of the Fourth I would enjoy lighting firecrackers, sometimes under empty vegetable cans to pop them into the air. Our dog was frightened of the firecracker noises and would hide under the back stoop. At night, I would shoot off some Roman candles and sparklers. Rockets were saved to enjoy the night of the Fourth. All of these pyrotechnics could be dangerous in the hands of a little boy. Luckily, I was never injured, but some children had fingernails blown off or burns on their hands or arms.

Fourth of July celebrations were commonly held in small towns. Chetek often had a parade down the flag-lined main street with the high school band and home-made floats of the American Legion, Masons lodge, other organizations, plus a few old tractors, cars, and local clowns. There would also be a horse pulling contest, weight lifting, various games of chance, and food for sale. A highlight for me was enjoying a hamburger and frosty mug of root beer at the A&W stand. The main event was speed boats racing in a big circle on the lake, something that seemed to me more noise than anything else and quickly got boring. In the evening they featured fireworks over the lake, something we missed, as we had to go home and milk cows, and Pa didn't want to drive back to town again.

Sometimes Sand Creek had a Fourth of July celebration in a park by the river. There were a large of number of booths with games of chance, hamburgers and pop, plate lunches from the Ladies Aid, and sometimes a special miniature attraction with people and machines that moved, or a collection of some unusual items not seen in Sand Creek. In the afternoon, they had some local entertainers singing or playing musical instruments on the stage, and sometimes a politician or a patriotic speaker. After dark, they shot fireworks off the little island in the river to end the day.

Often, a pilot would sell rides in his airplane which landed on a pasture behind the schoolhouse. One year, Clayton Saastad and I wandered away from the park to watch the airplane take off and land, a big event for us farm boys. Both of us thought it would be a thrill to ride in an airplane, but knew we could not afford it. The fare was $1 for a ride but Clayton and I had just over a dollar between us. Finally, I asked the pilot if he would take the two of us up for a dollar since we weighed less together than most adults. There were no other customers around so the pilot agreed to my proposal. Two excited boys squeezed into the single seat, the pilot strapped us in, and we bumped along the pasture and roared off on this sunny afternoon. It was thrilling to fly above our respective home farms as well as Sand Creek, seeing it all from the air! It was a short ride, but now we had bragging rights that we had actually flown in an airplane. Walking back to the park, we felt so important and excited. When I found Ma and Pa, I told them my news. Ma was horrified that I had done something so dangerous. Pa, who had never flown, thought it might have been fun. For me, it was my best Fourth of July!

Fairs and Circus

August was usually fair time for us in northern Wisconsin. Unfortunately, it also coincided with threshing time. We didn't just thresh our grain and do "change labor" with neighbors in our threshing run. Pa did custom threshing for many "runs" or groups of farmers so he threshed grain for around a month each year. That meant that sometimes it was difficult to work in a visit to a fair. Somehow we did get to at least one fair each year, and if threshing got rained out for a day, we might get to another. For me, fairs were a highlight and a taste of exotic places, events, and people.

The Colfax Free Fair, 15 miles away, had no charge to enter the grounds. The fairgrounds located along the Red Cedar River had show barns for animals, crops, household canning and sewing. Outside were displayed a few new farm implements, cars, and trucks. Most of the fairgrounds was devoted to the carnival rides, tent shows, and games of chance. Near the river was a stage with audience benches. Here polka musicians, singers, comedians, jugglers, acrobats, and speakers entertained the audience seated on plank benches. Master of ceremonies during the program was Sam K. Iverson, a local insurance agent who also was the spark plug in organizing the fair each year. S.K., as he was known, was a man of great energy, determination, enthusiasm, and with a marvelous gift of gab.

The small Midway with its ferris wheel, merry-go-round, bumper cars, tilt-a-whirl, and other rides was an exciting place for children and young people. A few tent shows tried to lure people in to see human freaks, wild animals, fun houses with mirrors of various shapes, and beautiful ladies. Games of chance were numerous. Poor quality hamburgers and hot dogs were sold by the carnival, but a substantial meal was served at the local Lutheran Ladies Aid building. I even sampled pink spun candy on a stick. That was a sickening disappointment and I never bought it again. The beer tent was a popular place for adult men, especially in the evening. It didn't take me long to use up my small fair allowance at 10 cents per ride and up to 25 cents for tent shows. Ma and Pa thought the Colfax Free Fair was a pretty poor event, but I was intrigued with it, especially watching the hawkers at each tent show or game of chance give their glowing pitch to the crowd. Boozy, dirty carnival laborers lounging around behind the tents or near trucks and small travel trailers seemed like a bad lot; so I stayed away from them.

Sometimes we were lucky enough to get to the Dunn County Fair in Menomonie. It was a larger event with more agricultural and home exhibits, farm machinery, and commercial stalls. The carnival was better than the ratty little one at the Colfax fair, having more exciting rides and tent shows. There was a large grandstand for spectators to view horse harness racing, stunt car drivers, and horse pulls. Afternoon and evening stage shows featured popular musicians, comedians, trapeze artists, and acrobats. Of course, all this entertainment cost money for tickets so going to the county fair was costly, and especially so for a large family. The few times I got there were big events in my life and long remembered.

There was a state fair in Milwaukee, but that was way down in southeastern Wisconsin where we never ventured. I had never visited Milwaukee or Madison. A few people got to the Minnesota State Fair, which was much closer at St. Paul. I got there once when Uncle Arnold took me on an all day adventure in his Model A Ford. It was awesome to enter the huge crowded fairgrounds with long rows of exhibit buildings, enormous amounts of farm machinery, a long Midway with amazing and perilous rides, lots of hot dog and hamburger stands, dining buildings operated by churches and other organizations, and all sorts of tempting tent shows. Scattered around the grounds were hawkers demonstrating and selling all sorts of new household appliances and gadgets that did marvelous things but probably were less useful at home. Watching these hawkers for free was almost as good as the shows. Uncle Arnold was just as excited as I was in going on rides and seeing many shows. We were so busy we didn't even take in the grandstand races and stage performances. Best of all, he paid for all our tickets! We had a wonderful day together.

Uncle Arnold also gave me one of the most exciting days in my childhood when he took me to an afternoon performance of the Ringling Bros, Barnum and Bailey circus tent show in Eau Claire. We got there early so we toured the big colorful animal wagons with lions, tigers, bears, big snakes, and monkeys; nearby were colossal elephants with one leg chained to a stake while they munched on hay. It was the first time I had ever seen these exotic animals. Hearing the roar of a male lion made me hold Uncle Arnold's hand even tighter. Just walking around this huge array of tents with side shows was better than anything at the Colfax fair! The main afternoon show was held in a huge tent with three rings featuring three simultaneous performances of various kinds. A colorful band played as the ringmaster wearing tails, boots, and a top hat directed the shows. The entry parade of the colorfully arrayed elephants with their riders, performers, and clowns set the stage for a great afternoon. There was so much to see all at once. Animal acts, acrobats, jugglers, high wire performers, strongmen, dancers, singers, dazzling costumes, a man being shot out of a cannon, and clowns kept us laughing with their antics. I felt I was the luckiest kid in Sand Creek to have been taken to the circus by Uncle Arnold; it was the greatest gift he could give me!

Other Summer Pleasures

Summer was a time for farm work like cultivating corn, haying, and threshing, but milking was less arduous as cows were drying up late in their lactation. It could be hot and mosquitos still tormented us, but they were less pesky by late summer. Most of all, summer offered more opportunities for seeing and doing more things off the farm.

As we prospered a bit during the late 1930s, Pa enjoyed taking us on one or two summer Sunday rides in northern Wisconsin lake country, visiting places like Amery, Hayward, Spooner, Hawkins, Park Falls, and Rhinelander. We enjoyed picnics by the lovely lakes but much of the landscape between them was depressing with abandoned farms and land going back to pine trees. Immigrants from Finland had struggled as dairy farmers on rocky, poor soils with a short growing season and given up. Tourism was growing, but that provided employment for only for a short season of the year.

By the late 1930s, Sand Creek was a bustling place on a Saturday night. Many people came to shop, the café was busy, and the barber shop was full of customers. Cassie Toycen and his wife Leah would drive to the café for ice cream cones during the evening. Their Model A Ford car dipped steeply to the passenger side, a result of her ample size and weak springs. The big attraction was a free show sponsored by local merchants. Each Saturday night, an old western or comedy movie was projected on a large screen by the Farmers Store south wall. Families would bring chairs and sit in the empty lot between the store and the bank. Viewers would loudly voice their feelings about an actor, making it a noisy performance. Pa and Ma never went to a free show and I only attended a few times when I had a ride with one of my Hanson cousins.

We enjoyed visiting neighbors and relatives on fine summer Sundays. Housewives always had a good supply of goodies to serve with coffee for their drop-in guests. Best-of-all for me was when Cora Peterson phoned to invite us when they were making ice cream. Cora, a pudgy, short lady with boundless energy and enthusiasm was a great hostess, along with her sunny talkative husband, Eddie. They had two children, Betty Lou, a quiet, pleasant girl nearly my age and Stanley, a boisterous, reckless fellow. Pa liked to go there as he and Eddie loved to share experiences with steam engines that they both had owned. Cora was generous as she served the hand-cranked vanilla ice cream, filling big soup bowls with this rich delight. Calories were not a concern of hers.

One of Ma's favorite cousins, from the Isakson clan, lived only about a mile from us as the crow flies, but since it was across the Red Cedar, we had to drive a circuitous route via Sand Creek to reach their farm for visits. Both Ma and her cousin had the same name, Caspara, and resembled each other. She was married to Rudolph Paulson, and they had two sons, Wesley, who was my age, and Gordon, who was two years older. Wesley, a tall, good looking fellow with a gentle disposition, and fine sense of humor, was a favorite of mine and I enjoyed his company. The family worked hard but had time to enjoy having guests in their home.

The Paulsons had moved to Sand Creek in 1934, trying to make a living on a drought-stricken sand farm with their dairy cows. Life was hard, and Rudolph struggled to start a small poultry egg operation which allowed them to survive. Later, he expanded with more chickens and started delivering eggs on a route to lake resorts and stores in the area. After a few years, the cows were sold, and the dairy barn was converted into several floors of laying hens which were fed from purchased feed delivered to the farm. Additional laying houses, an egg processing room, refrigerated storage, and more egg delivery routes eventually resulted in the largest farming business at Sand Creek. Wesley acquired it when his father retired. Rudolph and his family's dedication, hard work, frugality, and business sense had paid off during the Depression.

One of my favorite pleasures on summer Sunday afternoons was to walk along the stream bank or sit under a good shade tree along the Red Cedar near our farm. It was so peaceful to enjoy the sight of the slowly flowing river, which had a lush growth of aquatic plants in the shallowest places, giving a greenish cast to the water. Turtles and frogs croaked their distinctive language while birds filled the humid air with their songs. In the distance, the low, mournful "coo coo" cry of a mourning dove added to the choir. Bees buzzed while a few mosquitos reminded me that they still were interested in my blood. Aside from a rare fisherman floating down the river in a boat, I had all this to myself, and I could daydream to my heart's content. When I was lucky enough to have Billy Wick with me, we shared our fantasies and enjoyed this natural world together. Billy, knowing more about the native plants and animals than I did, helped broaden my education. He was fortunate that his father, unlike Pa, was interested in wildlife and shared his knowledge. Summer afternoons were times I treasured, a respite from the world of work on the farm. Summer was a good season of the year.

Autumn

Autumn is often described by poets and nature writers as having sunny bright blue weather to highlight the brilliant color of maple, birch, elm, and oak trees. Apparently they were not writing about typical autumn weather in northwestern Wisconsin during my childhood. We did get a few of those days and they were glorious! Bright sun is necessary to bring out the brilliant colors inherent in tree leaves for a couple of weeks in this northern clime. During the peak period, bright colored leaves of hardwood trees splashed their magnificent finery against the rich dark green of white pine and hemlock.

The Autumn Color Show

This kaleidoscope of color was provided by a wide variety of tree and shrub species. Usually, sumac was the first to herald autumn with brilliant scarlet or orange that later turned to dark red. Sugar maples followed with bright red-orange to scarlet. A bit later came fluttering pale yellow leaves of big leaf aspen (locally called "popple"), the bright yellow of quaking aspen, yellow birch, white birch, and elm. Adding to the show were red, orange, and yellow leaves of the abundant red maples and a few sugar maples. Latecomers were red and white oaks with dark red leaves that turned to a rich brown color in late autumn.

Walking home from school amid nature's glory was a treat to be savored, so I dawdled and stopped frequently to admire it all while late season bees added their sounds to the still cool air. Life was good as I slowly ambled home. On days like this, working outside on Saturdays was a treat. Flocks of wild geese flying south told us that temperature changes were coming. Even when the bright colors disappeared as leaves fell, oaks continued to give a late season color show of dark red to rich brown leaves on sunny days. The oaks continued to hold their leaves but announced that winter was on the way.

Autumn Farm Work

Unfortunately, too often autumn had long foggy mornings or low gray clouds with drizzle, and chilly winds. We used to call it corn husking weather as farmers were busy in the field harvesting mature corn ears from the husk on standing frosted corn stalks with a hand-held husking pin and throwing the ears against the bang board of a wooden box rack on a horse-drawn high wheeled Stoughton wagon. As farmers harvested the ears from two or more rows at a time, the horses moved ahead a few paces, punctuated by the banging of corn ears as they fell into the wagon box. As I recall, weather often was nasty for this finger-numbing task as cold wind and occasional spits of rain accompanied the low dark blue clouds. Just looking at those depressing clouds sent shivers through my body. As the season progressed, a few snow flakes added to the misery. Fortunately, I was at school all week. I only experienced foul weather corn husking on Saturdays. Bundling up in a sweater and mackinaw, this weather was the breaking-in period to get us ready for the rigors of winter. I always dreaded this time of year and seemed to suffer more from the cold of late autumn than I did in winter.

Depending on the year, sometimes pasture would be sufficient for the cows to continue grazing until mid-October. Farmers liked to keep them on pasture as long as possible to avoid the laborious indoor feeding and manure removal which allowed time for other autumn tasks. Fall plowing was desirable to have the land ready for early spring planting when wet weather could be a problem. People with big gardens had potatoes, Mother Hubbard squash, onions, and rutabagas to harvest and store. We had no garden produce to harvest except for rutabagas. Pa usually bought a wagon load of potatoes from Old Man Lundquist, who had a farm on the highest hill in our area. After we got them home, the potatoes were stored with the rutabagas in a cool part of our basement. Often, we bought cabbages, sliced them on a special board with a cutting knife, and fermented them in big crocks to make sauerkraut that Ma would preserve in Mason jars.

Wood needed to be cut and sawed in chunks for winter heating in our basement furnace. Oak was the preferred wood as it held a furnace fire longer, but we had little of it so used chunks of pine unsuitable for lumber. We had lots of pine slabs from the saw mill, but they burned fast and made a lot of ashes for me to carry out. We used a portable circular saw powered by a Fairbanks-Morse one-cylinder engine that popped away as we sawed the wood into short lengths. Our wood chunks or slabs had to be hauled to the house from the woods with the horses, thrown through a small window opening to the basement and then stacked neatly for winter use. This was another excellent Saturday job, regardless of weather. It took a lot of firewood, especially if it was white pine, to get through a winter, so much of the basement was stacked with wood. Pa bought coal a few times to hold a fire on extra cold nights, but Ma who didn't like the dust and smell of coal ended its use.

A Vacation Trip

In early autumn of 1940, Pa decided we should take a car trip to see Duluth-Superior and the iron mines of northern Minnesota. We returned by way of Ashland, WI to pick up Uncle Art who had been staying there for several weeks to escape the asthma-hay fever he suffered with during the goldenrod season at Sand Creek. It was the only time we had the luxury of a four-night trip away from the farm, and was so special I was excused from attending school that week.

Hotels in Duluth were too expensive for us so Pa was lucky enough to notice a sign, "The Same Old Place," a rambling old house that had been converted into cheap furnished efficiency apartments for tourists. We cooked and ate our meals in the room or on picnics. A shared bathroom was downstairs.

Duluth-Superior, known as the "twin ports," were lined with waterfront docks for the large Great Lakes ships which transported iron ore from the mines and wheat from the Dakota prairies. It was impressive to walk on the docks to view rows of tall grain elevators and railway cars on tracks above us noisily dumping ore into conveyors that filled the ships' holds. The ships looked enormous to me. Pa was fascinated with all the machinery and activity while Ma lost interest and was left to sit in the car and crochet.

Superior was an ugly little place and the lesser of the two cities but we had to visit Ma's Aunt Julia, the youngest sibling of Grandpa Noer. She was the widow of a high school principal and had lived alone for many years. Bookshelves lined the walls and stacks of old magazines littered the floor of several rooms. It was a strange house and Aunt Julia was unusual, using a hearing aid attached to a big box of batteries. Pa thought she was a peculiar lady and couldn't understand why she didn't clean up the place and get rid of all those magazines. For me, it was a wonderful place as I was envious of her books and stacks of old yellow-bound National Geographic magazines.

Duluth was a larger and more prosperous city, built on a steep slope coming down to the harbor. The result was many steep streets that must have been hazardous with ice and snow in winter. Crowning the city heights were elegant homes of the prosperous elite with fine views of the harbor. My biggest excitement was visiting the small Duluth zoo where we joined other visitors viewing the chimpanzees. One young man was taunting the caged animals when one chimp responded by picking up a handful of feces and tossing it between the cage bars. This fragrant, squishy, brown handful flew over my head, splattering the young man's shirt. Ma was scared while Pa laughed. I was pleased—the chimp got his revenge.

One day we drove northwest from Duluth to tour the iron mining cities of Hibbing, Chisholm, Virginia, and Eveleth. Here, rust-red iron ore was being scooped up with giant shovels from huge open pit mines and loaded on gondola rail cars for shipment to the lake port. Distances within the mine pits were vast and the mining equipment at work appeared to me like tiny toys. In several places, city buildings were being destroyed or moved elsewhere to mine the valuable ore beneath the old cities. It was a dirty, unattractive area with ugly buildings and probably even more so in winter. Pa was thrilled seeing all this equipment at work. I was excited to pick up and bring home pieces of ore to show fellow students at County Line School, something no one else had done.

Leaving Duluth-Superior we followed a lonely forested road eastward along Lake Superior, arriving at the impoverished fishing village of Cornucopia. Commercial lake fishing for trout, whitefish, and herring was the main occupation of the residents. My main recollection of this place is the ornate Russian Orthodox church. Nearby farms had been settled by Carpatho-Ukrainians in the early 1900s. Rounding a peninsula, we drove along a bluff to the insignificant little town of Bayfield which had scenic vistas of the wooded Apostle Islands. Tourists came here to fish in summer, furnishing a small income for residents and giving no indication of the luxury resort this town would become fifty years later.

A few miles farther south we stopped at Ashland, a grubby unattractive city, to visit another set of docks where ships loaded iron ore from mines in northern Wisconsin and Michigan. On the edge of town we stopped at a park to pick up Uncle Art who had camped for several weeks in a tent by the lake. He was feeling wonderful since breathing pollen-free air alleviated his asthma and hay fever problems. After frost killed the golden rod and other autumn pollen producers at Sand Creek, it was now safe for him to return.

About 25 miles farther south at Mellen we rented a typical "cabin" as the motels of that day were known. It was an unattractive frame structure with simple iron beds, a kerosene stove for cooking, a few hanging electric bulbs for light, a wood stove for heat, and communal toilets. These cabins were rented only during the short summer tourist season and then closed the rest of the year. Restaurants in small towns like Mellen were not known for their fine cuisine so cabin cooking as we did was a better choice.

White frost sparkled in the sun the next morning. It was definitely autumn up here and leaf color was impressive. After breakfast, we drove north to visit Copper Falls State Park where rust-brown foaming water gushed over the small rocky falls. I was not impressed with this tourist sight as I had expected a high waterfall, not realizing that the gentle topography of Wisconsin does not offer much opportunity for such a spectacle. From here, it was a two- or three-hour drive back to the farm.

It was our one and only vacation trip, something most of my school mates had never done. Ruth Harelstad, my teacher, thought I should give a talk about this big trip to the students. I was excited about all that I had seen so gave a "show and tell" presentation with photo snapshots from my box camera, samples of iron ore, rocks from along Lake Superior and Copper Falls State Park, and some junk souvenirs. I thought I had done well and was proud of the artifacts on display. One kid thought otherwise, saying, "We got better looking rocks on our farm!"

Birthday

My birthday was on October 25, a special day for me. Weather-wise, it was often a grim time of year. Except for some oaks selfishly clutching their dark red-brown foliage, trees were leafless. Skies were generally gray with low, dark blue clouds portending snow but often emitting only spits of icy raindrops or occasional snow flakes. Cutting winds added to the dreariness of this occasion. Once in a while this day would honor me with sunlight but still did not provide much heat. Mostly, it was the kind of day that attracted one to inside activities in a warm place.

Some other boys I knew had real birthday parties with other kids, games, and special stuff to eat. I got to enjoy this kind of party for a number of years at the home of Billy Wick who was my age and celebrated his birthday the next day. I never had such a birthday party. Mine was different as all the guests were adults. During my years at County Line School, Grandpa Hoveland would be waiting after school ended to give me a ride home in his old black Chevrolet touring car. I always liked to climb up high on the seat beside him as he beamed on me with his twinkling eyes and big smile. He was always interested to learn what I was doing in school. Of course, Grandpa had never gone to school; so he didn't know what it was like except through his children who had attended elementary school. I couldn't imagine how Grandpa could be so smart having never gone to school.

When we got home, Grandma Hoveland was there, and the dining room table was set with the special spice layer cake with white vanilla-flavored frosting that she brought every year. Ma poured fresh coffee for the adults and milk for me. Her spice cake was special and tasted better than those made by anyone else. Grandpa presented me with a dollar bill, a large amount for a little boy during the Depression. Ma always had a small wrapped gift for me to mark my special day. The conversation was mostly of the adult sort, although they did comment on my progress in school and how I was growing up. After we had our cake and coffee or milk, the conversation tapered off and Grandpa and Grandma drove home to arrive before twilight. The party was over for another year. It was time to change into my barn clothes and help milk the cows again.

Halloween

This was a big event in the Sand Creek area. Young men, generally in their mid- to late teens, played pranks on Halloween evening that provided a lot of entertainment for the community. Older folks eagerly awaited news the next morning on events of the previous night and what farms had been visited. Visits by these young fellows were late at night when most people were in bed. The most common prank was to tip over outdoor toilets on farms or in town. Generally, these buildings were not fastened down very well so it was an easy task to push them over.

Buckling horse harnesses on dairy cows in the barn, pulling wagons to block barn doorways, lifting a hayrack off a wagon and setting it on the ground, soaping windows of cars or town shops, blocking up and removing the rear wheels of a car which were then hidden elsewhere on the farm, hiding pails and stools used for milking cows, piling sacks of oats in front of the farm house doors, and pulling lighter pieces of farm machinery to another location were some of the common innocent pranks. Occasionally, they worked hard lifting disassembled old buggies or light farm implements with ropes to the top of a barn, then reassembling them to stand atop the building. Some of this took a lot of muscle power by the perpetrators, but the fun was worth it.

The same farmer victims received this special attention each year because they became upset and angry. Most farmers, like Pa, who thought it was all great fun did not have pranks played on them. Uncle Sophus was one who resented their antics and always was trying to catch the pranksters. One year he was determined to play a trick on them. As usual, they chose to push the toilet over. It was an especially dark night as they moved toward the toilet. All at once they discovered that Uncle Sophus had moved the toilet off its foundation a couple of feet, causing Toddy Hoveland to fall into the waste pit, which had not been cleaned out. Uncle Sophus was waiting nearby in the darkness and yelled at them, "Got you this year!" as he heard the commotion with Toddy crawling out of the foul pit as the others disappeared.

The worst Halloween trick occurred one year in Sand Creek. Townspeople awoke the next morning to the smell of cow manure. All along the main street, piles of fresh sloppy cow manure had been dropped in front of every business place and some of the houses. It was a nasty mess to clean up and in some places it stained painted wood surfaces. The big question was who did it and the source of the cow manure. The answer came the next morning when John and Gerald Harrington found their dairy barn gutters all cleaned out. The culprits turned out to be the two youngest Harrington children, Ernest and Mildred, along with several others who had worked hard that night cleaning the barn and hauling the manure to Sand Creek. This episode was not well received like the usual pranks that provided enjoyment for most residents.

Lutefisk

Hard slabs of lutefisk from Norway arrived in local stores during late October and November. Lutefisk is air dried cod treated with lye, then soaked in water before cooking. It forms a white gelatinous mess which is slathered in melted butter before eating. Because lutefisk stinks up the house and will damage silver, only steel cutlery should be used to eat it.

Poor Norwegians of the mid 1800s were grateful if they could afford a supply of dried lutefisk to eat during winter. Thus, immigrants to Sand Creek and other Norwegian settlement areas developed a tradition of eating this foul smelling and tasting fish in winter as a delicacy from the old country. It is interesting that per capita lutefisk consumption in states like Wisconsin and Minnesota is now much higher than in prosperous Norway where it is rarely eaten.

Ma prepared lutefisk for supper several times in late autumn and sometimes on Christmas Eve. Pa and Ma liked it, but I was not fond of eating this jelly-like white glop with a peculiar taste and smell that were somewhat masked by melted butter. Lutheran churches commonly hosted lutefisk dinners as fund raisers in late autumn. These dinners were popular, and people would often travel to several churches to enjoy bountiful meals. The menu would include boiled potatoes, green peas, mashed rutabagas, lefsa, lutefisk, melted butter, meat balls in brown gravy, and apple pie or røm-megrøt (cream mush). With good meatballs on the menu, I enjoyed these dinners even though the air in church basements was perfumed by lutefisk.

Thanksgiving

This national holiday was a home event where relatives or neighbors shared a big dinner in a home. Often there would be snow cover on the ground, making deer hunters glad as it was easier to track their prey then. Generally, it would be a cold gray day; so a warm house felt good. With no television or football game distractions, people enjoyed conversation and storytelling. Food preparation started early for the big feast, which might include roast turkey, but often baked chicken sufficed during the depths of the Depression. Lots of mashed potatoes and gravy, sweet potato casserole with marshmallows (a special treat), mashed rutabagas, canned green peas, pickled beets, sliced carrots in butter, homemade cranberry sauce, cucumber pickles, lefsa, and apple, mince meat, or pumpkin pie were on most tables.

Some years, when Uncle Sam and Aunt Ona Corbin drove up from Chicago the Hoveland families met for Thanksgiving dinner at Grandpa's and Grandma's house in Sand Creek. This was really was special as Aunt Ona was fancy and added special touches to the food preparation in the busy kitchen with its wood stove and bustling women. We cousins played outside, as the small house could not contain all of us except when we crowded around the dining table that extended into the living room. It was a noisy place when we were at the table eating, talking, and laughing. Uncle Oscar could eat more than anyone and amply demonstrated it at Thanksgiving as well as lutefisk dinners.

Autumn's End

Since December days were short, it was just getting light as I skied off to school, and the sun was low in the sky as I came home. It was easy to understand how our early Nordic ancestors developed their stories of the sun being captured by a god at this time of year. The landscape was stark with bare fields and leafless trees standing like lonely sentinels against the gray sky. It was a scene in black, gray, and white, broken in places by green pine trees.

Snowstorms continued to deposit more snow, so there was usually an ample supply on the ground by Christmas. As days got colder, it was evident winter was upon us. Most birds had flown south, leaving sparrows, crows, chickadees, and a few cardinals who didn't seem to know that worse weather was coming. It was a quiet time of year. Farm chores were reduced to caring for the animals, milking, and snow shoveling as needed. Life moved more slowly, with less pressure than at busier times. There was time for town visits to do Christmas shopping and stop for coffee with a neighbor. Although the calendar said that it was autumn, we already knew that winter had arrived in northern Wisconsin. The arrival of December 21, the shortest day of the year, was simply out of touch with our weather calendar.

Winter

Winter began with Christmas, the most exciting time of the year for me. Preparations for this event began several weeks earlier when Ma began baking Christmas cookies. Extra butter was delivered by our milk hauler for her to bake rich goodies. Sandbakkels, fattigman bakkels, krumkake, spritz, and flat yellow cookies in shapes of Christmas trees, stars, and bows decorated with red and green sugar were baked in quantity and stored carefully in wax paper-lined metal boxes. In addition, Ma made flat bread and fruit cake, but lefsa was supplied by Grandma Hoveland who made the best in our family. There was no way our little family could eat all this high-calorie food, but much of it was served to coffee guests we entertained during Christmas week and thereafter. This period of over-consumption of calories could be viewed as laying down fat reserves to cope with the rigors of winter. Of course, I did my share in eating too many of these sweets, giving me a sour stomach feeling at this time of year.

Christmas Tree

Pa and I would buy a spruce Christmas tree in Bloomer, Dallas, or Chetek and put it up on the wood stand a week before the holiday. Since the tree had no water, it did not take long in the warm dry air of our house for it to start shedding needles. The result was that by New Year's Day our tree was dropping needles like a Collie dog shedding hair in spring. Even so, I loved the tree and kept it up as long as possible each year. Trimming the tree was a big occasion. Our old string of electric lights was a continuing problem because when one bulb burned out, they all went out. That meant one had to patiently change each bulb until the dead one was found. Every Christmas we spent lots of time trying to find a dead bulb. Of course when two bulbs were out, it compounded the problem. Taking the old fragile colored balls and other ornaments out of tissue paper in boxes and hanging them on the tree was a much loved ritual. When I was little, Pa would hang the higher ornaments. Then we added icicles to the branches for that final touch. As a little boy, I would sit mesmerized by the sparkling lighted tree with its spruce fragrance in the corner of our dining room.

Local Towns

In the days before Christmas, I enjoyed accompanying Pa on errands to nearby towns as he seemed to have time for relaxation. The snow-packed roads were quiet as traffic was light except for an occasional milk truck. On a dark cloudy morning, lights shone in farm houses with smoke curling upward from their chimneys. Traveling through the snow-covered countryside, brown strips appeared on white fields from horse-drawn manure spreaders. Occasionally, one might see a farmer hauling wood with horses and sleigh to warm the house at Christmas. At some farms, a decorated Christmas tree might be outside, sometimes with food for the birds. A few others observed an old Norwegian custom and hung a grain bundle on a fence for the birds.

Each town would have the main street decorated with colorful Christmas lights that remained lighted all day close to Christmas. Bloomer had the best decorations, probably because it was larger and more prosperous than nearby towns. They had the busiest Farmers Store in the chain, and it was a bustling store at this time of year. I often bought my little family Christmas gifts here. Shopping at the store, one often heard a few customers speaking German, while on the streets were shops and mail boxes with names like Bauer, Sibel, Faschingbauer, Weiner, Steinmetz, Fink, Boese, Reetz, Rauscher, and Zwiefelhofer.

We usually made a stop at Kransfelder's meat market to buy liver sausage or blood sausage, neither one of which I cared for. The Bloomer brewery was a busy place at this time of year producing holiday beer for the local German clientele. A small hotel, several restaurants, drug stores, a bakery, gas stations, farm implement dealers, garages, various offices, and a number of taverns lined main street. Werner's on the Corner, a large hardware store, had the biggest collection of Christmas toys in the area and was the place where Pa and Ma usually bought my main gift. A large pea cannery and the Armour milk condensery were located on the north side of town. There were two small Lutheran churches in town, but it was overwhelmingly Catholic as indicated by the large brick church with a tall steeple facing the main street, offering daily masses and many on Sunday by the German-American priest. A parochial school taught mostly by nuns stood beside the church.

The village of Dallas was larger than Sand Creek and had two main stores, a Farmers Store with general merchandise and Jorstad's grocery store. We patronized the Farmers Store, buying groceries there when we were in Dallas. In contrast to Bloomer, Dallas was a Norwegian town, and one could hear Norwegian spoken in the store. A creamery by the river bridge anchored one end of the main street with a cluster of utilitarian little shops, restaurant, taverns, drug store, butcher, post office, tiny Methodist church, and a few offices, with the Lutheran church at the other end. Pa usually visited Harry McIntire's harness and shoe repair shop even when he didn't have any business as he enjoyed visiting with Harry, a colorful outspoken man. A pungent smell of leather pervaded the place, and new harnesses for sale hung on wall racks.

Sometimes we stopped at the railway depot for the arrival of the daily train as Pa liked the sound and smell of a steam locomotive. This short line called "The Blueberry" ran from Barron to Prairie Farm and hauled freight cars of various kinds along with a car at the end that was half for railway express packages and with half passenger seats that were mostly empty. Standing close to the train as it arrived and stopped with a squeal of brakes and hissing steam from the piston cylinders driving the wheels was fascinating, especially when the engineer waved to me and blew the whistle. Oh, how I wanted to ride this train even for a short distance! I often asked Pa about this, and he always put me off with, "Sometime when we have more time." The time never came.

Christmas decorations in Dallas were more limited than Bloomer, but on the day before Christmas the merchants usually sponsored a Santa Claus in red suit coming to town in a horse-drawn sleigh. Driving slowly along on the snow-covered main street, he would throw out candy treats to children along the way.

The ride to Chetek had a choice of roads, one through fairly good flat farmland or through the Dovre hills with small farms and forests on poorer land, which was the prettiest ride but it also had crooked, unpaved roads. This road went by the lovely white tall-spired Dovre Lutheran church set on a hilltop amid a cemetery. The City of Chetek was small, but a bustling place in summer with an influx of Chicago and Milwaukee tourists coming to stay at lake lodges and fish in the nearby chain of lakes. At Christmas, it was a tranquil place as tourists were absent, and the main customers were nearby dairy farmers.

The Farmers Store was the main business in town. Pa liked this store as they usually had a wheel of extra sharp cheddar cheese that they let him taste before he bought a hunk to take home. He ate this cheese alone as Ma and I found it too strong for our tastes. Downtown was Abramson's dry goods, a dime store, Hembrook Feed and Implement, Burnham undertaker, two drug stores, several restaurants and taverns, a bank, a physician, a dentist, a bakery, a movie theater, gas stations, and various offices. Near the Chicago Northwestern railway track was the passenger depot, a pickle plant, and a pea cannery.

Chetek was different from other towns in having a mixed ethnic population. The largest group was probably Norwegian, with some Swedes, followed by people of English-Scots ancestry. East of Chetek was a large Polish settlement and nearby some Bohemians.

By Christmas, the lake would normally be frozen over although the ice might not be thick enough for safe ice fishing. Clarence Hoveland, the Chevrolet-Buick dealer, owned the ice business, which cut lake ice in winter and delivered it to tourist lodges, taverns, and other businesses in summer. Chetek was our most exciting small town, probably a result of the tourists and diversity of residents. At Christmas they had it nicely decorated, and more things were going on in churches and clubs.

The little village of New Auburn was one we rarely visited as it had only a small Farmers Store. It was a depressing little place with a motley collection of business buildings housing a small bank, Hanson's butcher shop, Dr. McCormick's office and pharmacy, gas stations, and Moskowicz' junkyard where he also bought wild animal pelts. His business building usually had stacks of beaver, muskrat, fox, skunk, and other hides bought from local farmers who trapped. It all stank to high heaven, and I was glad when Pa's visit to buy a junk part ended. The Chicago Northwestern depot had one passenger train per day. The ethnic makeup of the village was mixed.

Driving 15 miles south to Colfax was a pretty ride through Trout Creek hill farms along the Red Cedar River, which opened up to flat dairy farms north of town where cigar filler tobacco was also grown. Holden Church, a typical rural Lutheran white board building with a tall spire, towered above the old cemetery. Colfax was a solidly Norwegian town. The old brownstone Norwegian Synod Lutheran Church was the main worship center in contrast to small congregations of Methodists and pietist Lutheran Brethren.

Downtown was dominated by the Farmers Store, the old opera house converted to a movie theater, Running and Martin Ford garage-undertakers, Noer Drugs, a restaurant, a butcher, several taverns, gas stations, Snyder Photography, offices of a physician and a dentist, and insurance offices of Dermont Toycen and S.K. Iverson. Off Main Street was a large creamery, a pickle plant, and the Soo Line railway depot where there was daily passenger service to Minneapolis. Near the railway tracks, Pa's Uncle Oscar Hoveland ran a junkyard where he bought scrap metal and sold it for processing. We generally stopped to visit him in his tiny office. He was a ruddy-faced, good-natured man with a smile that showed off his gold teeth. Colfax was a quiet little law-abiding town where not much happened, and one could commonly hear Norwegian spoken on the street. At Christmas, street decorations and lights brightened up the drab buildings and contrasted nicely with the snow-covered village.

Christmas Eve

The day before Christmas was a busy and exciting one, one of the best in the year for me. After we finished all the morning chores, Pa and I changed from our barn overalls into newer clean overalls for a trip to Sand Creek. We stopped first at Uncle Sophus Noer's so I could deliver a gift for cousin Swanhild and receive one from her. Quite often, we had to wait until she finished wrapping it. Our next stop was at Uncle Oscar's farm to deliver a big bag of mixed nuts or apples for the family. We did not exchange gifts with them as they were too poor for that expense during the Depression.

Sand Creek didn't offer any fancy street lights, but some stores put up wreaths or had colored lights in the windows, and a few milk haulers put wreaths on their truck radiators.

Stopping at the Farmers Store for a few grocery items, shoppers and clerks were in a festive mood, wishing one another, "Gladleg Jul" (Merry Christmas). If the skies looked like snow, people wondered if they might get snowed in tomorrow morning and not get to Christmas services at church. We depended mainly on the skies for weather prediction as weather forecasts in the newspapers or on the radio were about as reliable as those in the Farmers Almanac. Another stop was for coffee and to deliver gifts for Grandpa and Grandma Hoveland and receive their gifts for me. There were no surprises here, as every year I received socks and a handkerchief bought at the Farmers Store along with a laboriously written note from Grandma. The best gift she had for us was a big package of her marvelous soft thin lefsa, which was perfect for our Christmas Eve dinner.

In the afternoon, I would ski across the fields to Grandma Noer's house to deliver gifts for her and Uncles Arnold and Fritjof, getting packages for me in return. There were wonderful surprises here as they always bought interesting gifts. Uncle Arnold and Grandma had their gifts wrapped nicely, but Uncle Fritjof presented his to me in the brown paper or sack just as it came from the store. Of course, Grandma had special goodies for me to eat and a good Christmas story for me. On this day, Pa would do only the necessary cow feeding and spend extra time sitting in his leather rocking chair listening to Christmas carols that were sung or played much of the day on the radio. One of his favorites was to hear Ernestine Schumann-Heink, originally from Germany, sing "Silent Night" or "O Holy Night."

At home, Pa and I would go to the barn about 5:30 pm and do the milking while Ma prepared dinner. Walking back to the house after milking, I would look up at the black star-studded sky and think excitedly about all the wonderful things that would happen on Christmas Eve. Entering the warm house, wonderful smells of cooking filled the air and promised a special feast. Sometimes we had lutefisk and meat balls, but more likely it was salmon or halibut, along with boiled potatoes, melted butter, green peas, and sweet potatoes. For dessert, it might be rømmegrøt (cream mush) or hot rice in milk sauce with cinnamon butter.

After the dishes were done, we gathered around the lighted Christmas tree to read the Christmas story from St. Luke before we opened gifts. Gifts from relatives were opened first. A highlight was opening the box from Uncle Sam and Aunt Ona in Chicago as they always sent a big box of Mrs. Snyder's chocolates, very high quality candy with rich dark chocolate that Pa and I treasured. When I was little, I opened gifts from other people and some from Ma and Pa on Christmas Eve, but the big gifts from "Santa Claus" would be found by the tree when I crept down the stairs in the morning darkness. Ma and Pa would be in the barn milking. When I turned on the tree lights, it was as though a miracle had occurred.

Enjoying the warmth, I would sit by the furnace register, awed by the beautiful tree and gifts awaiting me; it was one of the richest experiences of the year for me! It was the one night of the year that my excitement was so great that sleep was interrupted by thoughts about the magic of this night when Santa would be coming to our house. I knew that Santa could not come down our chimney because he would have ended up in our furnace and burned his feet. Instead, I rationalized that at our house he probably came in by the unlocked door to deliver my gifts.

"Santa" did not wrap my packages with colorful Christmas paper, they usually had brown paper with blue lettering of "Werner on the Corner" hardware store in Bloomer. Apparently, "Santa" got my gifts locally and saved hauling them so far in his sleigh. One year I found a beautiful red sled. Another year it was a small stationary steam engine that actually ran when plugged into an electric outlet to heat water in the boiler. Unfortunately, that Christmas Eve a storm had caused a tree to fall over our power line so we had no electricity to operate my steam engine in the morning. Other years I received Tinker Toys, Lincoln Logs, and best of all, an Erector Set where I could build all sorts of structures with metal girders, nuts, and bolts. I hung on to belief in "Santa" later than most kids, as I did not want to give up the magic. Finally, when I was older and accepted the inevitable that Santa was a myth, we opened all our gifts on Christmas Eve, but Ma always had a little gift under the tree for me to enjoy on Christmas morning.

Even in the depths of the Depression with almost no money at home, there was always something from "Santa Claus." Little did I realize at the time the sacrifice my parents made for me from such limited resources. Ma and Pa gave me, in addition to the gifts, a rich treasure of Christmas memories that enriched my life. They seemed to derive a great deal of pleasure seeing me so happy at Christmas, but I doubt they realized the overwhelming joy that it gave me. Unfortunately, I was never able in later years to express my thanks adequately for their love and what they had given me so generously at Christmas.

Christmas Day church service was a big event and everyone imaginable was there. Even Fritz Nelson and other non-church goers would be in church that day. All the Myran family would dress up and attend Our Saviour's Church across the river. At Zion where we attended, parishioners were in a festive mood, some with new clothes, small children sometimes clutching a special toy, and excited to be in church. A tall tree with ornaments and lights stood in a corner. Bits of tree greenery decorated window sills, and the air was fragrant with spruce. Many carols were sung by the congregation. The choir would sing "Jeg er sa glad var Jule kveld" (I am so glad each Christmas Night) and sometimes do "Silent Night" in Norwegian. There was a sermon but those words were lost on me as I dreamed about the wonderful new gifts I had under our Christmas tree. It was a festive service and a highlight of the year, especially for some who attended church only once a year.

Christmas Week

The week between Christmas and New Year's was a time for visiting neighbors and relatives. Usually, farm work was limited to essentials like milking, feeding, and manure handling. It was time for rest and relaxation. People would take time to stop by for conversation, coffee and sandbakkels, krumkake, fruit cake, and other goodies. Some would invite guests for a special daytime meal. I always looked forward to such a party at Uncle John and Aunt Laura Hanson's house. Men were dressed in suits and ties, women in church dresses. With their seven sons, one could be assured of many stories, raucous laughter, and a good time as they met with other men in the two attached living rooms. It was fun as a child to listen to them as they talked. After dinner, clouds of cigar smoke filled the air. Sisters Ma and Laura would be busy working in the kitchen with other women who may have been present. Sometimes they served Jul øl (Christmas beer) which was homemade and not very good to my taste. The food was abundant with turkey or ham, potatoes, whipped cream salads, and included a heavy supply of Christmas baking.

Another event I liked was a Christmas party at Uncle Sophus' and Aunt Clara's house as one could be assured of eating well. Aunt Clara laid out a good table and added extra niceties. Uncle Sophus served adults a glass of sweet Mogen David wine to celebrate the season. Conversation was guaranteed to be exciting as the three brothers, Arnold, Fritjof, and Sophus, would argue on a variety of topics, providing great entertainment for a listener. Arnold would often take the lead, Fritjof usually agreeing, and Sophus quite often disagreeing. As the discussion continued, the noise volume increased. John Hanson was adept at introducing controversial viewpoints as he often took a devil's advocate position. Because Pa was matter of fact with a set viewpoint on a subject, he usually got the worst of it, especially with Uncles John and Arnold. Sometimes I played with Swanhild, but I hated to miss out on the excitement of the noisy debates.

Sometimes groups of young people from church would stop by and sing Christmas carols outside the house during the evening. It was so beautiful to hear them standing in the snow outside and then we each put on a coat and cap to stand on our porch to thank them for coming on a cold moonlit night. Occasionally, they welcomed a stop to have a cup of coffee or hot cocoa before they drove to other farms.

It was great fun when people came "julebukking" to our house in the evening. This was an old Norwegian custom dating back to pagan times when a bukk (male goat) was used in the ceremony to honor Thor. The Catholic church modified it into entertainment with the persons participating being known as a julebukk. Young men and women in the community would visit neighbors, dressed in various costumes, wearing a mask, and disguising their voices and body language. The object was to try and identify the persons in their disguises. Among others, the Hanson brothers could always be expected to furnish a good show. As a little child, I was scared by some of the people in their masks but I enjoyed it immensely as I grew older. It was all great fun, especially when it was difficult to identify an individual and a big surprise when they revealed their identity. The hosts would then offer the julebukk guests something to drink and eat before they moved on to another house.

New Year's

We didn't do anything special for New Year's Eve except eat a good dinner and go to bed early. New Year's Day we generally were at home. I was always sad then as it was the end of Christmas, and it would be a whole year before I could enjoy this grand season again. A visible sign of the end was watching the Christmas tree raining needles on the cloth floor cover. It was a sad day when we finally undressed the Christmas tree and dragged it outside a week or two later. Now there was nothing special to anticipate the rest of the long winter until mud season in the spring. Winter seemed like the longest season of the year.

Snowstorms

We got a lot of snow in northwestern Wisconsin during those years. One could tell when a snowstorm was coming. It would cloud up and get warmer for several days, then snowflakes would begin to fall. Since weather forecasts were often unreliable, we never knew how much snow to expect but we were prepared for the worst. Sometimes it would snow all day and night, piling it up in soft fluffy piles. Other times, strong winds would accompany the snow and produce hard packed high drifts many feet high that were tough to shovel or even to break through with snow plows. A foot or more of snow could pile up from a single storm. If winter continued without any significant periods of melting, the snow depth could reach several feet.

We had wood snow fences erected by our driveway to catch more of the snow as drifts in a field and thus reduce the amount we needed to shovel. The highway department also erected these fences in vulnerable places along main roads. Small snowstorms were no problem as milk truck drivers could usually get through using small plows on the front of their trucks to clean out farm driveways. We were fortunate in living close to a county trunk highway that was generally kept open. Huge four-wheeled drive Oshkosh or FWD trucks with winged plows would roar past during the night and day to get roads open after a snowstorm. Farmers living on small township roads were not so fortunate as those roads were plowed later after all county roads were open. Snow plows made one trip down each road to get them open; then later they would return to widen the road and wing the huge piles farther out.

When large amounts of snow accumulated, the snow banks on both sides were like high walls four to ten feet high with big clumps of frozen snow and ice rolling down on to the road. This made walking to school an obstacle course where one had to navigate between the solid clumps to avoid falling. As a result, skiing was a much easier way of getting to school. It was also a lot more fun, especially when the snow was crusted and so hard that one easily glided along effortlessly. Sometimes there was so much snow on fields that only the upper wires on fences would be visible.

Snow shoveling furnished plenty of exercise for Pa and me after each snow storm. Even if our driveway was plowed by the milk hauler, we still had to shovel access to each of our farm buildings. With Pa that meant cutting nice straight edges and throwing the snow back far from the walkway. Pa's insistence on leaving neat straight snow walls on our paths made no sense to me because when the snow melted all this extra effort would be wasted. My arguments were useless so we continued to construct straight snow walls, the best around Sand Creek. A continuing problem was at the entrance to our driveway where we would clean up the plowed snow left by the county snow plows. Then, at a later interval, the big truck would widen the road, leaving another big pile of snow in our clean driveway for us to remove with our snow shovels. There was one good thing about snow shoveling; it was good exercise and one kept warm even in very cold weather.

Once in a while we had a really big snowstorm along with a blizzard when screaming winds off the Canadian prairies gave us white outs with no visibility. Under these conditions, huge drifts built up in roads, and there was no car travel or attempts to plow the roads for a day or two. With no school, I enjoyed the opportunity to stay in the warm house except for essential barn chores. It was then that I spent hours enjoying my stamp collection, building model airplanes, constructing stuff with the Erector set, and playing with other choice Christmas gifts. It was a cozy feeling sitting there with the wind howling outside depositing piles of snow in deep drifts. Pa would sit in his rocking chair smoking a pipe and listening to the radio for news reports on the storm elsewhere while Ma enjoyed sitting with her coffee cup talking on the phone with neighbors.

Cold

January, the coldest month of the year, could be a cruel time. After a big snowstorm temperatures would drop as the dry cold high pressure air settled over us. The sun would come out, but there was no warmth in it during the few hours it appeared each day. If there was a wind along with the cold, it was even worse and all our bundling up with heavy clothes couldn't keep one warm walking to school. I wore long wool underwear, wool pants under my overalls, heavy wool plaid mackinaw, a wool neck scarf to keep the rough mackinaw wool from scratching my neck, a wool cap with big ear flaps, wool mittens covered by leather ones, and buckled rubber overshoes. Walking or skiing to school, my breath was visible, the cold air hurt the lungs, and the dry air made my skin crack and bleed. Eyeglasses, which I wore since fourth grade, were a nuisance since they fogged up when entering a warm building. It was also the season for colds, spread easily from child to child at school, so runny noses and dirty snot rags (handkerchiefs or rags) were the norm.

Pa kept close watch on the weather. He would listen daily to temperature reports on the radio from various parts of Wisconsin. At home, he checked our thermometer several times a day. At night before going to bed, when he went outside to pee and check the thermometer, he might come in and announce, "It's going to be cold tonight; it's already down to 10 below." By morning it might reach 20 or 25 below in January. Once in a while it would dip to 30 below or even lower. One time it hit 50 below. Things got serious when daytime temperatures did not rise above zero for one or two weeks. The only good thing about such an extended period of cold was that we didn't get much new snow to add to our misery.

There were substantial effects of these low temperatures over a period of time. The first involved keeping the house warm. We were lucky since we had a pipe furnace, although it did not have a fan to move the air all over the house. Our house was well built, had storm windows, and retained heat well, but, it took a lot more wood to feed the furnace in such cold weather. Pa had to get up during the night to add wood to the furnace so there would be a fire there in the morning. We were warm in our house. Folks with wood stoves in each room downstairs, especially in poorly constructed wood houses, usually suffered with drafts, cold floors and icy upstairs rooms. Even in our house during a prolonged period of extreme cold, ice would build up on upstairs windows so one could not see outside. When I went to bed at night upstairs, I would often carry a heated flat iron wrapped in a wool blanket to warm the icy sheets.

Barn chores were affected by the cold. Barn windows would also ice over, but the cows kept the temperature well above freezing. The hay mow was bitter cold as one pitched loose hay down the chute for the cows. Worse yet was getting corn silage out of the tower silo. Since it was frozen solid, one had to use a pick axe to dig it out, then pitch the frozen lumps down the chute where they were fed to the cows. The cows didn't find these lumps too appealing and usually allowed them to thaw before eating. Needless to say, milk production dropped during January. Cleaning gutters and filling the carrier tub was hard work where one might get sweaty, but one quickly got cooled off pushing the filled carrier on a cable outside in the frigid air to dump it on the manure pile. The open barn door soon let the cows know they were lucky to be standing in their stanchions with plenty of feed and water on a bitter cold morning.

Water was of concern on many farms in winter. We were fortunate to have an electric pump and well in our house basement. Many people suffered in the cold as they got house water from outdoor hand pumps that might freeze up in winter. Others might not have located underground water lines deep enough to prevent freezing. Pa had our water line to the barn and milk house buried seven feet deep; so we had no problems. Washing clothes during extreme cold was a miserable job. It was no wonder that this task was often delayed and people wore clothes longer before they were washed. Likewise, bathing was less frequent since steel laundry tubs kept outside had to be brought in and warmed before hot water from the wood stove water tank could be poured into them.

With less bathing and wearing clothes longer before washing, we no doubt smelled worse in January than other times of the year. Most men, and a few women, wore "long johns" which were one piece wool underwear with long sleeves and legs, buttoning from neck to crotch. After being worn daily for a week or so, sometimes also at night, the crotch and under arm areas got rather fragrant and discolored. Unfortunately, some people rarely washed these body areas, and underarm deodorants were an unknown commodity. We all smelled badly in January, the only difference was that some stank worse than others.

Car and truck engines had to be well maintained if they were to start in cold weather. I felt sorry for Uncle Art having to work on ice cold cars in winter even though he had some heat in his garage. Weak batteries showed up fast on a cold morning when the car starter wouldn't turn the engine over.

Battery sales went up in January. Another annoyance was brakes freezing up. Water in gasoline could result in frozen gas lines and prevent starting, necessitating thawing out gas lines to the engine. Smart farmers drove Fords and Chevrolets as they were more likely to start on a cold morning. Plymouths, Whippets, and a few other makes had a poor reputation for starting. Even so, it was common to hear someone grinding away helplessly on the car starter during a frigid morning. I suspect many vile words were spoken on those occasions.

Many of the older cars either had no heaters or simply a vent with engine heat flowing into the car interior. Heaters were an extra cost accessory when a new car was purchased, and some people did not think it was worth the additional money just for comfort in winter. Getting into a cold car that had been standing outside for several hours in sub-zero weather was not pleasant even if the engine started. Sitting on a cold car seat was akin to sitting on a block of ice and guaranteed to wake up a sleepy person. Unless the owner warmed up the engine for awhile before departing, there would be no heat from the heater until many miles down the road. Often, the windows fogged up from one's breath so they had to be wiped until the heater finally did its job. The unpleasantries of winter motoring no doubt caused people to stay home instead of visiting folks during bitter cold weather, especially at night.

It was easy to get stuck in loose snow with cars or trucks. Many drivers carried a small snow shovel either in the trunk or on the back seat floor if the car did not have a trunk. Tire chains were a necessity and carried in the car for emergency use. Once stuck, the driver would drape ice cold chains over the rear tires and attempt to hook them together near the base of the tires using bare cold fingers in zero weather. This was not an easy task and near impossible at night without the aid of a flashlight. The driver had to lie down under the car to reach the inside of the tire, hoping to find the needed hooks. A bit of melting snow water added to the torment of this job. It made it even better if one were dressed in a suit and overcoat. In periods of heavy snow, chains were left on the tires, but as roads thawed the snow, they had to be removed to prevent wear.

Another problem was that tires were not very durable, and flat tires were a common hazard. Changing tires on a country road in summer was simply an inconvenience compared to jacking up a car on snow and suffering at this miserable job on a cold winter night. A truly unlucky tire changer might drop wheel lug nuts in the snow and waste more time trying to find them with icy fingers, especially without a flashlight at night. These were tasks that tested the language of a good Lutheran.

Winter Fun

Winter, especially in January, was not fun for adults in Sand Creek. Children coped better as they enjoyed skiing, sledding, and skating. Skiing was mostly cross-country, as we had few hills for challenging downhill skiing. I enjoyed cross-country and found it exhilarating skimming along across fields. It was about the only sport in which I showed any athletic ability. Sledding down our small hills was fun for younger children and was common among them. Skating was less popular as the river ice was not dependable since the water level fluctuated and caused cracking of the ice. On small ponds it was different although one had to clear the snow off the surface to provide a smooth surface for skaters. I was not a skater.

One winter adventure stands out for me. During the winter that cousin Orville Hoveland lived with us, we would often go sledding or skiing on a Sunday afternoon. On this particular sunny cold winter afternoon, we decided to take our sleds and go sliding down on the steep Red Cedar River bank near our farm. We also took along a snow shovel to enhance the hill by making a tower of snow to create a jump area; the objective being to put the sled and occupant into the air so they would land on the river ice. Orville, five years older than I, was the originator of this great idea. This exciting prospect was not mentioned to Ma as she had previously instructed us to keep off the river ice because it was not safe.

At the river, Orville went to work with great gusto, shoveling snow and making a large jump part way down the slope. I was the first one to try this attraction. It worked splendidly lying on my sled as I became airborne and landed on the river ice, coasting a long way. Elated, I walked back and then watched as Orville followed on his sled. He came down, becoming airborne and landed on the ice, but because of his heavier weight, the sled broke through the ice along with Orville. He yelled, "It's cold!" as I stood there horrified at him in the frigid water. Somehow, I managed to pull him onto the ice so he could crawl out. We also rescued the sled.

Now we had a new problem. Orville was soaking wet and shivering in the cold air, but we didn't dare go home as Ma had ordered us not to do this sort of thing. Instead, we took a circuitous route around the house to the dairy barn. Orville stripped and wrung out his wet clothes; then I hung them to dry across the backs of cows standing in their stanchions while he stood naked trying to dry and warm himself next to a cow. Needless to say, the cows did not appreciate either the wet clothes on their backs or wet Orville next to them. As the afternoon progressed and I kept turning the clothes as they were drying, Orville was feeling better with several dry gunny sacks covering his body to stay warm. We finally got his clothes dried enough for him to get dressed again so we could go back to the house. It was a memorable afternoon. Ma didn't find out what happened until years later when I told her.

Late Winter

Winter was the longest season of the year. Barn chores were the same week after week. The snow-covered landscape, the dark green pines, and leafless oaks remained the same. A few rabbits left their tracks in the snow and crows announced themselves. We never saw deer in our area. An occasional passing car or milk truck broke the quiet. It was a lonely time of year.

There wasn't much going on. Valentine's Day was a minor event at school, with kids drawing names to send someone a funny card. As the winter wore on with days getting a bit longer, the extreme cold moderated, and sometimes there would be a time of real warmth and thawing of snow in February. This didn't mean the end of snowstorms since some of our biggest snow storms came in late February or even March. But by then we knew this snow wouldn't last as long and that the end of winter was in sight.

This was the time of year that Pa and I spent Saturdays in the snow-covered woods sawing down white pine trees and piling up logs to be moved by horses pulling skidder loads to our sawmill. Pa loved being out in the frigid woods cutting timber. I think it brought back memories of the winters he spent as a teen age boy working in a logging camp in northern Minnesota. Logging was not one of my boyhood joys. After weeks of Saturday work our late winter logging produced piles of logs to make lumber for sale. I was always glad when logging season was over.

By March, snow was melting down, although it usually still covered the ground. Farmers were getting around more and beginning to talk about spring planting of oats the following month. Still the ground was still frozen, melt water ran off in rivulets. Huge packed snow piles lined roadsides with melt water held on the frozen road, then froze at night into rough ruts. Due to the challenge of navigating frozen ruts and chunks of ice, walking to school in the morning was slow. It was easy to trip on one of these obstacles and fall. Ski snow on the fields was not good either; so the choices were difficult. It was warmer now, but weather was changeable with cold winds and snowstorms reminding us that winter was still here. At this time of year, we were tired of winter and ready for a better season. Eventually, the longest season would be over. It could not come too soon for me.

High School

By 1940 milk prices had improved substantially, and life for farmers was getting much better. This new prosperity resulted in Pa purchasing a milking machine, one of the best machines on the farm as far as Ma and I were concerned. We also got a Hedlund hay lift (manufactured at Boyceville) which was an electric motor-powered device that pulled a loaded hay fork up to the track and into the hay mow, replacing a horse and driver. Pa also bought a small Ford tractor with a plow and cultivator. Since our two horses were old and had to be put down, the new tractor replaced them for small jobs around the farm. We also traded our old 1934 Ford for a 1939 Chevrolet that had been owned by a rural mail carrier. Unfortunately, Pa still did not see the need for an indoor bathroom.

We followed the news of Hitler's invasion of Poland and later France and the low countries. The awful bombing of English cities and the courageous words of Churchill made people wonder when the United States would enter the war to help these desperate people. Local support for suffering Europeans was intensified in April, 1940, when Hitler's forces invaded first neutral Denmark and then Norway. We followed news reports on the radio each night as they described the desperate escape of the royal family, the Norwegian government, and the gold reserves as they moved northward, pursued by the Nazi army and air force. I had a map mounted on a plywood board where I used colored pins to track the Norwegian retreat through the mountains and the eventual escape to England of King Haakon and Prince Olaf on a British warship. It was a black day when news came that the Nazis controlled all of Norway. Some local young men volunteered for service in the army even though the United States was still neutral.

I graduated from County Line School in May 1941. Farmers were doing well, and factories in cities were hiring people so there were new job opportunities. Some local people with no farm prospects left Sand Creek permanently for jobs in Milwaukee, Chicago, and Detroit. As for me, I was looking forward to four years of high school with great excitement. I recall that Torphin Peterson, a gentle, impecunious farmer who eked out a living on a little dairy farm, was helping me with barn chores for a few days in winter when Pa was in bed with a bad case of flu. He was very impressed that I was going to high school and commented, "Carl, you'll finish high school and probably get a good job making $200 a month." For Torphin, $200 was a huge wage to earn in a month and beyond his dreams. Whatever my future earnings potential, I was eager for more education.

School Bus

The day after Labor Day in September, 1941, I started high school at Chetek. The snub-nosed GMC school bus, owned by Ingolf Hansen, came from Sand Creek and picked me up at our driveway. School buses used to be yellow but Governor Julius Heil, a wealthy Milwaukee industrialist, decreed that Wisconsin school buses would be repainted red, white, and blue to reflect our patriotism. It was probably the most significant thing Governor Heil did in office. The Sand Creek bus traveled a circuitous route past dairy farms south of Chetek, picking up students with Norwegian names like Gilberts, Paulson, Hendrickson, Hoveland, Knutson, Olson, Foss, Bergland, Thompson, Skoug, Harelstad, Carlson, Saastad, Peterson, Larson, Holter, and Lund. The Dallas bus brought in another load of students with similar names. The East bus was more mixed with some Swedes like Lenbom, Lundholm, and Osberg or eastern European names like Dobrowolski, Mickiewicz, Novak, Czerwonka, Lojewski, Bihun, and Modjeski.

Near Chetek the population was of mixed ancestry, often English or Irish names. Nicknames were common and some not so elegant. One such was a motherless boy by the name of Brown who lived with his father on a tiny farm south of Chetek. They supplemented their income by trapping muskrat, beaver, and other wildlife including skunks. As a consequence, the poor kid sometimes exuded a powerful skunk fragrance in the bus as he entered which earned him the nickname of "Skunk Brown."

Boys wore dress pants and shirt, sometimes with a sweater, to high school while girls had skirts and blouses or sweaters, saddle shoes, and bobby socks. When the weather got colder, boys had heavy jackets and caps while girls wore long wool coats and wool scarves over their heads. A few girls wore long heavy stockings, but most added wool pants under their skirts and removed them at school. Girls were forbidden to wear pants at school, regardless of weather. A big heater was at the front of our bus, but on a bitter cold morning with temperatures hovering at 30 below, it was a cold ride in a rear seat so one needed to be bundled up. Everyone wore rubber overshoes in winter to cope with the snow and cold.

During the bus ride, there was chatter and laughter, a few games of various kinds, and occasional pranks. A number engaged in low stakes gambling by matching pennies on the backs of their wrists. Don Larson, Wesley Paulson, and I often had such a game going which gave us a lot of fun but didn't do much to redistribute our wealth. The biggest excitement was when the bus got stuck in deep snow drifts and had to be pulled out by a farmer, resulting in us arriving late at school. Rarely was school closed because of snowstorms. In a few cases, when side roads were blocked by snow, farmers would deliver their children to the bus on a horse-drawn sleigh. Occasionally, when a heavy snowstorm was threatening, buses might be sent home early from high school.

It was a long day for high school students living on a farm. Like most of the boys, I was up by 5 am to help milk cows before breakfast and had to change clothes prior to boarding the bus. Girls had house jobs in the morning, and many helped with milking as well. Some kids, like Arlene Saastad (who later married my cousin Orville), worked especially hard at home before getting on the bus. On returning from school, I changed clothes and helped Pa milk cows before we ate our supper. I did all my studying at school and rarely brought textbooks home. Pa had never been to high school and thought one should be able to do all one's school work there during the day. However, I often brought home library books on travel, biography, history, and even novels to enjoy in the evening. Pa was not impressed with reading "story books" or novels as they did not supply factual material that might be useful.

Chetek High School

The two-story, brick high school building was located behind the old elementary school on the main street of

Chetek. The Farmers Store and drug store with a soda fountain were nearby. School started at 9 am and ended at 3:30 pm. It was quite an adjustment from County Line School, as each class was held in a different room, and free periods were spent studying in the large home room where one was assigned. Each student had a locker for clothes and books.

Most impressive was the huge, by my standards, library room where I was allowed to check out all sorts of wonderful books. I could hardly wait to enjoy this rich treasury of reading! A gymnasium was located in the basement along with a stage for theatrical productions. In the basement of the old elementary school was a room with a variety of hand and mechanical tools for shop classes. Next to it was the lunchroom presided over by Mrs. Atwood, an energetic, plump ruddy-faced lady with a big smile that showed off her glittering teeth.

Classes

Someone helped me get registered for a variety of classes, which I attended regularly. I soon learned there were some subjects that I loved and others that I did not like or had no aptitude for learning. English was one of my favorites. One year I was blessed with the finest teacher I was ever to have in my elementary, high school, and university education. Lillie Ahlgren, daughter of Swedish immigrants who farmed near Frederic, WI, was phenomenal! A tall, lean, attractive, brunnette lady with a winning smile, she had loads of enthusiasm, loved books, knew her subject well, and was intent on sharing it with us. She worked us hard, trying her best even with those who resisted learning much of anything. With me, I loved reading literature assignments and writing assigned themes. Recognizing soon that I was not being fully challenged, she gave me extra writing and projects to supplement the regular lessons. I eagerly responded and ended up doing more work than most of the students. She cleverly kept me from being bored as she prodded less eager students. She inspired in me a love for good literature and a desire to perfect my limited writing skills. I was spoiled by Lillie's talented teaching and thereafter judged the performance of other teachers by her.

There were other instructors at Chetek High who were good teachers and expanded my education. Paul Kinney, the band leader, taught world history and made this subject glow with excitement. It was one of my favorite subjects, and he encouraged me with extra readings that he thought I would enjoy. My cousin Frederick, seven years older, urged me to be in an extra-curricular activity like band and offered me the use of his trombone. Even though I had no musical talent, I thought it was a fine idea and mentioned the trombone to Mr. Kinney. Always looking for new band students, he offered to give me free trombone lessons on Saturday mornings during the summer. Excitedly, I told Pa about this free opportunity which Ma supported wholeheartedly. Pa replied that he just couldn't spare me from summer farm work to play a trombone, which was just entertainment. I was crushed as I thought it would have been exciting to wear a purple and white uniform and play trombone while marching at football games. So ended my band career.

Byron Van Hollen was looking for recruits in the Boys Chorus he taught; so I volunteered although I couldn't read a musical note. Amazingly, after an audition he accepted me, and I practiced with the group and enjoyed this activity as a freshman. We performed at a number of functions and received a second rating at the music finals for schools in our district that spring. Even though I enjoyed this group, realizing that I was no singer, I did not extend my shaky career in music. Mr. Van Hollen was a talented chemistry teacher and held in high regard by students. I had planned to take chemistry from him as a junior, but by then he had departed Chetek to study full time for a law degree at the University of Wisconsin. As a result, I ended up with a woman teacher who attempted to teach chemistry, a subject she apparently had never mastered and thus imparted little to her students.

My next venture in extra-curricular activities was as a reporter on the "Bulldog's Bark," the student paper that was cranked out on a duplicator in the commerce room where I took typing. I enjoyed typing class with Mrs. Isaacson, a fine teacher who also taught shorthand, and did well in the subject. Boys were not numerous in typing class, as this was generally considered a girl's subject. My tenure as a reporter was not a great success as I had trouble rounding up interesting stories. I had no social skills and thus was not knowledgeable about gossip that made good stories. A similar situation occurred with my venture into theater. I quickly found that I was scared to death in front of an audience, so could not perform on the stage. Instead, my highest achievement in theater was cranking the wind machine in a play that featured student-actors who loved performing on a stage.

I soon found out that my struggles with arithmetic in grade school were a good predictor of trouble ahead in high school mathematics classes. Algebra class was taught by Mr. E. L. Brown, the principal, who was reputed to be a good teacher. My lack of mathematical skills soon got me in trouble, but I managed to survive due to abundant help from two helpful girls, Jean Lindblad and Barbara Burnham, who breezed through this subject but patiently worked with me. The next mathematics course, geometry, was much worse. Mr. Beers, the teacher, was demanding, boring, and not very patient as he tried to explain details of geometry to dullards like me who had absolutely no interest in this subject. Somehow, I survived and passed the class. In contrast, I did very well in general science and American history with Mr. Simmelink.

I fared better than I deserved in Mr. Sauer's shop class where I made a bowl on a turning lathe, a doll bed for my little sister, and other wooden objects. My lack of mechanical skills resulted in less than perfect workmanship, but Mr. Sauer patiently encouraged me to try to do better. Since he was also the football and basketball coach, it is a good thing that he did not discover my pitiful lack of athletic skills. I also enrolled in a vocational agriculture class that was popular with many boys because it was easy and everyone got a good grade. After one semester I dropped the class as it was truly boring. I didn't see much sense in memorizing things like oat varieties adapted in our area when I knew this list would change in a few years. Mr. Vruwink, the teacher, was a fine fellow, but he failed to challenge students to think about principles rather than details in farming. Biology class sounded interesting to me. Unfortunately, since we were in World War II at the time, the teacher, Mrs. Blado, felt that we needed to learn first aid in case of wartime emergencies, so we spent half of our class time learning about bandages, splints, resuscitation, pulses, heart beats, cuts, bruises, broken bones, and stretchers. The result was that I had an abbreviated course in biology, a subject I loved.

I thought I would like to take a foreign language, but none was offered except for Latin, which sounded like a dead subject to me. There were no classes in art, public speaking, or economics. Students interested in improving their speaking skills would get some instruction if they joined the debate team. Of course, my shyness prevented me from volunteering for anything that required performance before a group.

Diversions

I was a shy kid with no social skills, liked most classes, and generally did not participate in the usual wide range of activities typical of most students. I would rapidly complete my lessons in the home room and then eagerly become lost in the pages of a library book until time for my next class. Recreational reading was my great love, and with an abundant supply of fascinating books in our library, I was completely contented. I suspect that I expanded my horizons more reading a wide range of subjects in the home room than I did in some classes.

It was in the home room that I discovered something about tolerance. Some rows were composed of double desks where two students sat side by side. One year I was assigned a seat adjacent to John Apker, a jolly fat boy with coal black hair who was a fairly good student. I immediately liked John but soon discovered that he was a devout Catholic. Based on the biases of what I had learned in church about Catholics, I was immediately suspicious of John. However, he turned out to be a kind, courteous fellow who spoke well of his parents and treated me with respect even though he was Catholic and I was Lutheran. Apparently, some Catholics were good people! Maybe some of the things I had learned about Catholics were wrong. It was a dilemma for me. Sitting beside John in home room that year and enjoying his company was a valuable lesson for me, learning to accept people with other religious persuasions.

One day I expanded my education in another way. It was lunch hour when students ate their sandwiches brought from home or bought a hot dish, sandwiches, and pastries from Mrs. Atwood at the school cafeteria. I had eaten my sandwiches and headed out to our Sand Creek bus parked by the school to retrieve a book that I had left on a seat.

Strangely, the bus door was open so I walked up the steps. Looking down the aisle on the floor I saw an amorous couple passionately sharing their semi-naked bodies with each other. I stared in disbelief, recognizing the couple who saw me. I beat a hasty retreat without my book, having learned more about human sexual activities that day than I knew before. The couple and I never discussed this romantic tryst.

Skipping school for part or all of a day was common among many students, particularly on pleasant days during autumn or spring. Chetek offered many opportunities for recreational outings such as canoeing on the nearby lakes, playing pool, romantic sessions, and hitchhiking rides to Rice Lake or Eau Claire. Occasional mishaps such as a spill in the water, sunburn, or getting back late and missing the bus created some problems but did not deter future adventures. Enjoying school, I was not greatly tempted by skipping school. One time, Don Larson begged me to go canoeing with him on a sunny afternoon. We had a pleasant time on the lake for several hours in our rental canoe, but I had a nagging feeling that maybe I was missing something at school. I was also afraid that I might get back late and miss the bus, creating a major problem in explaining this to Pa, who would not appreciate his helper missing milking that evening.

On Friday evenings, football or basketball games were played against other high schools in the area. During home games, the school buses would remain in Chetek until after the game. A few students who had to get home for farm work or other reasons were taken there after school in a small station wagon. As one would expect, Pa needed me at home for milking, so I missed staying in town for most of the games. When Pa allowed me to remain in town for the homecoming football game each year, I enjoyed the treat of eating a hamburger or grilled cheese sandwich and some ice cream during the homecoming festivities and game. I wasn't much interested in the game, but I enjoyed the band, cheerleaders, and the excitement of the crowd.

At the end of the school year, each class would have an all-day bus trip to a state park, lake, or some other entertainment place. Unfortunately, this was always a busy time on the farm; and Pa always needed me to work on some essential project. Thus, I never got to enjoy any of the bus trips with my fellow students. One year I was hard at work with Pa picking up stones and tree roots on a newly broken piece of land and loading them on a horse-drawn stone boat for removal. As I looked up from my miserable job, I was humiliated by students on the school bus waving to me as they drove by on their class trip. Farm work came first at our place.

War

Although war had raged in Europe from September 1939, it did not directly impact us. However, enlistments in the army and navy increased as Hitler's conquests increased and fears grew that there might eventually be a Nazi invasion of America. Farmers benefitted from the war as demand for food overseas increased and milk prices increased. To supply overseas markets, the Sand Creek creamery installed equipment to manufacture dried milk as well as butter. As a result of higher incomes, farmers bought new tractors to replace horses. New cars and trucks appeared on roads, and gas or electric stoves replaced many old wood stoves in kitchens. The advent of government REA (Rural Electric Administration) electricity lines made life much easier on the majority of farms that lacked power from private companies.

As we listened to the radio on Sunday afternoon, December 7, 1941, we were shocked to learn that Japanese planes from aircraft carriers had bombed and destroyed our Pacific fleet at Pearl Harbor, Hawaii. Soon after, the USA declared war on Japan and also Germany and Italy. The next day at high school a radio in the study hall provided continuing news on the losses at Pearl Harbor and new government policies as we changed from neutrality to a nation at war. We students were excited and wondered how this would change our lives. Classes that day spent time discussing current events with far greater interest than in the past. There was an immediate change in attitude as isolationist Republican politicians supported Democrats in increasing military expenditures. The USA was woefully unprepared to fight a war, and it took time to expand our armed forces and produce military equipment in factories.Large numbers of young men volunteered for military duty, and a national draft was instituted to provide more men.

Not much changed for us on the farm during the next few months, but later that year factories ceased production of cars and many other civilian goods to build military goods. Rationing was instituted for all sorts of consumer goods such as shoes, clothing, tires, gasoline, and many food items such as butter, meat, sugar, and coffee. A serious loss for us was no more imports of pickled herring from Norway. Farm machinery continued to be manufactured, but short supplies meant that farmers often had to wait for delivery. Sand Creek area residents found rationing of coffee and sugar the most painful as consumption of these items was particularly high among Norwegians. Gasoline rationing for cars was not a big problem for farmers as tractor gasoline was ample and some of it ended up in cars. Tire rationing was tough as all the rubber-producing areas of southeast Asia were now controlled by Japan. Synthetic rubber plants were started, but tires made from this product were of poor quality and did not last long. Thus, Pa put our car on blocks during the war, and we depended on the Ford pickup as our sole transportation.

As the war progressed, Karl Hansen in Sand Creek solved his lack of tires for the two-wheel car trailer he used to haul milk cans to the creamery by running the trailer wheels on their rims.The metal rims made an awful racket on the asphalt street as Karl made a daily trip to the creamery, announcing his contribution to the war effort.

School for me went on as usual. Since I was older, I was able to do more work on the farm and also some summer paid employment for neighbors. With most young men in the military or employed in expanded factories, farm labor was in short supply. Pa was astute enough to see that the future for our sawmill and threshing machine was not bright; so he sold them both at the beginning of the war. Combine harvesters were being used for harvesting grain, eliminating the labor of shocking bundles and hauling them to the thresher. Pa finally located and bought a used Allis-Chalmers combine, harvesting our grain and also doing custom work for other farmers. Pa also bought a new Ford corn picker that he used to harvest ear corn on many farms during autumn.

The Last Year of High School

By August 1944, Chetek High School Principal E. L. Brown had departed and was replaced by Mr. D. J. Huenink. Among other things, he rearranged bus routes, which resulted in my having to walk 3/4 mile from home to the Ness corner and wait for the bus. In contrast, Colfax High School was willing to pick me up at home. Pa was incensed at this change and decided I would not be returning to Chetek, but switch to Colfax High School. I protested that as a senior I wanted to be with all my old friends and was quite willing to wait in the cold for the Chetek bus. My protests were useless with Pa. Mr. Huenink made a visit to our farm to meet with Pa and me. It was a turbulent discussion with a stubborn Dutchman pitted against a stubborn Norwegian. Mr. Huenink tried to take my side, but Pa only replied that if Colfax could pick me up at the house, then so could Chetek. Mr. Huenink said that they were trying to conserve gasoline and keep the bus routes shorter, words that made no impression on Pa. I sat silently as they decided my fate. I ended up going to Colfax, riding a lengthy bus route that extended toward Bloomer. I was the first kid on the bus in the morning and last one off at night, a much longer day than if I had continued school at Chetek. Pa meant well in making another decision for me, certain that this would spare me the discomfort of waiting in the cold winter weather for the morning bus. Pa, having never attended high school, could not appreciate my feelings of being removed from the comforts of old friends and familiar surroundings to be thrust into an unfamiliar system for my senior year.

It was a miserable school year for me. I knew virtually no one, and my negative attitude didn't help. As a consequence, I made few friends and longed for Chetek High School. Sometimes I felt like quitting school. I had a dreadful English teacher, Lillie Gunderson, who appeared to be bored with her job and ground through Shakespeare's Hamlet with a total lack of enthusiasm for this fascinating play. At this time I was intrigued with the part time mechanical drawing occupation of Nordahl Trandhum, a Trout Creek farmer. I thought this might be interesting, so I signed up for a University of Wisconsin correspondence course in mechanical drawing that I worked at in school. I enjoyed the drawing but found there was more mathematics involved than I liked so I did not want to pursue it any further.

The only bright spot in school was Olaf Jensen, a basketball and football coach who was an excellent physics teacher. Even though my mathematical ability was limited, his teaching skills held my interest and I performed well. Adding to my woes that year was the deterioration of my teeth, which had seen virtually no dental care since my wisdom teeth were extracted. Pa and Ma decided I needed to have some fillings to eliminate toothache and save several teeth. I ended up spending many hours in the office of Dr. Krause, the sole dentist in Colfax. High speed drills were unknown and pain was inevitable, even with novocaine, since my teeth were in bad shape. He was not a gentle dentist, so I dreaded the sessions in his chair. To his credit, he eliminated my toothaches and saved a number of teeth.

When milking, Pa and I would carry on a conversation. This year, he would often talk about how we could farm together after I finished high school. He had plans for us to buy more machinery and expand our custom work for neighbors. As he spoke, I had visions of sitting on a tractor plowing or picking corn for hours in icy autumn winds day after day. It wasn't an appealing prospect. "Stubben" (Shorty) Anderson had an 80-acre farm near us by the river that was for sale at what I thought was an attractive price. I suggested to Pa that we needed more land and could expand our cow herd if we did. Milk prices were good. However, Pa felt the land was too run down from cropping by renters and thus would be unproductive. I replied that we could fertilize it and grow alfalfa to bring the land back again. He disagreed and said the land price was too high for such a poor farm. Later, neighbor Gerald Harrington bought the farm, renovated it with alfalfa, and made this land a highly profitable addition to his dairy farm.

Pa's love of machinery made him opt for more custom work instead of expanding our cow numbers. We had different objectives. Even at age seventeen, I recognized that Pa and I farming together meant that he would make all the decisions, and I would be the "hired man." I really didn't know what I would be doing after graduation from high school although cousin Fred Hanson and Ma wanted me to attend the University of Wisconsin at Madison where he was working on his master's degree in bacteriology. In the past year, Fred had me come down on the Greyhound bus to visit the university and take some aptitude tests. It was an exciting trip for me. The thought of attending classes on this beautiful university campus thrilled me. Unfortunately, I knew what Pa would say to that prospect, and he was the final authority in our family.

Leaving the Farm

In April 1945, the war ended in Europe but continued in the Pacific. Farming was profitable and some veterans returning early from the military were buying up available farms as they saw an opportunity. As for me, I was going to graduate from Colfax High School in May and didn't know what I would do then. It had been a bad year for me. I didn't want to attend the Baccalaureate service and graduation, but Ma and Pa insisted. I got through both events and ended up with a diploma. One day before school ended I rode the Chetek school bus to buy an annual from my old class that was graduating, visiting with many and having them write notes. It was the last time I would ever see most of them. I was not eligible to attend Chetek class reunions in subsequent years, and I had no interest in those of my Colfax graduating class.

A few days later, cousin Fred Hanson phoned and said he had returned from the university and wanted to come over and see us. Fortunately, we weren't busy on the farm that day. Pa, Ma, and I met Fred as he drove up in his old black Ford car. We stood outside and visited near our back door. Fred announced that he wanted to take me back to Madison with him for the summer semester at the university. Pa immediately told him that I was desperately needed on the farm this summer. They discussed this at some length while Ma supported Fred. I knew that my input didn't count. I remained silent except to say that I would like to go.

Finally, Ma said in a strong voice that Carl was going off to the university this summer. Pa retorted that Carl was needed for haying and other work. He didn't consult me. Fred waited patiently. Then, Ma firmly said, "Carl is going to the university!"

Pa said, "Who is going to help me in the hayfield?" Ma replied, "I'll take his place to put up hay! Carl is going to the university!" I stood there, amazed at how Ma had stood up to Pa and deeply touched by her taking my place in the hard work of haying. Pa sputtered some more, then agreed. I couldn't believe my good fortune!

Fred made arrangements for when we would travel to Madison and departed. He had accomplished his purpose. Now came the practical part of how I would manage financially at school. The outcome was that Pa gave me $100 and then it was up to me to find part-time jobs to support myself. I was so elated to be going that the prospect of working my way through the university didn't even concern me. It was the last school money I received from Pa. I worked three part-time jobs to support myself for three semesters until I enlisted in the Marine Corps Aviation section. I spent 20 months there and then used the GI Bill to support me through my B.S. and M.S. degrees. I left the farm and Sand Creek forever. A new life was beginning.

Epilogue

After leaving Sand Creek, I spent my life living and working as a professor of agronomy in the USA and in other countries. Over these years, I usually visited the Sand Creek area at least once a year. Now in my eightieth year, I do as old people usually do and that is to reflect on the past and the changes that have occurred in my childhood home. Wandering around Zion Lutheran cemetery looking at gravestones of beloved people who nurtured my childhood, it is easy to glorify the past and visualize Sand Creek as an idyllic place where all was perfect. Realistically, I know that it was not a perfect place but one with many hardships during the Great Depression; however, somehow, these people created a successful self-reliant rural community on land with limited resources that supported a large number of people in reasonable comfort *without large environmental inputs from other areas.* They developed homes where children could grow up with adequate nutrition, education, where they learned responsibility, good work habits, and were given the moral training to cope with life wherever they went. For this, I am deeply grateful as I contemplate what these wonderful people did for me.

Change is inherent in nature and human life; we cannot maintain the status quo. Even the Amish farmers who have moved into nearby areas with their lifestyle based on horsepower, no electricity, and simple living have had to make some concessions to the modern world. For me the questions are how the landscape, economy, and people of Sand Creek have changed, why these changes occurred, and their viability in the future.

After all these years living away from Sand Creek, I am an outsider who lives with vivid memories of what used to be sixty-five or more years ago. The experiences of living in other places have no doubt changed my views compared with people who never left this community. Thus, my views on the present status of my childhood community may differ from those who presently reside there. I simply offer them as how I see Sand Creek today.

The Landscape

During my childhood, the Sand Creek area was a vibrant community of small family-operated dairy farms. Driving through the countryside today, it seems empty and depopulated compared with the past. Large expanses of corn, soybean, potato, or other crops cover the best farmland. Pastures and alfalfa hayfields are gone.Today, dairy farms are rare. The colorful, well-kept dairy barns of the past have disappeared, some collapsing into a mass of rubble, many completely removed, and a few maintained by affluent people who appreciate their nostalgic charm. On many of these farms, the houses are vacant and decrepit or else have been torn down. A few are lived in and poorly maintained by newcomers who need cheap housing. Mobile homes, junk cars, and trucks litter some farms. The tidy, one-room schools are gone or converted into cheap family housing. It is a lonely place with few cars on the roads, the land empty of cows and people. The diversity of farm scenes and beauty of well-kept farm yards is gone.

Our old family farm is no more. Most of the farmland was sold to a large farming company and the fences removed to facilitate planting the acreage to corn or soybeans. The dairy barn with its beautiful stone basement is gone as well as most other farm buildings. An ugly modern steel machine shed and the old car garage remain. The gray stucco house, now painted white, is unchanged except for a small addition at the rear that houses a bathroom and extends Ma and Pa's tiny bedroom. The old maple trees still line the driveway and others shade the house. New owners enjoy a few acres in the country, not knowing the history of the family that once lived in this house.

The little hamlet of Sand Creek has changed greatly. The former neat little town of the past is less attractive today with many run down houses and with junk piled in some yards, contrasting with newer well kept homes, mainly on the edge of town along the river. The central area of town is despoiled with rows of new and used cars and pickup trucks, courtesy of the main business, a busy Chrysler sales and service agency. The creamery has been gone for decades, and the volunteer fire department building stands on that site. The Farmers Store is empty. Seversons Grocery is gone, and the IGA (later Red and White) grocery store is boarded up. The formerly busy Home Oil station is empty and deteriorating. The elementary school has been closed for many years with local children being bused to Chetek. The old brick school-house, with an ugly concrete block addition, houses the post office, library, a leather craft store, and arts center. On the south side of town are subsidized low-rent apartments for old folks living on Social Security checks. The bank continues to operate in a new building. A Cenco store sells gasoline and convenience foods but no beer as the township of Sand Creek still votes dry.

The café is the local meeting place where people come to eat and visit. Fortunately, the café retains its old familiarity with a marble-topped soda fountain and walls hung with an engraved picture of 19th century King Oscar of Sweden-Norway, some mounted local wildlife, antique household items, and various local pictures. Cece Hagan Cruse, raised on a farm in Dovre, operates this busy place, which serves a substantial plate lunch as well as the best malted milks and hamburgers in the area, all at attractive prices. The prominent tall-spired white board Zion Lutheran church is gone, along with Our Saviour's church west of town, a result of amalgamating the two parishes to build the brick New Hope Church that is part of the Evangelical Lutheran Church of America. A number of parishioners departed to join a dissenting Lutheran group in Running Valley but later left to form an Independent Lutheran church that meets in a building on the east side of town.

The Land

After laborious clearing and plowing of the cutover pine lands around Sand Creek, the Norwegian immigrants developed a cash crop system of wheat farming. This system flourished for several decades, but a combination of declining soil fertility, pests, and low wheat prices brought ruin to the farmers and townspeople. It was not a sustainable farming system. The introduction of dairying in the late 1890s and early 1900s transformed the area. Dairy cows furnished manure to restore soil fertility. Red clover and crop rotation enhanced it and followed a low-input farming system that produced a reasonable level of milk production. It was a low-input, sustainable farming system that furnished sufficient income to support a high population density on this sandy soil. The system continued to operate well until the 1970s, enhanced by inputs of limestone for alfalfa which furnished higher yields than red clover.

During most of this dairy farming era, horses were the main power source, and cows grazed on pasture from May to October with hay and corn silage used the rest of the year. Purchased inputs were low. The big change came when farmers, using university extension recommendations, began confined feeding of cows all year to increase milk production per cow, requiring more silage and hay. The old system grazed cows as much of the year as possible and depended on cow manure and legume-fixed nitrogen which resulted in lower milk production per cow but it was a low-input system with low expenses. Keeping cows confined all year resulted in no wasted forage from trampled pastures and the ability to maintain forage quality at a high level all season. Thus, cows did not waste energy walking in pastures and would consume larger amounts of uniform quality forage during their entire lactation which resulted in more milk per animal. Cows were stressed with more grain to utilize their full genetic potential.

Unfortunately, the new confined feeding system increased costs. Purchase of more silos, tractors, silage harvesters, and feeding equipment was costly.Cows were stressed by the heavy feeding regimes and had to be replaced after fewer lactations than in a pasture system, requiring more replacement heifers. Much more fertilizer was purchased to increase silage yields as farmers expanded their farms to feed more cows. Confined feeding increased waste disposal costs as compared to spring-summer grazing when cows were their own manure spreaders. While milk prices remained the same or declined, farmers experienced a profit squeeze as equipment and land prices increased. Debt grew sharply on many farms. Older farmers retired and quit farming. Sons and daughters were not tempted to remain on the farm to milk cows twice a day all year while wrestling with a huge debt burden and low profits. Young people were leaving the land and commuting to jobs in nearby cities or leaving Sand Creek forever.

As dairy farming disappeared, the land was farmed with cash crops like corn, soybean, and potatoes. With no manure for the land, crop farming with no alfalfa in a rotation required larger inputs of fertilizer. Irrigation from wells increased crop yields on these sandy soils now deficient in organic matter. Because profit margins were low, small farmers could not afford the heavy equipment costs. As a result poorer land was rented to the government for conservation reserve payments or planted to pine trees. Higher quality land was accumulated into larger units either by rental or purchase and farmed by large farming companies that could spread their equipment and other costs over more acres to make a profit. Fences and trees along fence lines were ripped out to allow large farming equipment to operate efficiently in big fields. The result was miles of the same cash crop along roads that once contained large numbers of picturesque small dairy farms with contrasting fields of bright green alfalfa and corn, ripe golden oats, and lush pastures with contented cows.

Few people are needed to farm cash crops; so the land provides little local employment. The large farming companies have little positive economic impact on the area as they purchase little or nothing locally and profits go elsewhere unless the land is farmed by a local farming company. The destructive impact of the cash crop system can be seen in Sand Creek. There is no creamery, the milk haulers are gone, there are no milk trucks to service, there is no longer a grocery store, and the feed mill has little business. Except for the Chrysler garage, Sand Creek is economically distressed, populated by retirees, younger people who commute to jobs elsewhere, and poor people living on limited incomes. The economic vibrancy it once exhibited is gone. It is likely that some of this loss could be expected, as residents now shop at large stores in nearby towns, a result of better transportation and roads. However, the enormous reduction in local income from the land with the demise of dairying has contributed to the present lack of economic activity in Sand Creek.

Is the present cash crop farming system sustainable? For the short term, the answer is yes. The sandy soils of the Sand Creek area have little inherent fertility, but with soil testing and large inputs of lime and fertilizer, high yields of continuous corn and other row crops are possible without alfalfa as a rotation crop. There are a number of risks that could change this outlook over the long term. Corn requires large inputs of nitrogen fertilizer made from natural gas, a fossil fuel resource with declining USA production. Costs of natural gas will surely rise as more of this commodity is imported by tanker vessels, creating more problems for our national balance of payments. Thus, nitrogen as well as phosphate and potash fertilizer costs can be expected to increase in the future. Presently, corn prices are highly subsidized by government ethanol payments, a practice that may not be politically possible in the future. Equipment prices will continue to increase as manufacturing costs rise. Continuous cropping without using a perennial rotation legume like alfalfa eliminates a rich source of cheap biological nitrogen and also risks the possibility of new destructive pest problems.

Other land uses are apparent. Much of the poorest land is now in forest or grassed government land rental. Small tracts of old farmland have been bought by affluent city people to build nice homes for weekends, vacations or retirement. Many of these old farms have land that is reverting to trees and grassland. With improved wildlife habitats, populations of whitetail deer, fox, turkeys, and bear have increased over what they were during my childhood. Growing up, I never saw fox, turkey, bear, or bald eagles, but now they add interest to the environment. With more hill land forested, watersheds have increased to capture rainfall, furnishing water so small streams flow with greater regularity than in the past.

Tourism is likely to increase in the future. Dovre, Trout Creek, and other forested hill areas along the Red Cedar River offer lovely natural scenery. Driving, bicycling, or walking on quiet, uncrowded roads amid dense hardwood and pine forests is an enjoyable experience. Autumn leaf color can be stunning, and an attractive venue for city visitors. Visitors can camp in Myran Park. This 40-acre white pine and hardwood forest area between our old farm and the Red Cedar River was given to Dunn County by Andrew and Annie Myran. In addition to well equipped camping spaces, it also contains an old log house and a collection of old farm machinery and steam engines. A boat landing is available for fishing enthusiasts to launch their boats. Forested land along the river has become valuable as building sites for vacation cottages of city people.

Lifestyle

Residents of the area today may live on the land, but not from the land. Aside from mechanic jobs at the Chrysler garage, there is little local employment available. The Sand Creek community appears to be a bedroom community where people commute to jobs in surrounding towns like Menomonie, Eau Claire, Rice Lake, and even Minneapolis-St. Paul. Commonly, both husband and wife are employed, often in different towns. Thus, most of these families own two vehicles of which one is most likely a large pickup truck. It would seem that vehicles and fuel to operate them must consume a considerable percentage of their personal incomes. The attractions of lower cost housing and rural living appear to be worth the time and cost of commuting to jobs elsewhere.

New Hope Lutheran Church, with a woman pastor, is an active parish. In addition to the regular worship services, they have women's circles, a men's group, a young people's organization, a quilting club, and also furnish meeting space for various other community activities. The volunteer firemen hold an annual chicken barbecue dinner, attracting a large crowd, to raise money for needed equipment. Local people travel a lot more than in the past, enjoying movies in nearby towns, theater, and concerts of popular entertainers, as well as trips to various parts of the United States. Some have made trips to Norway and other areas of the world. Community spirit appears to be alive, and neighbors continue to care for one another when needed. Volunteers are usually available to transport infirm or older persons for medical attention or other needs. This tradition of caring for others appears to have been adopted by newcomers to the community.

A striking change has occurred in people's clothing. Bib overalls are much less common having been replaced by blue jeans. Print dresses have disappeared as women also wear mostly blue jeans. Church attire was formerly suits and ties for men and print dresses and hats for women. Today, few men wear suits and ties, but appear in sport shirts and dress pants or jeans. Women usually wear pant suits and occasionally jeans to church. Children of both sexes are overwhelmingly dressed in blue jeans and shirts.

The People

The makeup of the population in the community has changed greatly. There are no descendant residents with the name of Hoveland or Myran, early settlers of the Sand Creek area. Many other names common during my childhood such as Eyk, Noer, Gregarson, Hendrickson, Svalestun, and Thornby are no longer represented. However, many old Norwegian family names remain such as Anderson, Lofthus, Gilberts, Gustum, Peterson, Berg, Larson, Nelson, Hanson, Dahl, Omtvedt, and Severson. The big change is a shift to non-Norwegian names such as Smith, Schuler, Moore, Schoen, Robinson, Lyrek, Sparks, Vlcek, and Killoren. The Norwegian language has died out, with only a few old people able to converse haltingly.

In the early 1930s very few went off to college unless it was for two years of teacher's training. A number of young women enrolled in hospital nursing schools to become registered nurses. Some never finished high school. Education was not a high priority in most families. Increasingly over the years, more and more young people left their Sand Creek area homes to attend college. Since there were no jobs for them here after college graduation, they moved away permanently to other parts of the state or nation. Many have distinguished themselves in various professions such as public school teachers, university professors, business careers, military officers, social services, nurses, and Lutheran pastors. In this way, Sand Creek has given this educated elite of their youth to benefit other areas of our country but received little in return.

A New Land Ethic

Over the years, the area has lost descendants of the original settlers, and been replaced to some extent with new people from other areas. For me, few people remain from my era and understandably, I do not know the children who have grown up here. For me Sand Creek is becoming a foreign place with new people, new landscapes, new lifestyles, and few things reminiscent of my childhood. The livelihoods of people living there today do not come from the land but are dependent on employment elsewhere. It is a place where most of the residents use the land as a place to live and for recreation, a very different place than I knew. We lived and worked in close harmony all year with the land, the forage plants, and the dairy cows, each contributing to the life of the other components. Most farmers found satisfaction in preserving the land and improving it for future generations. As a result, most proudly left their land in better condition for the next owner when they retired from farming.

The demise of family-operated small dairy farms has affected the people now living here. The close relationship to the land as a necessary part of one's life is gone. The smells of moist plowed soil, newly mown hay, chopped silage corn, and fresh pine sawdust that were a part of our everyday life are missing for most of today's residents raised on the combustion smells of fossil fuels. Children growing up in the area today cannot be expected to understand this love for the land and working in harmony with it and their animals to feed themselves and preserve the land for the future. Earnings today come not from the land but from a job in some occupation at another location, with the wage earner often doing something from which they get little satisfaction other than a paycheck. This job, often unreliable as businesses change their employment needs, provides income to live on a bit of land to enjoy nature and escape from the work day world. The land may provide a vegetable garden, but it is more likely a place on which to live and hunt, fish, snowmobile, ski, or enjoy other recreational activities.

Living in the country has some costs that may pose problems in the future. The cost of transportation to and from the place of employment was cheap at one time, but as vehicle and fuel costs rise, this system of lengthy commuting in individual vehicles, especially to low wage jobs, is likely to pinch workers in places like Sand Creek even more in the future. Taxes will continue to rise as people, especially new home owners, expect more of the services that they had living in urban surroundings. Credit cards and other forms of debt have replaced the frugality of the past, raising concerns about the stability of their lifestyle. The old order is ended. The generations of frugal people who lived off the land, and their dairy cows are gone. One hopes that the new economy will be as successful and sustainable.

My Legacy from a Sand Creek Childhood

The people who nurtured me during childhood had a profound impact on, and to a large extent, molded me into what I am today. My parents and the community provided not only the necessities of food, clothing, and shelter but also a loving environment with good role models to mentor a growing child. I was exceedingly fortunate to have these opportunities during the privations of the Depression era. The legacy I inherited was not monetary wealth but things that were much more valuable for a successful life.

The strong genetic stock of my ancestors contributed to the good health that I have enjoyed all these years. They were generally long-lived folk who seemed to be too busy to get sick. Pa had only minor health problems in spite of abusing his body with hard work and survived to age eight-four. Grandpa Hoveland lived to the age of ninety-three and never spent a day in a hospital. Ma lived an even longer life, four months short of one-hundred, still mentally alert although in a nursing home. Obviously, for long life and good health one needs to choose one's ancestors well!

Under the tutelage of my disciplined, hard-working father, I learned to work. I learned to like work, although some miserable jobs taught me only that I wanted to escape them in the future. Having learned to cope with tough jobs on the farm, I found that most work I did during my career was relatively easy. Many people were smarter, but I could usually compete with them because of the disciplined work habits that Pa taught me. Pa had an enormous capacity to perform hard physical work and took pride in being able to do more in a day than most other people.

I learned self-discipline and responsibility early as a child at home. This was easily reinforced by the attitudes and actions of neighbors around us. We were responsible for what we did and how it affected others. We did not try to blame others for our misdeeds. I developed a sense of pride in being responsible so that people could trust me. For example, as a small child, I learned the importance of closing a fence gate when I opened it as a gate left open could be serious and allow livestock to enter a corn or hay field.

Honesty, speaking the truth, and not stealing were values easily learned, as they were the norm at home and among neighbors in our community. I doubt if the church had much influence in fostering these virtues as they were already part of the culture, even among people who did not attend worship. People did not lie, cheat, or steal. A person's word was accepted in a business arrangement. If a problem arose, it was easily settled in discussion. I doubt if lawyers got much business from people in our area. Crime was not a problem and murder was unknown. There were no police. When Ma learned of someone in another community stealing, she described them as having "long fingers." Houses generally remained unlocked, our car keys remained in the vehicle, and tools or small farm machinery could easily be borrowed from a neighbor when needed. Being raised among upright people, it was discouraging for me to learn after I left home that some people commonly cheated, lied, or stole.

Frugality and saving were commonplace. At home, string and brown wrapping paper from the store were saved for future use. Pa would save scraps of lumber or metal because "they might be needed sometime." We didn't waste anything. Ma saved old worn overalls and used good parts for patches on other overalls, holes in socks were darned, holes in shirts were sewn up, and pieces were cut from old clothes to make patchwork quilts for beds. During the worst of the Depression, chicken feed sacks made of colorful print cotton cloth were commonly used to sew dresses for girls and women. At home, nothing was bought on credit. One saved money in order to purchase something. For Pa, debt was a sin. As a small child I had a savings account at the bank. I learned at an early age to save and invest money, a valuable lesson to be practiced the rest of my life.

Concern for neighbors and assisting them when in need was commonplace in our community. Illness or death promptly brought food and help from others. A farmer suffering injury or illness would soon have neighbors helping with milking or other farm work. Immediate neighbors would dig the grave for a deceased farmer or wife. Our next door neighbors, the Myran family, were typical of the area as they freely gave of themselves to others without any thought of receiving anything in return. It was a loving community for a child to grow up in and experience the Golden Rule in action.

Sand Creek gave me a rich childhood legacy that has paid rich dividends throughout my life.The people who mentored me as a child were not perfect but could be expected do the right thing toward their neighbors.They were honest, humble, hard-working, loving people. I was fortunate to grow up in their midst.